NATHALIE DUPREE'S

Southern Memories

NATHALIE DUPREE'S
Southern Memories

RECIPES
AND
REMINISCENCES

PHOTOGRAPHS BY TOM ECKERLE
DESIGN BY RICHARD FERRETTI

Clarkson Potter/Publishers
New York

ALSO BY NATHALIE DUPREE

Cooking of the South

New Southern Cooking

Nathalie Dupree's Matters of Taste

*Nathalie Dupree Cooks for
Family and Friends*

Published by Clarkson Potter/Publishers, 201 East 50th Street, New York, New York 10022.
Member of the Crown Publishing Group.
Random House, Inc. New York, Toronto, London, Sydney, Auckland
CLARKSON N. POTTER, POTTER, and colophon are trademarks of Clarkson N. Potter, Inc.

Manufactured in Japan

Library of Congress Cataloging-in-Publication Data
Dupree, Nathalie.
Southern memories / by Nathalie Dupree.
p.   cm.
Includes index.
1. Cookery, American—Southern style.   2. Southern States—Social
life and customs—1865–   I. Title.
TX715.2.S68D86   1993
641.5975—dc20   92-27342
                                                            CIP
ISBN 0-517-59062-X
10 9 8 7 6 5 4 3 2 1
First Edition

This book is dedicated

to my dear former husband, David Dupree,

who shared with me his family and his life.

He also paid for my year at the

London Cordon Bleu, for which I am grateful.

Contents

Introduction

$\mathcal{T}_{0}$ *many Americans,* all of the area south of the Mason-Dixon line and east of Texas makes up a vast, slightly mysterious, vaguely rural, and steadfastly folksy place called "the South." In fact, the South is larger than Europe and as diverse, a loose conglomeration of distinctly differing regions. My South is not the Gulf south, although it is a south too, or all of the counties of Florida, Texas, and Louisiana, where Southerners also live and breathe in batches, as they do in Illinois and Indiana. My South ranges from the Eastern Shore of Maryland through the District of Columbia and Virginia, taking in the Carolinas, weaving its way around West Virginia, embracing Georgia, Tennessee, Arkansas, Alabama, and Mississippi.

My South is the South where I ate fried fish for my wedding supper on the island of Ocracoke in the Outer Banks. It is memories of the massive black babysitter who tenderly cradled me between vast bosoms while she played the piano and crooned the blues and I ate an angel biscuit smeared with jam. It is the sweet-smelling aroma of vines and gardenias and magnolias, the flowers tucked in the hair and decolletages of vain and beautiful women, wafting through screened windows, floating in glass bowls, and the smell of the oysters—fecund and earthy, as Pat Conroy says in *The Prince of Tides*, a dank smell of darkness and secrets, prejudices and kindness. It is poverty and swimming pools.

My South encompasses the rice fields I helped seed

from a small plane, the grits I saw ground from dried corn in a small mill next to a powerful stream, the small towns and cities of Covington and Social Circle, Georgia, where I made my home and started my first restaurant. It is the South of a million small memories, pieced together over the nearly forty years I've lived here, the South whose dogwoods, azaleas, and redbirds greet me as I open my door each morning, where I sit outside eight months of the year and drink iced tea and sip Coca-Cola from sweaty glasses. It is putting up tomatoes for tomato conserve, the tangle of zucchini vines, and the dance of garlic flowers on their tall winding stalks. It is the place where with pigs and some turnip greens you could last out the hard times, where a kitchen garden made the difference between living well and barely living. A place where the soil may put out only enough nurturing to keep collards or turnips going, or where its lush lands support fields of melons. It is the place where food is always kept on hand for family and visitors.

I came to Virginia when I was in the first grade. We lived under the shadow of Mount Vernon with its gardens and kitchens and I was a frequent visitor there. I married a Georgia man, and even as we lived in London and Spain, we missed the South's ways. And so we returned and so I have stayed.

While I love all of the United States, the South is my soul. It is the part of me I can't change, can't get rid of, even should I want to.

P i c k - u p s

SOUTHERNERS DON'T LIKE TO BE FAR FROM their food. Pick-ups, as opposed to appetizers, can be eaten at any time—they needn't precede a meal, are not a first course, but rather are something that is always "just there." A pick-up can be as simple as boiled peanuts to offer to a dirty child coming straight from the sandbox or as elegant as those delicacies offered on a silver tray. All that matters is that there is something plentiful and tasty, ready to eat with hand or fork.

This imperative always to have something to eat can be traced back to the tradition of unfailing hospitality and endless enter-  taining established by Martha Washington at Mount Vernon. It is also a response to those impoverished times that followed both The War Between the States—when Scarlett O'Hara's vow, "I'll never go hungry again," was a universal sentiment—and the Depression; Southerners feel that as long as you have

LEFT: *A casual pick-up buffet offers Pepper Jelly Turnovers, Marinated Okra, filled Finger Rolls, and Stuffed Cherry Tomatoes.* RIGHT: *Modern Angels on Horseback.*

something, no matter how modest, to offer a guest, you're not dirt poor. Pick-ups don't tend to be elaborate—wrapping bacon around an oyster with a basil leaf for "modern" Angels on Horseback is about as complicated as they get—for they must be ready to serve at a moment's notice. We slice up ham or turkey to put inside a small biscuit or roll around asparagus, and voilá, by golly, there's a pick-up! We can answer the doorbell's ring and pull out something to eat in an instant!

Every town has a caterer renowned for "the best" cheese straws, and well-to-do Southerners are rarely without a supply. They remain in their white boxes, tied with string, and are stored on top of the refrigerator until ready to use. But everyone knows the best are made at home and kept in an airtight box or even the freezer, to be pulled out for drop-ins and fancy parties alike.

Nuts are also standard pick-up fare. My mother still sends me pecans from the big tree in her backyard for Christmas. The recipes for toasted pecans are legion, closely guarded secrets that are passed on from generation to generation. Whether buttered, spiced or plain, toasted in the oven or the microwave, only choice halves, not pieces, will do. Roasted peanuts are frequently spiced as well, though boiled peanuts, whether cooked at home or scooped up from a pot next to the vegetable truck pulled up on the street, are a welcome snack anytime.

Of course, sometimes extravagance is called for, even on informal occasions. Shrimp dips, seafood kebabs, and crab cakes made to be eaten with fingers or a tiny plate and fork are all easily assembled and make a gathering memorable.

MISSISSIPPI CAVIAR
SERVES 10 TO 12

This wonderful make-ahead dip is made from the South's caviar—black-eyed peas. The colorful name's been around awhile, but I always associate it with the party at which I first tried it, held in conjunction with the National Chicken Cooking Contest in Jackson, Mississippi. It can be refrigerated for 4 to 5 days and can easily be doubled for large parties. Hot peppers spice up many Southern dishes. Jalapeño peppers are used extensively in Texas. Tabasco peppers are hotter. But most Southern peppers are finger and cowhorn peppers.

  3 16-ounce cans black-eyed peas,
      drained
  ½ cup finely chopped green bell pepper
  ½ cup finely chopped red bell pepper
  ¼ cup finely chopped hot peppers
  ¼ cup finely chopped onion
  ¼ cup drained and finely chopped
      pimiento
  1 garlic clove, chopped
  ⅓ cup red wine vinegar
  ⅔ cup olive oil
  1 tablespoon Dijon mustard
      Salt
      Tabasco sauce
      Tortilla chips

In a large mixing bowl, combine the peas, bell peppers, hot peppers, onion, pimiento, and garlic. In a separate bowl, whisk together the vinegar, oil, and mustard and pour over the bean mixture; mix well. Season to taste with salt and Tabasco. With a wooden spoon or potato masher, mash the bean mixture slightly.

Refrigerate until ready to serve. Drain the caviar well and serve with tortilla chips.

MODERN ANGELS ON HORSEBACK
SERVES 6 AS A FIRST COURSE

When I was growing up, everybody's mother had a recipe for baked oysters wrapped in bacon, called Angels on Horseback, which was served at cocktail parties throughout the South. This version, skewered, wrapped in basil leaves, and grilled, is an update and it's incredible how fresh tasting the basil is, encasing the plump, juicy oysters under the crunchy bacon skin.

  24 fresh oysters, drained
      MARINADE
   2 tablespoons olive oil
  ¼ cup lemon juice
   1 garlic clove, finely chopped
      Salt
      Freshly ground black pepper
      Dash Tabasco sauce
   4 skewers
  24 basil leaves
  12 thin slices bacon, cut in half

Place the oysters in a medium bowl. In a small bowl, whisk together the olive oil, lemon juice, garlic, salt, pepper, and Tabasco to taste, and pour over the oysters. Marinate for ½ hour to 2 hours, stirring once or twice. If using wooden skewers, soak them in hot water for 30 minutes to prevent burning.

Preheat the broiler or a charcoal grill. Drain the oysters well, discarding the marinade. Wrap each oyster with a basil leaf and then with a piece of bacon. Thread 4 oysters onto each skewer. Grill or broil on a baking sheet for 3 minutes, or long enough to crisp the bacon. Serve on the skewers for a casual occasion, or remove from the skewers and arrange them on a platter.

HOT HAM
OR TURKEY ROLLS
MAKES 60

Horseradish mustard and grated onion add tang to these petite treats. The rolls themselves may be store-bought or homemade.

> 60 Finger Rolls (page 130)
> ¼ cup (½ stick) butter, softened
> 2 teaspoons horseradish mustard
> 2 teaspoons grated onion
> 2 teaspoons poppy seeds
> 1 cup shredded ham or smoked turkey
> 1 cup grated Swiss cheese

Preheat the oven to 400°F.

Split the rolls in half. In a small bowl combine the butter, mustard, onion, and poppy seeds and spread on both sides of the split rolls. Place some of the shredded meat on the bottom halves, and top with the Swiss cheese. Replace the tops of the rolls. Bake for 10 minutes. These freeze very well.

ABOVE: *Hot Ham Rolls.* OPPOSITE: *Cheese Straws, rolled out and ready to cut.*

CHEESE STRAWS
MAKES 80 TO 100

No self-respecting Southern host or hostess would ever be without a ready supply of cheese straws, perhaps the best loved of our pick-up foods.

These marvelous Southern delicacies are short crust strips baked with butter and cheese and fired with red pepper. Serve them whenever a crowd is gathered, as well as when a few friends or family drop by for a glass of iced tea. Traditionally they go through a cookie press or pastry bag, but I find it easier simply to roll out the dough and cut it in strips.

> ½ pound imported Parmesan cheese,
>   very finely grated
> ½ pound sharp Cheddar cheese, grated
> 1 cup (2 sticks) butter, softened
> 3¼ to 3½ cups cake or all-purpose flour
> 1 tablespoon salt
> ½ to 1 teaspoon cayenne pepper

Preheat the oven to 375°F.

Lightly grease 2 or 3 baking sheets.

Beat the cheeses and butter together until very smooth. (If the mixture is not well beaten, larger pieces of cheese may clog up your cookie press.) Mix in the flour, salt, and cayenne pepper to taste. Put the dough into a cookie press with a cheese straw blade, and press onto the greased baking sheets in 2½- to 3-inch strips. Alternately, roll out the dough ¼ inch thick on a floured surface. With a pastry wheel or sharp knife cut the dough into strips 2½ to 3½ inches long and ¾ inch wide. Place on the baking sheets.

Bake 8 to 10 minutes, reducing the heat if the straws start to get too brown. Remove them to a rack to cool completely.

Store in a tightly covered container for up to 1 week or freeze for up to 3 months.

STUFFED CHERRY TOMATOES
MAKES 2 TO 3 DOZEN

Cherry tomatoes are easily grown in planters on Southern patios and decks and I am particularly fond of them. I make these tasty tomatoes ahead of time for parties or casual gatherings. Their bite-size shape makes them ideal for stand-up eating.

24 to 36 cherry tomatoes
½ pound cream cheese, at room
    temperature
5 scallions or green onions, including
    green tops, finely chopped
3 tablespoons capers, finely chopped
5 or 6 radishes, finely chopped
2 to 3 tablespoons finely chopped fresh
    parsley
2 to 3 tablespoons finely chopped
    fresh basil
¼ to ½ teaspoon Tabasco sauce
½ to 1 teaspoon Worcestershire sauce
    Sprigs of dill or fennel fronds,
    for garnish

Cut the tops off the tomatoes and scoop out the insides with a small spoon. Combine the cream cheese, scallions, capers, radishes, parsley, basil, Tabasco, and Worcestershire and beat together well. Fill the tomatoes with the mixture using a pastry bag or small spoon. Garnish with sprigs of dill or fennel fronds, if desired.

PEPPER JELLY TURNOVERS
MAKES 2 TO 3 DOZEN

Flaky pastry encasing a sweet peppery jelly makes an unusual appetizer that I keep on hand in the freezer for last-minute guests and cocktail parties. Homemade pepper jelly adds dash to the recipe.

5 ounces sharp Cheddar cheese,
    cut into ½-inch cubes
1 cup all-purpose flour
½ cup (1 stick) butter, cut into
    ½-inch cubes
3 to 4 tablespoons ice water
½ cup or 1 4-ounce jar Hot Pepper
    Jelly (page 92)
2 tablespoons chopped smoked or
    country ham (optional)

Preheat the oven to 375°F.

In a food processor or in a bowl using a pastry blender, roughly cut the cheese into the flour. Add the butter. Process or blend until the butter is about the size of garden peas. Add the ice water and process briefly until the dough starts to come together.

Turn the dough out onto a board and shape it into a flat round. Roll it out (between sheets of wax paper if necessary) ⅛ inch thick and cut into rounds with a 2-inch biscuit cutter. Place approximately ⅓ teaspoon hot pepper jelly and ¼ teaspoon chopped ham, if using, in the center of each round and fold over; with a fork, crimp the edges well to seal or the jelly will run out.

Place the turnovers on a baking sheet, and bake 10 to 15 minutes. The turnovers may be frozen before or after baking. Defrost and bake or reheat before serving.

BARBARA MORGAN'S HALF DOLLAR HAM BISCUITS
MAKES 9 TO 10 DOZEN

The first time I had these easy-to-handle and tasty half dollar–sized ham treats was at my friend Barbara's home. I begged the recipe from her when I learned they could be frozen filled with the spread and ham, re-heated in foil, and still taste incredibly fresh and delicious!

> 9 to 10 dozen baked biscuits, each
>   the size of a 50-cent piece
>   (page 58)
> 1¼ cups (2½ sticks) butter, softened
> 2 small onions, finely chopped
> 2 tablespoons poppy seeds
> 5 teaspoons Dijon mustard
> 2 pounds shaved ham

Split the baked biscuits.

In a small bowl, mix together the butter, onions, poppy seeds, and mustard. Spread the mixture on the bottom halves of the biscuits. Top with the shaved ham, then replace the top halves of the biscuits. Arrange the biscuits in a basket or on a platter.

You can store the finished biscuits, tightly covered, in the refrigerator up to 2 days. To freeze, wrap the biscuits in foil and put them in a plastic bag.

CRAB CAKES
MAKES 36 PATTIES

Serve these tiny crab cakes with a fork or toothpicks if you aren't in the mood to handle fried foods with your fingers; they'll be the hit of a stand-up or cocktail party. There could be another war about breadcrumbs and saltines with crab cakes—in Maryland they are heresy! I don't use them for delicate entrées, but for a tasty pick-up food they are necessary.

> ½ cup toasted breadcrumbs
> ½ cup crushed saltine crackers
> 2 eggs
> 6 tablespoons mayonnaise
> 1 tablespoon Dijon mustard
> 3 green onions or scallions, chopped
> 1 tablespoon chopped fresh parsley
> 2 teaspoons horseradish
> 2 teaspoons capers
> 1 teaspoon celery seed
> 2 teaspoons dry mustard
> 1 to 2 teaspoons Old Bay or other
>   seafood seasoning
> 1 pound lump crabmeat, picked over
> 3 tablespoons vegetable oil, for frying
>   Lemon wedges, for garnish

Combine the breadcrumbs and cracker crumbs. In a large bowl mix together ½ cup crumb mixture, the eggs, mayonnaise, Dijon mustard, green onions, parsley, horseradish, capers, celery seed, dry mustard, Old Bay seasoning, and crabmeat. Divide into 36 small patties, roll in the reserved crumb mixture, and refrigerate for 1 hour.

In a large skillet heat the oil and fry the crab cakes in batches until golden brown, about 2 minutes per side. Drain on paper towels and garnish with fresh lemon wedges.

ASPARAGUS WITH HAM
SERVES 4 TO 6

Lightly cooked asparagus drizzled with vinaigrette and slivers of country ham is a refreshing first course. Called "sparragus" in *Martha Washington's Booke of Cookery*, then "sparrow-grass" in popular terminology through the eighteenth century, asparagus has long been one of the South's favorite vegetables. It is blessedly easy to prepare and adds a feeling of grace and refinement that far exceeds its cost.

2 pounds asparagus
¼ cup red wine vinegar
1 teaspoon Dijon mustard
¾ cup vegetable oil
Salt

Freshly ground black pepper
4 ounces thinly sliced country ham

Cut off the thick ends of the asparagus. If the stalks are large, peel them from the bottom up to the first of the little offshoots. Place them in a large frying pan with enough boiling water to cover. Cook until the spears are no longer raw but are still rigid, usually 3 to 5 minutes for small spears, 5 to 8 minutes for large spears. Drain.

In a small mixing bowl, combine the vinegar and mustard. Whisk in the oil. Season to taste with salt and pepper. Place the asparagus in a serving dish, and top with the thinly sliced ham. Drizzle the vinaigrette mixture over the dish or pass it separately.

SEAFOOD KEBABS
SERVES 8

This incredibly flavorful dish is light in calories and bursting with taste and color. Whenever anyone sees it, they exclaim, "Ah, what a good idea!" as if it were a stroke of genius.

¾ cup olive oil
1 tablespoon white wine vinegar
1 tablespoon fresh lime juice
   Grated peel of 1 lime
      (no white attached)
1 to 2 tablespoons finely chopped
      fresh mint
1 to 2 tablespoons finely chopped
      fresh parsley
1 garlic clove, finely chopped
2 tablespoons freshly grated ginger
1 pound large shrimp, peeled
      and deveined
1¼ pounds sea scallops
8 skewers
2 to 3 green or yellow peppers,
      cut in 1-inch pieces
32 cherry tomatoes
32 small mushrooms, stems removed
2 red onions, peeled and cut in
      1-inch pieces

In a large bowl, whisk together ½ cup olive oil, the vinegar, lime juice, lime peel, mint, parsley, garlic, and ginger. Add the shrimp and scallops and stir to coat. Cover and refrigerate for 2 to 3 hours.

If using bamboo skewers, soak them in hot water to cover for 30 minutes.

Prepare a charcoal grill.

Drain the shrimp and scallops, reserving the marinade. Place the seafood on the skewers, alternating with the peppers, tomatoes, mushrooms, and onion pieces. Brush with the remaining ¼ cup oil. Place on a hot grill and grill 3 to 5 minutes, until done, turning frequently and brushing with the reserved marinade. Serve hot or at room temperature.

OPPOSITE: *A collection of antique silver asparagus servers and tongs enhances Asparagus with Ham.*
ABOVE: *Seafood Kebabs are quickly grilled.*

Okra

Early one morning we flew to southern Georgia to do a TV shoot on okra. I wasn't prepared for the beauty of row after row of the tall hibiscus esculentus that produces okra. The pickers wore brimmed straw hats to keep off the sun. As we looked across the fields all we could see were the hats bobbing over the beautiful flowers.

MARINATED OKRA
SERVES 8 TO 10
AS AN APPETIZER OR 4 TO 6
AS A SALAD

This amazingly refreshing crunchy okra has a lovely orange flavor. It's very unusual and very well liked. Leave the stem on as a tiny handle.

> 2 *pounds whole okra (about 90 pieces)*
> ¼ *cup red wine vinegar*
> ½ *cup olive oil*
> 1 *tablespoon Dijon mustard*
>   *Grated peel of 1 small orange*
>   *(no white attached)*
> 3 *tablespoons fresh orange juice*
> ½ *teaspoon cumin*
>   *Salt*
>   *Freshly ground black pepper*

Steam or blanch the okra for 3 to 5 minutes; refresh under cold water. Set aside in a mixing bowl to cool. Combine the vinegar, oil, mustard, orange peel, juice, cumin, salt, and pepper. Whisk well, pour over the okra, and marinate several hours or overnight. Drain and arrange on a serving platter to be eaten as a finger food or on individual salad plates.

FRIED TURNIP GREENS
SERVES 6 TO 8

These crisply fried leaves are snacking good, either on their own or as an accompaniment like potato chips. I invented this recipe for Nathalie's restaurant many years ago, and they've always been a great conversation starter.

> 2 *pounds turnip greens, washed,*
>   *stemmed, and sliced ½ inch wide*
>   *Peanut oil*
>   *Salt*
>   *Freshly ground black pepper*

Dry the cleaned greens well. Pour enough oil to reach the halfway mark of a deep fat fryer or large frying pan and heat. When hot, add the dry greens by batches; they really boil up and sizzle so be very careful. Fry until crisp. Remove with a slotted strainer and drain on paper towels. Repeat until all the greens are cooked. Add salt and pepper, if desired.

BOILED SHRIMP
SERVES 4 TO 6

When all is said and done, the simpler ways of cooking shrimp are often the best loved. Perhaps it's the conviviality that comes from eating them in the shell or sitting on the ground and peeling them, then dipping them in sauce, making a mess on the newspaper, before popping them in one's mouth.

2   *pounds large shrimp, in the shell*
1   *lemon, sliced*
2   *to 3 teaspoons Creole seasoning*
      (optional)
1   *cup clarified butter (see Note)*

Bring a generous amount of water to the boil in a large pot. Place the shrimp, lemon slices, and seasoning, if using, in the boiling water and cook until the shrimp turn pink, usually 1 to 2 minutes. Drain well and serve with clarified butter.

NOTE: To clarify butter, melt 1 cup unsalted butter over low heat. Remove from the heat and let stand several minutes until the milk solids settle on the bottom. Remove the top layer of foam, then carefully pour off the clear butter, discarding the bottom layer of milk solids.

SHRIMP DIP
SERVES 4 TO 6

This famous old Georgia recipe, adapted by my talented friend, Candy Sheehan, is a lovely finger food for any occasion. I particularly like it for stand-up parties.

1   *pound large cooked shrimp*
⅓ *cup mayonnaise*
¼ *teaspoon Tabasco sauce*
2   *teaspoons grated onion*

2   *tablespoons dry sherry*
2   *tablespoons fresh lemon juice*
     Salt
     Freshly ground pepper
     Toast points or crackers

Chop the shrimp very fine by hand or in a food processor and place in a bowl. Add the mayonnaise, Tabasco, onion, sherry, and lemon juice and blend thoroughly. Season to taste with salt and pepper. Serve on toast points or crackers.

CHEESY PECAN TOASTS
MAKES 30 TO 40 TOASTS

I make this cheese mixture and freeze it, pulling it out and spreading it on toast for a last minute pick-up for drop-ins. Before chopping, toast the nuts on a baking sheet in a 350°F. oven for 5 to 10 minutes, stirring every few minutes. Alternately, toast according to microwave directions.

2   *pounds rat cheese or sharp*
      Cheddar cheese, shredded
¼ *cup (½ stick) butter, softened*
¼ *cup mayonnaise*
1   *tablespoon fresh lemon juice*
2   *cups lightly toasted pecans,*
      finely chopped
     Salt
     Tabasco or hot sauce to taste
8   *pieces toasted white bread,*
      crusts removed

Preheat the broiler.

In a small bowl, mix together the cheese, butter, mayonnaise, lemon juice, pecans, salt, and Tabasco to taste. Spread the mixture on the toast. Broil until bubbly and puffed, 1 to 2 minutes. Cut into bite-size pieces.

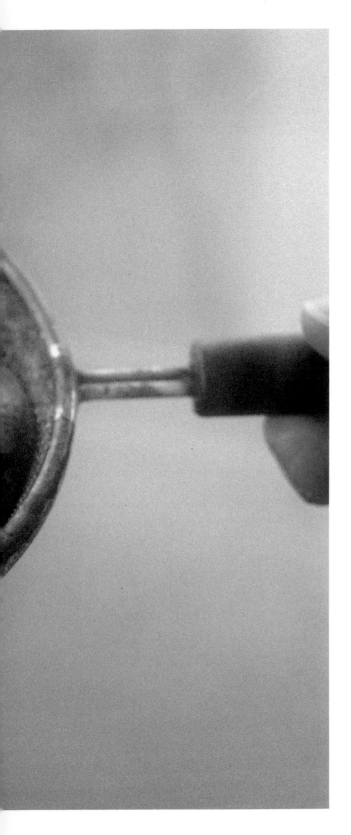

BOILED PEANUTS
MAKES 2 POUNDS

It's an amazing thing to pull up a peanut plant and find dozens of these oddly shaped little legumes attached to the roots. George Washington Carver is credited with propelling them into the mainstream, and we owe him a debt of gratitude for all the ways they are fixed. Although Southerners like them roasted, as they are eaten at ballparks and zoos, eating them boiled in the shell is more likely to stir memories of country life and our roots. Cooking them yourself is not difficult. Expect a peanut that's a little soft and salty.

> 2 *pounds raw peanuts in the shell*
> 1 *gallon water*
> 1¼ *cups salt*

If the peanuts still have dirt clinging to them, wash and rinse them until the water is clear. Place the peanuts in a large saucepan. Mix the water and salt to make a brine. Cover the peanuts with the brine. Bring to the boil, cover, and boil until the shells are tender, about 45 minutes. Remove from the heat and let stand for 15 minutes, then drain well. Crack open the shells and start eating, or refrigerate in the shell for up to a week.

BEIGNETS
MAKES 3 DOZEN

Although I'm not always sure we should view New Orleans as the South—it seems a different world to me—who doesn't think of Beignets, those fried puffs of air sprinkled with confectioners' sugar and served everywhere in New Orleans with strong, hot coffee, as Southern? You can find them from Georgia to Mississippi and Louisiana.

> 4 to 6 cups shortening or vegetable oil
> 2 eggs
> ½ cup milk
> 1 cup flour
> ¼ teaspoon salt
> 2 tablespoons sugar
> 2 teaspoons baking powder
> 1 tablespoon butter, melted
> 1 teaspoon vanilla extract
> 2 egg whites
> Confectioners' sugar
> Cinnamon

In a deep fat fryer, heat to 360°F. enough shortening or oil to fill the fryer halfway.

In a mixing bowl, beat the eggs until light. Add the milk, flour, salt, sugar, baking powder, butter, and vanilla, and beat until it forms a smooth batter.

In a separate bowl, beat the egg whites until stiff but not dry and fold into the batter. Let the batter sit for 5 minutes. Drop the dough by tablespoons into the hot fat, taking care to not crowd the pan. Remove after several minutes when golden brown and puffy, and drain on paper towels. Sprinkle with confectioners' sugar and a little cinnamon and serve immediately.

PECAN MINI MUFFINS
MAKES 6 DOZEN

These mini muffins would be a wonderful surprise for breakfast in bed, along with a bowl of fresh fruit. They are also good for a main meal accompaniment or even a picnic. The recipe was sent to me by a fan, Neeley Oliver.

> 1⅓ cups (2⅔ sticks) butter
> ¾ cup brown sugar
> 1 tablespoon baking powder
> 1 cup all-purpose flour
> ¾ to 1 teaspoon salt
> 1 cup whole wheat flour
> 2 eggs
> 1 cup milk
> 1 teaspoon vanilla extract
> ½ cup ground pecans
> ¼ cup chopped pecans

Preheat the oven to 400°F.

In a mixer bowl beat the butter and sugar together until light. Sift together the baking powder, all-purpose flour, and salt, then add the whole wheat flour to the dry ingredients.

In a small bowl beat the eggs with the milk and vanilla.

Combine the butter, flour, and egg mixtures, stirring just until incorporated, then mix in the ground and chopped nuts thoroughly. Do not beat—you'll get air bubbles. Fill mini muffin tins two-thirds full.

Bake 15 to 20 minutes. Serve hot. These may be made ahead and reheated or frozen.

PEANUT NIBBLES
MAKES 3 CUPS

This is a great pick-up to be eaten in front of the TV, or at a stand-up party, or with a Coca-Cola—or anytime.

> 3 cups raw peanuts, shelled
> 2 tablespoons butter, melted
> 2 tablespoons soy sauce
> ½ teaspoon sesame oil
> 1 teaspoon ground ginger
> 1 tablespoon honey
> ½ teaspoon red pepper
> ½ teaspoon garlic powder
>   Salt
>   Freshly ground black pepper

Preheat the oven to 250°F. Place the peanuts on an ungreased baking sheet.

In a small measuring cup, mix together the butter, soy sauce, sesame oil, ginger, honey, red pepper, and garlic powder. Pour evenly over the peanuts and bake for 1 to 1½ hours, tossing every 15 minutes. Remove the peanuts from the oven and place on paper towels to drain. Salt and pepper to taste. Store in an airtight container.

DENICE'S TOASTED SPICY PECANS
MAKES 4 CUPS

These hot and tangy pecans compel you to eat "just one more." They're devilish!

> ¼ cup (½ stick) unsalted butter
> 3 tablespoons soy sauce
> ½ to 1 teaspoon cayenne pepper
> ½ teaspoon garlic powder
> 4 cups pecan halves

Preheat the oven to 300°F.

Place the butter in a large baking dish or jelly roll pan and put in the oven for a few minutes until the butter is melted. Remove from the oven and stir in the soy sauce, cayenne pepper to taste, and garlic powder. Add the pecan halves and toss until they are well coated.

Return to the oven and bake for 15 minutes. Stir the pecans and bake for another 10 minutes, or until the pecans are toasted. Remove the pecans to paper towels to absorb any excess butter. When cool, store in an airtight container.

TRIPLE CHOCOLATE PEANUT CLUSTERS
MAKES 3 POUNDS

Peanuts glued together with a marvelous mixture of three different kinds of chocolate—now how bad could that be?

> 6 ounces white chocolate
> 6 ounces semisweet chocolate chips
> 6 ounces milk chocolate chips
> 1 12-ounce jar unsalted dry roasted peanuts

Melt the white, semisweet, and milk chocolate chips over low heat in a heavy pan. Cool slightly and stir in the peanuts. Let sit until mixture thickens slightly. Drop by tablespoons onto wax paper. Let cool and harden completely. Wrap in plastic wrap and keep in the refrigerator or freezer until ready to serve.

Ladies' Lunches

ALTHOUGH SOUTHERN LADIES' lunches are a time for exchanging sentiments and stories, celebrations of friends and families, troubles and joys, loves and losses, they are also a symbol of the strength of the Southern woman. For the kitchen was always the domain in which the Southern woman could exercise control and indulge creative impulses when all other avenues were closed to her. When the audience for her culinary endeavors was other women, her efforts and results tended to be even more spectacular.

LEFT: Sterling tea caddies, fine china, and lacy linens complement a late lunch of figs with ham. RIGHT: Pecan and raspberry-topped Lemon Tassies.

And no Southern woman would try to win support for a project dear to her without offering something to eat. For food to us is the great convincer, the great mediator, the way of saying, "I want to please you," as well as to say, "You are welcome, wanted here."

Ladies' lunches are still special occasions in the South, whether at garden club meetings with a spring garden cake bedecked with candied violets and pansies, charity organizational meetings, fund-raisers, showers, bridge clubs, or simply a gathering to fuss over an out-of-town guest. On these occasions the fare is sophisticated, men are banished, and women reign supreme.

*I*ndeed, the tradition of ladies' lunches is not the exclusive province of elegant women with time for leisure; it might just as easily be that of employer and employee, sharing a chicken salad and a long talk, a young woman and her beau's mother eating crab salad and tassies under the dog-wood blossoms, or old friends relishing fresh figs with country ham in the shade of the fig tree.

There is no particular mandate for what or how one eats at these functions, except that even in these harried times we still try to provide a touch of grace. In the spring, my mother-in-law, Celeste, borrows knock-up tables from the Baptist church next door to her house (even though she is a Methodist) and sets up for company outdoors. With great pleasure she uses her antique linens and plates—the older the better. Frankly, she has just about the best garden in town.

*W*hether a simple meal of corn bread and Piperade, or an elaborate outdoor party with Minted Melon Ring or Grits and Goat Cheese Timbale—linens and silver, sparkling glasses and flowers everywhere—the ladies' lunch is worth fighting for, even in busy times when many women are working both inside the home and out.

MT. PLEASANT FIGS WITH COUNTRY HAM AND LIME VINAIGRETTE
SERVES 4

My first restaurant, Nathalie's, was in a renovated warehouse at Mt. Pleasant Village, on the site of the Mt. Pleasant Plantation. The old homestead is now owned by Mrs. Oby (Ann) Brewer. Ann had the fig trees, well over 200 years old, moved from the side to her backyard, where she will often entertain a friend in the afternoon for a late lunch or hot or cold tea and figs. I think lush figs filled with slivers of country ham and drizzled with a light vinaigrette is one of the most beautiful of Southern marriages.

> 4 *large ripe figs*
> 4 *very thin slices country ham*
>   *or baked ham*
>
> LIME VINAIGRETTE
> ¼ *cup fresh lime juice*
> 2 *teaspoons balsamic vinegar*
> 1 *teaspoon Dijon mustard*
> 1 *shallot, minced*
> 1 *teaspoon grated lime peel*
>   *(no white attached)*
> ½ *teaspoon sugar*
> ⅔ *cup peanut oil*
> 1 *tablespoon freshly chopped chives*
>   *Salt*
>   *Freshly ground black pepper*

Cut the figs into 6 wedges, slicing through the flower end into, but not through, the stem end. Open out like the petals of a flower. Fold the ham slice in half to resemble a triangle. Holding one corner, gather or bunch the ham together in a spiral pattern. When rolled, open up the edges and separate slightly to form a rose pattern. Place a ham flower in the center of each sliced fig.

In a small bowl, whisk together the lime juice, balsamic vinegar, Dijon mustard, the shallot, lime peel, and sugar. Add the peanut oil in a slow stream, whisking constantly to form an emulsion. Add the chives. Adjust the seasoning with salt and pepper.

Drizzle the vinaigrette over the figs or serve on the side.

CHUTNEY CHICKEN SALAD
SERVES 10

This recipe is very similar to Coronation Chicken, the famous London Cordon Bleu dish seen everywhere in England. It's not surprising that it has shown up in the Southern repertoire, as so many of our earliest recipes are of English origin.

> 6 *cups roughly chopped cooked chicken*
> 1½ *cups finely chopped onion*
> 1½ *cups finely chopped celery*
> 1 *17½-ounce can apricots in*
>   *heavy syrup, drained*
> 2 *tablespoons chutney, preferably*
>   *Major Grey's*
> 1 *cup mayonnaise*
> 1 *tablespoon fresh lemon juice*
> 1½ *teaspoons soy sauce*
>   *Salt*
>   *Freshly ground black pepper*
> 1½ *cups chopped toasted pecans*

Combine the chicken with the onion and celery. In a blender or food processor, puree the drained apricots with the chutney. Add the mayonnaise, lemon juice, and soy sauce and combine. Season to taste with salt and pepper.

Fold the dressing into the chicken mixture. Fold in the pecans or sprinkle them over each portion when you serve.

GRITS AND
GOAT CHEESE TIMBALE
SERVES 6

Grits and eggs take well to each other, and this very graceful, pretty, light-tasting custard is particularly nice for a special party. It is typical of the kind of meal my mother-in-law, Celeste Dupree, serves for a lawn party luncheon in her garden in Social Circle, Georgia. I like the way it combines traditional grits with an upscale local ingredient (there is a goat cheese farm within ten miles of Celeste's home) in a dish that will cause some conversation.

½ cup grits, cooked in milk
  according to package directions
7 ounces goat cheese
1 egg
2 tablespoons finely chopped
  fresh thyme
Salt
Freshly ground black pepper

SORREL SAUCE
½ cup heavy cream
½ cup sour cream
2 bunches sorrel, watercress, or basil
Salt
Freshly ground white pepper

Preheat the oven to 350°F.

Generously butter 6 half-cup molds or ramekins. In a bowl, combine the hot grits, cheese, egg, thyme, salt, and pepper. Spoon into the prepared molds and place them in a large baking dish; add enough hot water to reach halfway up the sides of the molds. Bake for 30 minutes. Remove from the oven and cool slightly before unmolding.

To make the sauce, combine the heavy cream and the sour cream in a heavy saucepan.

Bring to a boil over medium-high heat. Reduce the heat and simmer until reduced by about half, about 10 minutes.

Meanwhile, bring a large pot of water to the boil. Wash and stem the sorrel, watercress, or basil, drop into the boiling water, and blanch for about 1 minute; drain well then pat dry with paper towels.

When the cream has reduced, place it in a blender or food processor and add the sorrel. Process until well pureed and smooth. Sea-son to taste with the salt and white pepper. Serve hot with the warm timbales.

NOTE: The timbales are best made just be-fore serving, but the sauce can be made a day or two ahead. If fresh sorrel and basil are out of season, substitute a good tomato sauce.

OPPOSITE AND ABOVE: *Grits and Goat Cheese Timbale is a delicate starter for an outdoor luncheon party.*

Asparagus
Martha Washington's Booke of Cookery *offers a recipe for pickling "green sparragus." It instructs the reader to "hould ye roots in your hands and dip in ye green ends whilst ye water boyls. Soe doe by every bundle you have, & when yr sparragus is cold, put it into a glass with verges & salt, and it will keep all ye year." Verges is an acidic sauce based on unripe grapes with lemon or sorrel juice; vinegar would be the modern equivalent.*

GRILLED ASPARAGUS
SERVES 4 TO 6

This is a particularly modern, fresh-tasting way to serve an old-time Southern vegetable. Use leftovers cold in a salad. If only the larger, thick-stalked asparagus are available, you might want to blanch them first.

1 pound fresh asparagus
½ cup olive oil
1 tablespoon chopped fresh basil leaves
½ teaspoon chopped fresh thyme
2 teaspoons chopped fresh parsley
1 green onion, finely chopped

Prepare a grill.

Snap off the tough asparagus bottoms. Place the asparagus in a large plastic bag or in a shallow glass dish. In a small mixing bowl, combine the olive oil, basil, thyme, parsley, and green onion and pour over the asparagus. Marinate for at least 30 minutes, then drain the asparagus and grill the spears about 5 to 7 minutes, turning 2 or 3 times.

GRILLED MARINATED CHICKEN BREASTS OR CORNISH HENS
SERVES 6

Herbs grow outdoors at least nine months of the year in the South and many grow year round. This wonderful marinade incorporates ingredients used since Colonial days, contrasting the cool tang of lemon juice with the heat of the spices. The marinade gets spicier the longer it sits, so if you plan on making it ahead to use later, watch out.

¼ cup vegetable or olive oil
¼ cup fresh lemon juice
1 tablespoon chopped fresh oregano
1 teaspoon ground coriander seed
1 teaspoon red pepper flakes
4 garlic cloves, finely chopped
  Salt
  Freshly ground black pepper
6 boneless, skinless chicken breasts or 2 Rock Cornish hens, cut into quarters

In a large bowl, whisk together the oil and lemon juice. Add the oregano, coriander, red pepper flakes, and garlic. Whisk again to blend and season to taste with salt and pepper. Add the chicken breasts or Rock Cornish hens to the marinade, cover, and marinate at least 30 to 45 minutes before grilling. Remove the chicken from the marinade, reserving the remaining marinade, and place the fowl, skin side to the heat, on a hot grill or under a broiler. Cook 5 to 10 minutes on each side. While the chicken grills, transfer the marinade to a small saucepan and bring to a rolling boil; set aside.

Serve the chicken warm or cold, with the sauce on the side.

PIPERADE
SERVES 6 TO 8

Since few of us eat eggs every day anymore, the Vidalia onions, sweet peppers, and country ham wrapped in tenderly cooked eggs make this a special treat. It has been included in Southern recipe books, like the *Virginia Housewife*, for centuries. I use this as a starter, summer lunch, or light supper.

3 tablespoons butter or drippings
2 onions, chopped
4 garlic cloves, chopped
3 large red bell peppers, seeded and
    cut in ¼-×-3-inch strips
2 small hot green chiles, seeded and
    chopped
1 pound tomatoes, seeded and chopped
2 tablespoons chopped fresh oregano
16 eggs, lightly beaten
¼ pound baked or country ham,
    cut in ¼-inch strips
    Salt
    Freshly ground black pepper
6 to 8 slices bread, toasted and brushed
    with butter or oil and garlic.

Heat the butter in a heavy frying pan. Add the onions and garlic, and cook over medium heat until soft and golden, about 5 minutes. Add the bell peppers and chiles, and cook until soft, about 15 minutes. Add the tomatoes and the oregano. Cover, and cook until very soft. Remove the cover, and add the eggs and ham. Stir gently for a few minutes until the eggs are lightly cooked and scrambled, but not hard. Season to taste with salt and pepper. Serve over toast.

SUMMER SQUASH SOUFFLÉ
SERVES 6 TO 8

Tender summer squashes—yellow crookneck and zucchini—are very suited to fluffy soufflélike side dishes that are good for lunches as well as family dinners.

2 pounds yellow crookneck squash or
    zucchini, sliced ½ inch thick
1 medium onion, coarsely chopped
½ cup water
2 tablespoons butter, melted
3 eggs, lightly beaten
¾ cup half-and-half
¾ cup cracker crumbs
¼ cup freshly grated imported
    Parmesan cheese
    Salt
    Freshly ground black pepper
¼ cup finely chopped pecans

Preheat the oven to 350°F.

Place the squash, onion, and water in a medium saucepan. Cover and cook over medium heat until tender, about 10 minutes. Mash with a spoon, potato masher, or in a food processor; you should have 1½ cups. Transfer to a large bowl and add the melted butter, eggs, half-and-half, ½ cup cracker crumbs, and the Parmesan cheese. Season to taste with salt and pepper. Pour into a well-buttered 2-quart baking dish and bake 30 minutes. (The soufflé may be made ahead to this point and reheated.) Combine the pecans and the remaining ¼ cup cracker crumbs. Sprinkle over the casserole and bake 15 minutes more. It is best served right away but may be made ahead several days or frozen and reheated.

MINTED MELON RING

SERVES 6

It's hard to think of a summer garden party or church supper without a "congealed salad"—the unglamorous name for the cool, soothing gelatin concoctions for which the South is famed.

  2 envelopes unflavored gelatin
  2 cups fresh orange juice
  ½ cup sugar
  ½ cup fresh lemon juice
  ¼ cup finely chopped mint leaves
  3 cups melon balls (cantaloupe,
       honeydew, or a mix)
  HONEY LIME DRESSING
  ¼ cup honey
  ¼ cup lime juice
  1 cup sour cream or plain yogurt
       Fresh mint leaves, for garnish

Place the gelatin, 1 cup orange juice, and the sugar in a small saucepan. Place over low heat and cook until the gelatin and sugar are dissolved; it may simmer, but don't let it boil. Remove from the heat and add the lemon juice, the remaining 1 cup orange juice, and the chopped mint. Place over a pan of ice water

and stir 5 to 10 minutes, or until the gelatin starts to thicken. Gently fold in 1 cup melon balls. Turn into an oiled 4-cup ring mold and refrigerate until set, about 4 hours.

Meanwhile, blend the honey, lime juice, and sour cream in a small bowl and chill.

To serve, unmold the ring onto a chilled plate, fill the center with the remaining melon balls, and garnish with fresh mint leaves. Pass the Honey Lime Dressing separately.

CRAB AND EGGPLANT SOUFFLÉ

MAKES EIGHT ½-CUP SERVINGS

This very pretty soufflé is light and fluffy. The unusual combination of ingredients and textures produces a perfectly delightful starter or side dish. For more drama, add 2 extra egg yolks and whites and prepare as for a soufflé.

  1 large or 2 small eggplants
  ½ pound fresh lump crabmeat,
       picked over for shells
  2 tablespoons butter
  2 tablespoons all-purpose flour
  1 cup half-and-half
       Salt
       Freshly ground black pepper
  2 teaspoons Creole seafood
       seasoning (optional)
  1 teaspoon Worcestershire sauce
  1 teaspoon grated onion
  ½ cup freshly grated imported
       Parmesan cheese
  2 eggs, separated

Preheat the oven to 375°F.

Cut the eggplant in half lengthwise. Place, cut side down, on a lightly oiled baking sheet

and bake 30 to 45 minutes, or until soft. Let cool. Scoop out the flesh and discard the skins. Chop the eggplant and place it in a mixing bowl with the crabmeat. Refrigerate until needed.

While the eggplant bakes, make the white sauce. Over medium-low heat, melt the butter in a saucepan. Add the flour and cook briefly, stirring. Add the half-and-half and bring to the boil, stirring constantly until thickened. Remove from the heat and add the salt, pepper, Creole seasoning, if using, Worcestershire, grated onion, and cheese to the hot mixture. Set aside to cool.

Stir the egg yolks into the sauce. The souf-flé may be made ahead several hours to this point, covered, and refrigerated. When ready to serve, add the crab and eggplant. In a separate bowl, beat the egg whites to stiff peaks, then fold into the cooled soufflé mixture.

Place the mixture in 8 buttered individual ramekins or a buttered 4-cup casserole dish. Bake 15 to 20 minutes for small soufflés, 30 minutes for a large one.

OPPOSITE: *A cooling Minted Melon Ring garnished with fresh mint.* ABOVE: *Individual Crab and Egg-plant Soufflés.*

CLOVERLEAF ROLLS
MAKES 24 ROLLS

Special meals deserve these pretty, light, flavorful yeast rolls, shaped in cloverleafs so pieces can be broken off and buttered. (The dough may be made ahead 1 or 2 days and kept in the refrigerator, then shaped, doubled, and baked.)

> 5 to 6 cups bread flour
> 2 packages rapid-rise yeast
> 1 cup milk
> ½ cup sugar
> ½ cup (1 stick) butter
> 2 teaspoons salt
> 3 eggs
> Melted butter (optional)

Preheat the oven to 400°F.

Grease two 12-cup muffin tins.

In a large mixing bowl, combine 3 cups of the flour and the yeast. In a saucepan, heat the milk, sugar, butter, and salt to 120°F., then add to the yeast mixture. Mix in the eggs. Beat or process in a food processor for 1 minute. Add enough of the remaining flour to make a stiff dough. Turn out on a lightly floured surface and knead until smooth and elastic. Place in an oiled plastic bag or in a lightly greased bowl and turn to coat. (At this point the dough can be refrigerated, to be shaped at a later time.) Seal or cover with plastic wrap, and let rise in a warm place until doubled. Punch down the dough, cover, and let rest for 10 minutes. To shape into cloverleafs, divide the dough in fourths, and form each portion into eighteen 1-inch balls. (Roll each ball to make a smooth top.) Place 3 balls in each greased muffin cup. They should fit easily. Let rise until doubled. Bake 10 to 12 minutes, until golden brown. Brush the tops with melted butter, if desired. Cool on a wire rack.

NOTE: The rolls freeze well. Simply reheat them in the oven for 5 to 10 minutes at 350°F.

BAPS
MAKES 20

In my classes at the London Cordon Bleu I was amazed that these rolls I thought of as Southern—for they'd been in many a Southern cookbook—were of English origin. They were the only roll I served at my restaurant in Social Circle, Georgia, in the seventies. I like this dainty size but they can be made much larger.

> ¾ cup warm water
>   (105°F. to 115°F.)
> 1 package active dry yeast
> 1 teaspoon sugar
> 1 teaspoon salt
> ¾ cup warm milk
> ¼ cup (½ stick) butter
> 4 to 5 cups bread flour

Preheat the oven to 350°F.

In a mixing bowl, combine ¼ cup warm water with the yeast and sugar. When the yeast is dissolved, add the rest of the warm water, the salt, milk, and butter. Stir in enough of the flour to make a soft dough. Turn out onto a floured surface and knead until elastic and smooth as a baby's bottom. Place in an oiled plastic bag or bowl and turn to coat. Let stand until doubled, about 1 hour. Punch down the dough and shape into 20 small rolls. Place the rolls on a greased baking sheet. Let rise until doubled. Dust with flour and bake 20 minutes, or until very lightly browned on top and cooked through. The baked rolls freeze well.

SPRING GARDEN CAKE
MAKES 1 CAKE

A garden club meeting would be a perfect place for this beautiful bicolored cake trimmed with sugar-dipped pansies. It combines an angel food cake batter with a limed yellow batter to make a wonderfully delicate but flavorful cake. A variation of the most popular cake in my television series, *New Southern Cooking*, this nearly fat-free cake is a grand dessert for a birthday as well as an I'll-bring-the-dessert occasion. It takes a bit of organization but is simple if you do it step by step, and it freezes well. *Do not* use a nonstick or greased tube pan, as the cake will fall.

WHITE BATTER
1¼ cups cake flour or soft wheat flour
1¾ cups sugar
1¾ cups egg whites (12 to 14 large eggs)
1½ teaspoons cream of tartar
¼ teaspoon salt
1½ teaspoons vanilla extract

YELLOW BATTER
5 egg yolks
2 tablespoons soft wheat flour
2 tablespoons sugar
1 tablespoon grated lime peel
(no white attached)

JEWELED LIME SAUCE
½ cup sugar
2 tablespoons cornstarch
1 cup water
2 teaspoons grated lime peel
(no white attached)
2 tablespoons fresh lime juice
1 tablespoon butter

*Candied Violets and Pansies
(page 28), for garnish*

Preheat the oven to 375°F.

For the white batter, sift the flour and ¾ cup sugar together 3 times on a piece of wax paper. Set aside. In a large mixing bowl, whisk the egg whites, cream of tartar, and salt until soft peaks form. Gradually beat in 1 cup sugar, and continue to beat until very stiff peaks form. Sift about one-quarter of the flour mixture over the egg whites, and gently fold it in. Repeat with the remaining flour mixture, a quarter at a time. Fold in the vanilla. Transfer a third of the white batter to another large mixing bowl and reserve.

For the yellow batter, in a separate bowl, beat the egg yolks, flour, and sugar until thick and pale yellow. Stir in the lime peel. Fold in ½ cup of the reserved white batter to soften. Pour the egg yolk mixture over the reserved white batter, and gently fold until blended.

Ladle the white and yellow batters alternately into an ungreased tube pan. Run a knife gently through the batter to eliminate air pockets and to swirl the two batters. Bake in the lower third of the oven until lightly brown, about 35 to 40 minutes. Invert the pan until cool. When completely cool, run a thin knife up and down between cake and pan to loosen, and turn onto a cake plate. (The cake can be frozen at this point.)

To make the glaze, cook the sugar, cornstarch, and water over medium heat until just boiled, smooth, and thickened. Add the lime peel, juice, and butter; heat until warm. Pour the glaze on top of the cake to drizzle down the sides or serve it warm on the side. Garnish with candied violets and candied pansies.

CANDIED VIOLETS AND PANSIES
MAKES 2 DOZEN

There are a few tricks to candying flowers successfully. First, cut your flowers the day before you intend to candy them, leaving some stem on the flower. Place the cut ends of the stems in a small vase of water, and refrigerate overnight. This will stabilize the flowers so they hold their shape. Dry weather makes more predictable candied flowers than humid.

1 *egg white, lightly beaten*
2 *dozen violets and/or pansies,*
    washed and dried
    Granulated sugar

With a pastry brush, paint the flowers all over with the egg white.

Sprinkle the flowers with plain granulated sugar, being careful not to let the petals stick together, and place, stem down, on a small grid-type cooking rack to hold up the flower heads while they dry. This will take about 2 days. Store the candied flowers up to a year in paper candy cups in an airtight container.

Spring Garden Cake sprinkled with candied flowers is a fitting finale for a garden club meeting.

RASPBERRY TART
MAKES ONE 9-INCH TART

To me, raspberries are near the top of the list of nature's delights. With new varieties available, they now come down fresh from the Georgia/Carolina mountains several times a year. I especially love them in this simple tart casing. The tart may be assembled and refrigerated several hours in advance.

1 recipe Basic Piecrust (page 192)
1 egg
1 3-ounce package cream cheese, softened
½ cup sour cream
2 tablespoons confectioners' sugar
   Grated peel of 1 orange
      (no white attached)
2 tablespoons Framboise or Chambord
      (raspberry liqueur) (optional)
2 pints fresh raspberries
⅓ cup red currant jelly
1 tablespoon water or Framboise

Preheat the oven to 350° F.

Roll out the pie dough to fit a 9-inch pie pan. Line the pastry-lined pan with crumpled wax paper or foil and add beans, rice, or pie weights to weigh down the bottom and sides. Bake until the crust loses its translucent quality, about 15 minutes, and remove from the oven. Remove the paper and weights and cool.

Mix together the egg, cream cheese, sour cream, confectioners' sugar, orange peel, and liqueur, if using, in a food processor or mixer until smooth. Spread over the bottom of the tart shell and bake 15 to 20 minutes, until just set but not brown. Cool.

Arrange the raspberries in the tart shell. Heat the jelly and water in a saucepan over low heat until melted and smooth. Brush over the top of the tart, coating the berries well. Serve chilled or at room temperature.

TASSIES
MAKES 24

These tiny tartlets with a cream cheese crust are called tassies, particularly in the Deep South near Florida and south Georgia. They are equally delicious filled with the golden pecan mixture or the tangy lemon chess filling topped with raspberries—a favorite of President Clinton's.

PASTRY DOUGH
1 3-ounce package cream cheese,
      softened
8 tablespoons (1 stick) butter, softened
1 cup sifted all-purpose flour

PECAN FILLING
1 egg
½ cup dark brown sugar, packed
1 tablespoon butter
1 teaspoon vanilla extract
⅛ teaspoon salt
⅔ cup chopped pecans

LEMON CHESS
FILLING
½ cup sugar
1 egg
2 tablespoons butter
2 tablespoons heavy cream
½ teaspoon vanilla extract
   Juice and grated peel of ½ lemon
      (no white attached)
24 raspberries

Preheat the oven to 325°F.

Mix together the cream cheese and butter in a small bowl or food processor. Add the flour and blend thoroughly. Chill if hard to handle. Divide the dough and roll into 24 balls, wrap the balls in plastic wrap, and chill again briefly. Place each ball in a tiny, ungreased fluted tart pan or miniature muffin cup and press the dough with your fingertips against the bottoms and sides—or use a "tart

Tassies

These delightful little tarts figure prominently in my recollections of a luncheon I prepared many years ago for the mother of the man I was seeing at the time. My good linens were on the table, the china was flowered, and the tiny vases held softly draping flowers. I wanted beauty, and grace, and charm to be in each part of the meal, but in reality I hadn't been able to plan as I had wished; I had to rely on what was in the freezer: frozen golden tassies and the shells for the raspberries, all done at the last minute.

"Golden tassies!" the older woman exclaimed. "I wasn't going to eat any dessert, but you've tempted me down memory lane." The flowering tree above the deck added shade and the summer heat had faded into a welcome fall breeze. The ice melted in our glasses as we slowly ate the tarts, relishing the caramel-wrapped pecan inside the tender tiny crusts and spoke softly, sweetly, carefully of the man we both loved.

tamper" gadget if you have one. Place the pans in the refrigerator to chill while you prepare your preferred filling.

For the golden tassies pecan filling, beat together the egg, brown sugar, butter, vanilla, and salt in a mixing bowl until all the lumps are gone. Place half the pecans in the dough-lined pans and top with the egg mixture. Dot with the remaining pecans. Bake 25 minutes, or until the filling is set. Cool 5 minutes on a rack, and remove from the pans before they are cool.

For the raspberry tassies chess filling, beat together the sugar, egg, butter, cream, vanilla, lemon juice, and peel. Spoon into the prepared pans. Bake 25 to 30 minutes, or until the filling is set. Remove from the pans before they cool completely and finish cooling on a wire rack. Place a raspberry in the depression in the center of each tart and refrigerate until serving.

These tassies will keep several days closely wrapped or 3 months in the freezer.

SUSAN'S COCONUT CUSTARD PIE
SERVES 8

Susan Rice served this to us in her 1830 home on Edisto Island. It's light and melts in your mouth.

> 6 tablespoons (¾ stick) butter
> 3 eggs, beaten
> ¼ cup buttermilk
> ½ cup sugar
> 1½ teaspoons vanilla extract
> 1 cup flaked coconut
> 1 recipe Basic Piecrust (page 192)

Preheat the oven to 375°F.

Melt the butter. Mix together the eggs, buttermilk, sugar, vanilla, and coconut and add to the melted butter. Pour into the unbaked piecrust. Bake for 10 minutes, reduce heat to 300°F., and bake for 35 minutes or until the middle is set.

Dishes of Fishes

THERE IS NOTHING QUITE LIKE FRESH FISH, whether catfish caught by a boy sitting on the side of a pond, string tied to a pole, or shrimp pulled in by nets, or crabs pulled out of pots down our Southern seashore. The South is defined by its waterways, from coastal tide pools to the Florida Keys and the venerable Mississippi River. And each yields up its own distinctive bounty.

The importance of fish in Southern cuisine is evident even in the earliest Colonial cookbooks. We're known for our fried fish and shrimp, but we also love our crabs steamed and our fish grilled, and who can top boiled shrimp and crawfish in their shells?

The fish that was served when I was young was local trout or perch, caught fresh

LEFT: *Frogmore Stew, a favorite dish from the Carolina coast.* RIGHT: *A shrimping fleet.*

by a fishing friend or relative. My mother was never enamored of the fish sticks that came along later or the narrow packages of frozen

fish that were nearly tasteless when defrosted and cooked. (Now, of course, we can get frozen fish that smells and tastes fresh, and salmon is seen on Southern tables as often as amberjack, scamp, flounder, or redfish.)

Of course a meal of seafood or fish often involves more than a trip to the fishmonger. As a child my mother told me of slipping out with her sister early in the morning, returning home about 5 A.M. with a line of fish from the river, ready to be scaled and fried for breakfast. My father, a Yankee, often spoke of overlooking the river from his parents' house on the cliffs where nets had been set for shad next to the ferry boat station. In my pursuit of fresh fare from the waters I've gone gigging for flounder, caught crabs off a dock, and stood all day staring into the shallow water of the Florida Keys looking for signs of (sadly inedible) bonefish. I've watched Florida tuna get weighed and graded to be shipped all over the world. And I've gone out on shrimp boats, those vessels that move through the early morning light like pirate ships hovering offshore. The spoils of my efforts, whether simply boiled and drenched in butter or served up in more elaboate fashion, never fail to satisfy.

SHRIMP AND OKRA IN A TANGY BUTTER SAUCE
SERVES 6 TO 8

This recipe was developed for some German guests who called at the last moment when their plane was delayed at the airport. I wanted to serve them something Southern, so I served this along with Corn Bread with Red Peppers and Rosemary (page 102). Let your guests peel their own shrimp, but be sure to provide plenty of clean napkins.

1¼ pounds okra, tipped and tailed to
    make 1 pound
1 cup (2 sticks) butter
3 large garlic cloves, chopped
1 teaspoon cayenne pepper
½ to 1 tablespoon chopped fresh
    marjoram
½ to 1 tablespoon chopped fresh
    rosemary
2 pounds large shrimp, in the shell
    Salt
    Freshly ground black pepper

Bring a pot of water to the boil, add the okra, and boil 2 minutes. Drain and refresh under cold water. Drain again and set aside. Melt the butter in a large skillet. Add the garlic, cayenne, marjoram, and rosemary and cook over medium heat for a few minutes without browning. Add the shrimp and cook until they are pink on one side, about 2 minutes; turn. Add the drained okra and cook until the shrimp are pink on both sides and cooked through and the okra is reheated, about 3 minutes. Season to taste with salt and pepper and serve immediately.

GRACE'S FRIED SHRIMP
SERVES 6 TO 8 AS A STARTER OR 4 AS AN ENTRÉE

I hate to tell this story on my dear friend Grace Reeves, who passed away last year, but she told it on herself, and it may help a novice cook. As a bride nearly sixty years ago, she knew nothing about cooking seafood. Truth be told, she never ate shrimp. But her husband loved them, and she aimed to please him, so she dutifully bought her first pound of shrimp, frying them so they would be just right when he walked in the door of their trailer. He burst in eagerly, smelling them. Then he spied what she was doing. He stopped short. "Grace," he said, "what ARE you doing?" "What do you think I'm doing?" she queried, "I'm frying shrimp for your supper!" "Aah, Grace," he cried, "you must *peel* them FIRST, honey."

2 pounds medium or large shrimp,
    peeled and deveined
¾ cup all-purpose flour
2 teaspoons salt
½ cup milk, or more as needed
1 egg
¼ cup cornmeal
½ to 1 teaspoon cayenne pepper
    Peanut oil for frying

In a medium bowl, mix together the shrimp, flour, salt, milk, egg, cornmeal, and cayenne pepper, adding an additional tablespoon or two of milk if needed to make a nice batter. Fill an iron skillet no more than half full of oil and heat to 350°F. Add the shrimp, in batches if necessary, to the hot oil. Do not crowd the pan. (The oil should cover the shrimp.) Fry until golden, about 2 to 3 minutes, turning once. Remove and drain on paper towels. Serve hot.

Boiled
Crawfish

I've been to many a wonderful crawfish boil, but perhaps the best was one I attended while doing a segment on rice and crawfish for the New Southern Cooking *series. Many rice farmers also cultivate crawfish once their rice has been harvested; the crawfish eat the rice stubble, making a second crop for the farmer. That day we planted rice from a crop duster. The rice, dyed pink to indicate it has been chemically treated, contrasted vividly with the blue waters flooding the fields below. Next, we toured a pond in which crawfish had been seeded after harvesting the rice.*

It was a beautiful, magical day.

For lunch we went to a crawfish boil. Our hosts had prepared a monumental meal, the focal point of which was, of course, the crawfish. On a large fire built in the shade they had a tall red steamer-type kettle in which water was boiling vigorously. They added a commercial crab boil or Creole seasoning to the pot, then potatoes. When the potatoes were nearly done, fresh corn and finally the crawfish went into the pot.

We sat at a large picnic table inside a screened porch and dipped our crawfish in butter as we peeled them. They were perfectly cooked (an overcooked crawfish is hard to peel) and we ate with gusto.

BOILED CRAWFISH
SERVES 8 TO 10

Since you should plan on 2 to 3 pounds of crawfish (yielding ½ pound of tails) per person, it's hard to cook them all at once. Instead, cook them in batches, removing the barely cooked crawfish to a Styrofoam ice chest, which allows them to continue cooking to just the right degree.

16 *pounds crawfish in the shell*
½ *pound commercial crab boil or Creole seasoning*
24 *small new potatoes, unpeeled but well scrubbed*
12 *ears corn, shucked*

Wash the crawfish. Bring a large pot (preferably one with a drainer) of water to the boil with the crab boil. Add the potatoes and boil until nearly tender, about 15 minutes. Add the corn and then the crawfish and cook for 3 to 4 minutes, then drain and transfer to a large Styrofoam container to finish cooking.

Alternate method: Cook the crawfish first in the seasoned water, cooking them in batches until nearly done, then removing and keeping warm in the cooler. Place the potatoes in a string bag, put it in the simmering water, and cook for 15 minutes. Add the corn in another string bag and cook approximately 5 minutes longer. Drain the corn and potatoes and serve with the crawfish, plenty of napkins, and a good dose of laughter.

STUFFED CATFISH
SERVES 6 TO 8

Most commercially available catfish is now farm-raised and devoid of the muddy taste for which it was known, which suits most people better. The flesh of the farm-raised fish is more delicate in texture as well. However, it is still an ugly fish, with a big head and catlike whiskers. We chop off the head as fast as we can, serving just the sides, cut into fillets or left on the bone, according to size and personal preference.

Now that catfish is a dressed-up fish, there are many ways to serve it. Of all of Mary Hataway's recipes that we serve at the Richmond Marriott, this is the most popular. It's tender, moist, delicious, and very different.

STUFFING

2 tablespoons unsalted butter
2 tablespoons vegetable oil
½ cup finely chopped onion
½ cup chopped scallions
1 cup finely chopped mushrooms
½ cup breadcrumbs
½ cup plus 2 tablespoons grated
    Swiss cheese
½ cup plus 2 tablespoons freshly
    grated imported Parmesan cheese
½ cup well-packed chopped parsley
¼ cup heavy cream
1½ teaspoons dried tarragon
¼ teaspoon salt
¼ teaspoon freshly ground black pepper
    Vegetable oil for deep-frying

6 to 8 catfish fillets, pounded lightly
1 to 2 eggs, lightly beaten
1 to 2 cups Italian seasoned
    breadcrumbs

To make the stuffing, heat the butter and oil in a sauté pan. Add the onion and scallions and sauté over medium heat until they begin to soften, about 5 minutes. Squeeze the liquid out of the chopped mushrooms, add them to the pan, and sauté until dry. Remove the pan from the heat and add the breadcrumbs, Swiss cheese, Parmesan, parsley, cream, tarragon, salt, and pepper. Mix well.

Preheat the oven to 400°F.

In a deep pan, heat 2 to 3 inches of vegetable oil to 350°F. Place about 2 tablespoons stuffing in the center of each fillet and roll up. Brush the fillets with the beaten egg and lightly roll in the seasoned breadcrumbs. Deep-fry in the hot oil just long enough to brown the breadcrumbs, then transfer to a baking dish and place in the oven for about 10 minutes to finish cooking.

FLOUNDER OR CATFISH WITH PECAN SAUCE
SERVES 4 TO 6

Delicate, special, and very simple, this is a lovely treat. If the fillets are very thin, fold them in half, skin side inside, to keep the flesh moist.

1½ pounds flounder, catfish, or
    red snapper fillets
1 tablespoon fresh lemon juice
PECAN SAUCE
6 tablespoons butter
½ cup chopped pecans
2 heaping tablespoons chopped
    fresh parsley
3 tablespoons fresh lemon juice
1 teaspoon Worcestershire sauce
½ teaspoon grated lemon peel
    (no white attached)

Preheat the oven to 400°F.

Lightly grease a baking dish large enough to hold the fish in a single layer and arrange the fillets in the pan. Add enough water to come halfway up the fish, then add the lemon juice. Cover with a greased piece of wax paper. Bake 10 minutes for every inch of thickness. Transfer the fish to a hot platter.

While the fish is baking, prepare the Pecan Sauce. In a small frying pan, melt the butter over low heat. Add the pecans, parsley, lemon juice, Worcestershire, and lemon peel and cook for 1 to 2 minutes, until the sauce is heated through and the nuts are toasted. Spoon the Pecan Sauce over the hot fillets and serve immediately.

GRILLED BARBECUED AMBERJACK
SERVES 4

Amberjack, a firm fish that is becoming increasingly popular in the South, is one of those fish that used to be tossed back when we went deep-sea fishing. "Throw it back," the fisherman among us would say, "it's a trash fish." We would stare forlornly into the deep blue, wondering why on earth we couldn't just *try* cooking it. Now, it turns out, there was no reason except ignorance. Any firm fish can be substituted, such as grouper or scrod. This is yet another of Margaret Ann's wonderful creations.

½ cup "N.C.-Style" Barbecue Sauce (page 171)
¼ cup soy sauce
1½ to 2 pounds amberjack fillets

Combine the barbecue sauce and soy sauce. Mix well. Add the fish fillets, and marinate up to 30 minutes.

Preheat the broiler or grill.

Grill the fish 10 minutes per inch of thickness, measured at the thickest point, turning the fish halfway through the cooking time.

While the fish is grilling, place the marinade in a heavy saucepan over high heat and bring to the boil. Boil until reduced by about half. Remove from the heat.

Serve grilled fish with the sauce.

BAKED FISH DAUFUSKIE
SERVES 4

Carl Campbell's family has called South Carolina its home for many generations. A fine chef as well as home cook of his regional cuisine, Carl went north to seek his fame and fortune, but has returned home to hang his toque at The South Carolina Yacht Club. Daufuskie is an island known for its Gullah dialect—and good cooking.

4 grouper fillets (about 1½ to 2 pounds)
1 medium onion, thinly sliced lengthwise from root to stem
½ cup mayonnaise
2 tablespoons Dijon mustard
1 tablespoon fresh lemon juice
Paprika to taste

Preheat the oven to 400°F.

Pat the fish fillets dry, and place them on a greased baking sheet. Cover the fillets with the sliced onions. In a small mixing bowl, combine the mayonnaise, mustard, and lemon juice and stir until smooth. Spoon the mixture over the fish and the onions.

Bake 10 minutes per inch of thickness. Remove from the oven, and place under the broiler for 2 minutes. Sprinkle with paprika and serve.

EASY OYSTER STEW FOR A
WINTER'S NIGHT
SERVES 4 TO 6

Although storms have wreaked havoc on our oyster beds in recent years, South Carolinians still swear they can tell the difference between each cove's bounty—and Apalachicola Floridians also swear their oysters have the best flavor. What could be more satisfying on a cold night than this elegant rich soup we call a stew? The jolt of bourbon zips up the dish and warms up the diner!

> 1 cup chicken broth or stock
> 2 cups heavy cream
> 1 tablespoon bourbon (optional)
> ½ tablespoon freshly ground
>   black pepper
> 36 oysters with their liquor, strained
>   Salt
>   Finely chopped fresh flat-leaf
>   parsley, for garnish

In a medium saucepan, bring the broth or stock to the boil over high heat. Boil until reduced by about a third, about 5 minutes. Lower the heat, add the cream, bourbon, and black pepper, and simmer very slowly 30 to 45 minutes to mellow the flavor. Do not boil.

When ready to serve, add the oysters and as much of their strained juice as desired and heat just until the edges of the oysters curl. Season to taste with salt. Serve immediately, garnished with the chopped parsley.

GLORIOUS SEAFOOD STEW
SERVES 4 TO 6

Stew is an inglorious name for delicious thick broth full of shrimp and scallops and studded with tomatoes and herbs. Saffron is expensive these days, but then so are scallops and shrimp—also worth the cost.

- ¼ teaspoon saffron threads
- 1 cup white wine or seafood stock
- ¼ cup olive oil
- 1 to 2 large onions, cut in ½-inch pieces
- 2 to 4 garlic cloves, finely chopped
- 1 1-pound, 12-ounce can peeled plum tomatoes, coarsely chopped
- 1 bay leaf
- 1 to 2 teaspoons sugar (optional)
  Salt
  Freshly ground black pepper
- 2 to 3 tablespoons finely chopped fresh basil
- 2 to 3 tablespoons finely chopped fresh oregano or thyme
- 1 pound fresh shrimp, peeled
- 1 pound fresh sea scallops

Soak the saffron in a little of the wine and set aside. Heat the oil in a large Dutch oven over medium heat, add the onion and garlic, and cook until soft, about 5 to 7 minutes. Add the wine, saffron, tomatoes, and bay leaf and simmer, uncovered, until thickened, about 45 minutes. Season to taste with sugar, if using, salt, and pepper. Add the basil and oregano or thyme, and continue cooking about 10 minutes more to blend the flavors. (The stew may be made ahead to this point and refrigerated or frozen.) When ready to serve, bring the sauce to the boil; add the shrimp and scallops, reduce the heat to a simmer, and cook 2 to 3 minutes—just until the shrimp are pink and the scallops are opaque. Serve immediately.

GEORGIA CRAB SOUP
SERVES 8

Blue crab dominates Southern seafood cuisine. Because the meat must be carefully picked through for shells, lump crab is expensive and therefore considered a treat. If you are lucky, the crabmeat will come with a tiny, bright orange-yellow sprinkling of roe, a lovely garnish for this rich, luscious soup.

- 6 tablespoons (¾ stick) butter
- 2½ cups sliced fresh mushrooms
- 3 tablespoons all-purpose flour
- 3 cups homemade chicken stock or canned chicken broth
- 1½ cups heavy cream
- 12 ounces cooked crabmeat, fresh, canned, or frozen (about 1½ cups), picked over
- ¾ cup freshly grated imported Parmesan cheese
- ¼ cup good-quality dry sherry (optional)
  Salt
  Freshly ground black pepper
  Chopped fresh parsley, for garnish

Melt 3 tablespoons butter in a 10-inch skillet over medium heat; add the mushrooms and cook until soft, about 5 minutes. Remove from the heat and set aside. Melt the remaining 3 tablespoons butter in a heavy 3-quart saucepan over medium heat. Add the flour and stir until blended and smooth. Pour in the chicken stock and cream and cook, stirring, for 8 to 10 minutes, until the mixture thickens and comes to the boil. Reduce the heat and add the crabmeat and sautéed mushrooms. Cook and stir 2 to 3 minutes longer until just heated through. Remove from the heat and stir in the Parmesan, sherry, if using, salt, and pepper. Serve garnished with chopped parsley.

The
Southern
Crab

The blue crab lives up to its unwieldy formal name, Callinectes sapidus, which means "beautiful swimmer" and "tasty"; it truly is the most beautiful and flavorful of the approximately 1,000 crab species. It thrives all along the eastern shore of the United States and, to my mind, the farther south it grows, the better it tastes.

It is an enormous pleasure to throw on a pot of crabs for a casual evening with good friends: papers out on the floor, bowls of mayonnaise and butter, piles and piles of napkins and, just as essential, a large trash can. Everyone joins in hacking and cracking and eating until the crabs are all gone. I also love eating crabs in restaurants that are low-down and dirty and have holes in the center of round tables, with a giant repository for the discarded shells underneath, or buying cooked crabs off the wharfs. A top crab picker can pick a whole crab in under a minute, but I relish the languorous process of drawing the crab swimmers through my teeth, sucking the last drop of flesh from the hardened claws.

A very different but just as enjoyable eating experience is fresh lump crabmeat, separated from the muss and bother. It is a heady indulgence, delicate and yet full of the flavor of the sea, whether in a crab cake or a stuffed crab, or better yet a crab salad or a crab tart, or any of the other infinite variations to which the succulent flesh lends itself.

And don't forget the soft-shell crab. I have watched with awe as the blue crab sheds its shell, backing out of the old garment and leaving it on the sandy floor of the ocean containing nothing of the essence of the exhausted crab lying beside it. In a brief twenty-four hours the crab's new shell hardens; if the soft-shell crab is to be eaten, it must be captured in that twenty-four hours. The "dead men," also called the gills, are frequently (and preferably) removed at the packing house, as are the inedible sand, mouth, and eyes. The rest of the soft-shell is edible and delicious sautéed in butter or broiled or deep-fat fried. If a soft-shell is shipped live it will tend to harden within twenty-four hours as well. Soft-shell crab season is from mid-May to mid-September.

Steamed Hard-Shell Crabs

The first time I went crabbing I was a young woman, very much in love. My sweetheart and I had spent part of the day wandering amidst the fishing boats on the South Carolina coast, talking to shrimpers and fishermen, holding hands in the sun. When we returned to our condo we passed a small boy sitting on the dock, pulling up a crab in his net. He showed us how to bait a piece of string with a bit of fish, and following his example, we caught enough for a delectable supper.

I don't stand on much ceremony on the cooking; I just bring a large pot of water to the boil, add some crab boil (bought in the grocery store), and then the crabs. I keep the water at a simmer until the crabs turn bright red-orange. A grown man can eat up to a dozen, but my limit is about six, and planning on three or four per person is not considered skimpy if it's just a starter. Always have plenty of napkins and melted butter on hand.

LEMON-FRIED SOFT-SHELL CRABS
SERVES 2

These are the crispiest, crunchiest, tangiest, zippiest battered soft-shell crabs you'll ever eat. In making the tartar sauce, always dice the red onion by hand rather than chop it in the food processor to prevent its "bleeding" into the sauce and discoloring it.

JALAPEÑO TARTAR SAUCE
1 cup mayonnaise
¼ cup finely diced red onion
2 tablespoons finely chopped capers
1 to 2 jalapeño peppers, finely diced
1 teaspoon Dijon mustard
* Tabasco sauce*

3 lemons, juiced, plus enough water to equal 1 cup
* Grated peel of 1 lemon (no white attached)*

1 cup all-purpose flour, plus additional for dredging
3 cups vegetable oil or shortening
4 to 6 soft-shell crabs, cleaned and dried

To make the tartar sauce, combine the mayonnaise, onion, capers, jalapeño peppers, mustard, and Tabasco to taste in a medium bowl. Stir until well combined and refrigerate for several hours before serving to develop the flavors.

Combine the lemon juice and water mixture with the lemon peel in a wide, shallow dish. Gradually sift in the 1 cup of flour, whisking constantly.

Pour one inch of oil into a heavy 10-inch skillet and heat it to 350°F. Dredge the crabs in flour, shaking off the excess. Dip the crabs in the lemon batter. Slip them into the hot fat and fry until brown and very crisp, about 2 minutes per side. Drain on paper towels and serve immediately with Jalapeño Tartar Sauce.

FROGMORE STEW
SERVES 8 TO 10

When I visit my brother and his wife in Charleston, South Carolina, they often plan a special treat like this stew for me. It is best saved for a time when you don't mind getting covered with the food you are eating—it's a sloppy, papers-on-the-floor-and-table or beach food, a messy group "eat-with-your-fingers" orgy! I remember fondly one special evening, when the sun setting over the ocean provided a great display of pink and gold, and a group of us sat on the beach, watching and eating, in awe of nature and quietly appreciative of being alive.

Frogmore Stew is named after the place it was first served, "Frogmore" on St. Helene's Island, in Beaufort County, South Carolina. If you want to jazz it up, spread some of the red pepper mayonnaise or dill mayonnaise on the shrimp as you serve it. I do not use the seasoning mix, but my brother and his wife do. I add it as an option for you.

2 pounds hot country sausage,
    preferably links
16 new potatoes (1½ inches in
    circumference), still in their
    skins but scrubbed
30 garlic cloves, peeled
16 medium onions, peeled, halved
    or quartered, roots intact
4 finger-sized hot red peppers, chopped
8 lemons, halved
2 tablespoons seasoning mix,
    such as Old Bay (optional)
6 stalks fresh parsley, leaves removed
1¼ cups apple cider vinegar
    Salt, about 2 teaspoons
    Freshly ground black pepper,
    about 2 to 3 tablespoons

16 ears fresh corn, husked and broken
    into 2 pieces
2 tablespoons hot sauce or Tabasco
    sauce (optional)
6 pounds shrimp in the shell

OPTIONAL CONDIMENTS
    Cocktail Sauce
    Dill Aioli Mayonnaise
    Red Pepper and Chive Mayonnaise
    Sour cream
    Butter

In a skillet, cook the sausages over medium heat until done; set aside, reserving the drippings separately.

Fill a 12-quart stockpot or water bath canner with 5 quarts of water. Bring the water to the boil over high heat. Add the sausage drippings, potatoes, garlic, and onions and return to the boil. Cover and cook for 15 minutes. Add the sausage links, hot peppers, lemons, seasoning mix (if using), parsley stalks, and vinegar. Cover and simmer 15 minutes longer. Add the salt, pepper to taste, and corn and bring quickly back to a rapid boil. Taste and add the hot sauce or Tabasco if desired. Add the shrimp and poach until the shrimp are just done, no more than 5 minutes. Remove and discard the lemons and, if desired, the onions and garlic. Heap the rest into a large bowl, or drain and dish out into individual plates. Serve the broth separately, as a soup.

If desired, serve the stew with the Cocktail Sauce, Dill Aioli Mayonnaise, or Red Pepper and Chive Mayonnaise for the shrimp; the sour cream for the potatoes; and/or the butter for the corn.

COCKTAIL SAUCE
MAKES 4 CUPS

For shrimp or Frogmore Stew, you'll find homemade cocktail sauce is better than store-bought.

2 *cups chili sauce*
2 *cups ketchup*
6 *tablespoons prepared horseradish*
2 *tablespoons Dijon or coarsely
    ground mustard*
1 *teaspoon celery seed*
¼ *cup lemon juice*
3 *tablespoons red wine vinegar
    Salt
    Freshly ground black pepper*

In a large bowl, mix together the chili sauce, ketchup, horseradish, Dijon mustard, celery seed, lemon juice, and red wine vinegar. Adjust seasoning to taste with salt and pepper. Chill for at least 2 hours before serving.

DILL AIOLI MAYONNAISE
MAKES 3 CUPS

This is a marvelous accompaniment for cold shrimp as well as Frogmore Stew.

4 *egg yolks*
½ *teaspoon salt*
½ *teaspoon freshly ground black pepper*
¼ *cup fresh lemon juice*
8 *garlic cloves, crushed*
½ *teaspoon dry mustard*
¼ *teaspoon cayenne pepper*
1½ *cups olive oil*
½ *cup fresh chopped dill
    Salt
    Freshly ground black pepper*

In a food processor, whisk the egg yolks with the salt, pepper, and lemon juice. Add the garlic, dry mustard, and cayenne pepper, and puree until smooth. In a slow steady stream, add the olive oil a little at a time until the mixture becomes thick. Whisk in the chopped dill and season to taste with additional salt and pepper.

RED PEPPER AND CHIVE
MAYONNAISE
MAKES 2 CUPS

This mayonnaise is good for a cheese sandwich as well as Frogmore Stew.

1 *slice white bread*
¼ *cup bottled clam juice*
¼ *teaspoon cayenne pepper*
3 *egg yolks*
½ *head garlic, about 5 cloves,
    peeled and crushed*
¾ *cup olive oil*
1½ *large sweet red bell peppers, roasted,
    peeled, and seeded (page 99)*
¼ *cup chopped chives*
1 *tablespoon lemon juice
    Salt
    Freshly ground black pepper*

Combine the bread and clam juice in a small bowl and sprinkle with the cayenne pepper; let sit until the bread has absorbed the juice. In a food processor, whirl the egg yolks until thick and lemon colored. Add the moistened bread and combine, then blend in the crushed garlic. With the processor running, slowly add the olive oil in a thin steady stream until the mixture becomes thick. When the desired consistency is reached, add the red peppers, chives, and lemon juice. Puree. Season with salt and pepper.

RICHMOND PEPPERED SHRIMP
SERVES 4 TO 6

Occasionally I am sent very special recipes like this one, which combines a number of traditional Southern ingredients with our beloved shrimp. Soybeans are one of our important rotating crops and ginger has been used since Colonial days; it, like horseradish, grows easily here.

6 scallions or green onions, sliced, green and white parts reserved separately
1 tablespoon chopped fresh ginger
1 tablespoon soy sauce
1 tablespoon prepared horseradish
¼ cup tomato sauce
½ teaspoon red pepper flakes
1½ tablespoons peanut oil
1 pound large shrimp, shelled and deveined
Salt
Freshly ground black pepper
Tabasco sauce

In a small bowl, combine the white part of the scallions with the ginger, soy sauce, horseradish, tomato sauce, and red pepper flakes.

Heat the oil in a large sauté pan over moderately high heat. Add the shrimp and cook, stirring, just until pink, about 3 minutes. Add the sauce mixture and cook a few minutes longer, stirring frequently, until the sauce is heated through. Season to taste with salt, pepper, and Tabasco. Serve hot or at room temperature. Garnish with the sliced scallion tops.

NOTE: This dish can be prepared ahead and refrigerated, covered. Reheat quickly before serving.

BROILED SHAD
SERVES 2

Shad is a highly prized fish, with the male being preferred to the female, as the fish is tastier and has more flesh when not carrying roe. Usually, when shad is sold boned it is sold by the side—a wide center piece attached to the skin and two narrow side pieces. It freezes well when fresh. I feel simple broiled shad is the best.

1 side shad
1 teaspoon chopped fresh tarragon
1 teaspoon chopped fresh thyme
1 teaspoon chopped fresh parsley
Salt
Freshly ground black pepper
Lemon juice
Lemon wedges for garnish

Heat the broiler. Place the shad, skin side down, with the 2 smaller pieces enclosed in the center flap, on a broiler pan 6 inches from the heat. Measure the fish, and broil for 10 minutes per inch of thickness, turning once. Sprinkle with tarragon, thyme, and parsley. Season with salt, pepper, and lemon juice. Serve immediately with lemon wedges.

ABOVE: *Richmond Peppered Shrimp.* OPPOSITE: *A carefully boned shad fillet is broiled with herbs and lemon.*

SHAD ROE

SERVES 2 TO 4 DEPENDING ON
THE SIZE OF THE ROE

Available only in the spring when the shad swim up inland rivers like the Ogeechee and Altamaha to spawn, shad roe is prized by connoisseurs of good food. The female fish yields a double roe divided by a thin membrane; when purchased as a double roe, gently separate it into two single roes. It freezes well when fresh. Aficionados agree the best way to cook roe is also the simplest, yielding a moist, tender roe.

4 tablespoons (½ stick) butter
1 double shad roe
    Salt
    Freshly ground black pepper
    Juice of 2 lemons

Heat the butter in a large heavy frying pan until very hot. Season the shad roe with salt and pepper and add to the pan. Slash with a knife to prevent blistering, reduce the heat to low, and cook for 5 minutes. Turn and cook the other side until brown, about 5 minutes longer. The roe should still be pink inside. Pour the lemon juice over and serve.

BENNE AND ORANGE SALMON

SERVES 8 TO 10

Benne (the African word for sesame seed) combines with orange juice to give an extraordinary flavor and texture to this spicily marinated fish. Chill the leftovers and serve on lettuce for an elegant salad.

MARINADE
    Juice of 3 oranges (1 cup)
2 tablespoons ground cumin seed
2 medium onions, coarsely chopped
1 tablespoon coarsely ground fresh
        black pepper
1 teaspoon red pepper flakes
1 teaspoon salt
1 teaspoon Worcestershire sauce
2 teaspoons chopped or grated
        fresh ginger
1 tablespoon chopped fresh thyme

1 3- to 5-pound whole salmon
    Juice and grated peel of 3
        oranges (no white attached)
½ cup toasted sesame seeds

Mix the orange juice, cumin, onions, pepper, red pepper flakes, salt, Worcestershire, ginger, and thyme in a mixing bowl or large plastic bag. Add the salmon and marinate for 45 minutes to 1 hour, refrigerated, turning 2 to 3 times.

Preheat a charcoal grill or the broiler. Measure the thickness of the fish. Grill the salmon 10 minutes per inch of thickness, turning halfway through. Remove from the heat. Meanwhile, heat the orange juice and zest together in a saucepan. Pour the warm juice over the salmon and sprinkle with the sesame seeds. Serve hot.

CRAB TART
SERVES 6 TO 8

This thick tart is creamy and rich, yet delicate at the same time. Although we call it a tart, it is made in a large metal pan, then cut before serving. The unusual pastry recipe is geared for hot weather when butter would melt. This recipe can be multiplied very easily to serve a crowd. A note of warning: For one tart, you can stir together the onion, crab, and cream mixtures and then place the filling in the tart shell. However, if you multiply the recipe, this won't work because the crab will not be evenly divided, so prepare filling separately for multiple tarts.

TART PASTRY

2½ *cups all-purpose flour*
   Rounded ¼ teaspoon sugar
½ *teaspoon salt*
½ *cup (1 stick) unsalted butter, cut into small pieces and kept chilled*
6 *tablespoons vegetable oil*
5 *tablespoons ice water*

CRAB FILLING

2 *tablespoons unsalted butter*
1 *cup chopped scallions, both white and green parts*
⅔ *cup dry vermouth*
10½ *ounces backfin crabmeat, picked over*
10½ *ounces claw crabmeat, picked over*
10 *eggs*
1 *tablespoon salt*
1 *teaspoon freshly ground black pepper*
¼ *cup tomato paste*
4 *cups heavy cream*
¾ *cup grated Swiss cheese*
2 *teaspoons finely chopped fresh tarragon*

Combine the flour, sugar, and salt and mix well. Cut the butter into the flour mixture until the butter is in small flakes. Stir in the oil and ice water. Gather the pastry into a ball and knead several times on the counter until the mixture comes together. Flatten and shape into a rectangle. Wrap in plastic wrap, refrigerate, and let rest for at least 1 hour. Flour a board or the counter. Roll the pastry out into a rectangle to line a 9 × 13-inch metal pan and press into the pan, leaving a slight overhang on the sides. Chill until firm.

Preheat the oven to 350°F. Line the pastry-lined pan with crumpled wax paper or foil and add beans, rice, or pie weights to weigh down the bottom and sides. Bake the tart crust until it loses its translucent quality, about 15 minutes, and remove from the oven. Remove the liner and weights and cool.

To make the filling, melt the butter in a frying pan. Add the scallions and cook 2 or 3 minutes, until slightly softened. With a slotted spoon, transfer the scallions to a bowl and reserve. Add the vermouth to the butter remaining in the pan and stir. Toss in the crab and sauté over the medium-high heat for 2 to 3 minutes, or until the liquid has evaporated. In a bowl, beat together the eggs, salt, pepper, and tomato paste, incorporating the tomato paste thoroughly. Beat in the cream.

Spread the scallions over the partially baked tart crust and top with the crab. Pour the cream and egg mixture over the crab. Stir with a fork to make sure that the mixture is well incorporated into the crab, or the filling will cook in layers. Toss the cheese with the tarragon, and sprinkle over the tart, stirring a little with a fork to ensure that the cheese does not just sit on the top.

Bake until the tart is firm around the edges and fairly firm in the center, about 45 to 50 minutes. The center will finish cooking as the tart cools. Cut into squares when the tart has settled and cooled slightly.

Comfort Foods

AT THE CORE OF SOUTHERN CULTURE IS A culinary tradition of foods cherished not only for the nourishment they provide, but also for what they represent. These comfort foods are inextricably entwined with memories of home in nearly every Southern psyche.

Many of the best-loved comfort foods hearken back to a time when the region could hardly sustain itself agriculturally in the aftermath of a brutal war, when there was no cash to supplement the meager offerings of the farms and smokehouses; these foods satisfied the body and comforted the soul. From necessities, these dishes have come to symbolize the strength and resilience of the South.

Turnip and collard greens, hog jowls (which portend good luck), and black-eyed peas are all traditional New Year's fare. But perhaps even more important, black-eyed peas when combined with

LEFT: *Clabbered corn bread is served in an antique pewter bowl.* RIGHT: *Fried Green Tomatoes with Tomato Conserve.*

rice in Hopping John provide a complete protein that nourishes hard-laboring bodies. Turnip greens flavored with hog jowl meat supply calcium and potassium, as well as a pleasant tartness that adds flavor and zing to a poor man's meal. We dip breads in the potlikker—preferably corn bread—and it soothes us. The meat juices give us energy for the cold, just as they gave energy for working in the fields and sustaining Southerners in the unheated homes of another era, when the first snap of cold came.

These foods are frequently thought of as soul foods and considered ethnic-black oriented. In truth, during the lean times everyone cooked the same thing—the foods that were in season or that they put up themselves. We didn't use our cash crop money for daily eating if we could avoid it. You could walk down the streets of any small town and find a similar meal in every pot, rich or poor. Even now, when economic prosperity and such modern innovations as refrigeration bring the world to our tables, these are the foods Southerners return to again and again.

When I was in England at the Cordon Bleu, I would yearn for good Southern food and fantasize about a bowl of potlikker and corn bread. And biscuits—ah, our biscuits—feathery, light, split with butter melting inside, or perhaps topped with cream gravy!

One fabled comfort food, fried green tomatoes, is hard to find on a restaurant menu, for their preparation requires loving hands. As Idgie noted longingly in the movie *Fried Green Tomatoes*, they are "the thing to be missed," piled high on a plate, perhaps topped with tomato conserve. Like all Southern comfort foods they are a sign of love and caring expressed in a tangible and delicious way.

HOE CAKES
SERVES 6

Hoe cakes can be eaten anytime—but the best time is a leisurely breakfast or a Sunday night supper. These are the heavier kind as opposed to the lacy type. Serve with sorghum syrup.

1½ cups cornmeal mix (page 102)
¼ teaspoon baking soda
1¼ cups buttermilk
1 egg, lightly beaten
⅓ to ½ cup shortening or vegetable oil

Combine the cornmeal mix and baking soda in a medium bowl. Stir in the buttermilk and beaten egg.

Heat ⅓ cup shortening to 365°F. in an electric skillet or over medium-high heat in a large heavy skillet. Pour 1 tablespoon hot shortening into the batter, and stir just to combine. For each hoe cake, pour ¼ cup batter into the skillet. Fry 1 or 2 minutes, or until golden brown on each side. Drain on paper towels. Add additional shortening to the pan as needed. Serve immediately.

FRIED GREEN TOMATOES
SERVES 4

These delicious, tart, thick slices of green tomatoes with their crusty brown exterior are a particular favorite of mine for spring and fall late breakfasts or suppers. Cynthia Jubera, who worked as the food stylist on this book, was also the food stylist for the movie *Fried Green Tomatoes*, which has catapulted this homey dish into national recognition. However, here they are done my way since, truth be told, I didn't care for the movie version as much as my own.

3 to 4 green tomatoes
Salt
Freshly ground black pepper
1 cup flour or cornmeal
½ to 1 cup (1 to 2 sticks) butter
¾ cup Tomato Conserve (page 87), optional

Slice the tomatoes ¼ to ½ inch thick and season them with salt and pepper. Spread the flour or cornmeal out on a plate, season with additional salt and pepper, and add the tomato slices, coating each side evenly.

Meanwhile, melt the butter in a heavy skillet until it sings. Reflour the tomatoes if necessary, and add to the pan in one layer, taking care not to crowd the pan. When dappled golden brown, turn the tomatoes and lightly brown the second side. Drain on paper towels. Proceed to add in batches, 3 or 4 slices at a time, until all are done. Serve immediately, with the Tomato Conserve spooned on top, if desired.

Grits Is!—or Are They?

There are those, like Craig Claiborne, who feel that grits is a plural noun. In his delightful book Craig Claiborne's Southern Cooking, however, he offers a letter from a fellow Mississippian who chides him for subscribing to the Yankee ignorance that inspires even editors of dictionaries to refer to grits in the plural. "Never mind what these Yankee dictionaries say," his friend implored, "come back home where grits is IT, not them." I stand with Craig's friend. To me grits, too, is the most singular of nouns, and is used so here. But, then, it certainly is hard to remember to say it right!

QUICK GRITS
SERVES 4

At one time grist mills dotted the Southern landscape. Powered by waterwheels, the mills' huge stones ground dried corn successively finer. The coarsest grind was, and is, known as grits. Although I love the texture of stone-ground grits, it takes half an hour or more to cook it right. I prefer quick grits for everyday cooking. I like my grits creamy, so I cook it longer than the 5 minutes indicated on the package. For economy, grits was traditionally cooked with water, but now it is cooked with all sorts of liquids. A combination of milk and cream is my favorite.

> 3 cups water, cream, milk, or broth
> ¾ cup quick grits
> ¼ teaspoon salt

In a heavy, preferably nonstick saucepan, bring the water, cream, milk, or broth just to the boil. Stir the grits and salt into the hot liquid, and return to the boil. Cover, reduce the heat to low, and cook for 7 minutes, stirring occasionally. Serve immediately.

NOTE: Cooked grits can be reheated in the microwave in an appropriate container.

FRIED SAUSAGE AND APPLES
SERVES 4

I love the contrast of sharp and sweet, soft and crunchy in this dish. I've substituted pear for the apple and it's nearly as good. This recipe multiplies very well; make it ahead and reheat it for parties.

> ⅔ pound sausage links or bulk sausage
> 2 cooking apples, red or green, cored
>   and cut into ½-inch wedges

Place the sausage in a skillet and fry, turning as necessary, until nearly done. Add the apple wedges and sauté in the sausage fat until almost soft but not mushy. Drain the sausage and apple quickly on paper towels, then arrange on a platter and serve hot.

A breakfast spread of Fried Sausage and Apples with Fried Green Tomatoes.

BUTTERMILK SKILLET CORN BREAD OR CORNSTICKS

SERVES 10 TO 12

Buttermilk is found in many corn bread recipes, contributing a pleasant, slightly acidic underlying flavor. Corn bread and "clabber," as buttermilk is now colloquially called, is a favorite rainy night supper or late night snack for children and grown-ups alike. Just crumble up the corn bread in a bowl and pour buttermilk over it.

> 5 tablespoons butter
> 1 cup yellow cornmeal
> 1 cup all-purpose flour
> 1½ teaspoons baking powder
> 1 teaspoon salt
> ½ teaspoon baking soda
> 1 cup buttermilk
> 2 eggs

Preheat the oven to 425°F.

Place the butter in an 8-inch cast-iron skillet, 8-inch square baking pan, or cast-iron cornstick molds and heat in the oven until melted. In a medium bowl, mix together the cornmeal, flour, baking powder, salt, and baking soda. In a small bowl, stir together the buttermilk and eggs. Mix 2 tablespoons melted butter into the buttermilk mixture, then gently stir into the dry ingredients. Pour the batter into the hot pan with the remaining butter and bake in the middle of the oven until the top of the corn bread is golden brown, 18 to 20 minutes for corn bread, 12 to 15 minutes for cornsticks. Run a knife around the outside edge and invert onto a plate. Serve warm.

CRACKLIN' CORN BREAD: Brown 2 ounces diced fatback in a skillet. Remove with slotted spoon and add to the batter. Proceed as above.

SHIRLEY CORRIHER'S COUNTRY BUTTERMILK BISCUITS

MAKES 12 TO 18

Shirley Corriher is a very talented Southern cooking teacher and cookbook author who specializes in knowing why food works the way it does. Her grandmother, Nanny, taught her to use a big wooden biscuit bowl to turn out these feathery and delicate biscuits, but she's adapted it to modern measures and equipment.

> 2½ cups self-rising flour (if self-rising
>   flour is not available, combine 1
>   cup all-purpose, teaspoon salt, and
>   1½ teaspoons baking powder)
> ⅛ teaspoon baking soda
> ½ teaspoon salt
> 1 tablespoon sugar
> 3 tablespoons shortening
> ⅞ cup buttermilk
> 2 tablespoons butter, melted

Preheat the oven to 450°F.

Spray an 8-inch round cake pan with nonstick spray.

In a medium mixing bowl, combine 1½ cups flour, the soda, salt, and sugar. With your fingers or a pastry cutter, work the shortening into the flour mixture until there are no shortening lumps larger than a small pea.

Stir in the buttermilk and let the dough stand 2 or 3 minutes. It will be very wet. This dough is so wet that you cannot shape it in the usual manner. Pour the remaining cup of flour onto a plate or pie pan. Flour your hands well. Spoon or scoop with a small ice cream scoop a biscuit-sized lump of wet dough into the flour and sprinkle some flour on top. With your hands, shape the biscuit into a soft round,

Corn Bread and Clabber

Not long ago, my friend Elliott Miller was hospitalized. During his recovery, one of the first meals he ordered from the hospital menu was buttermilk and corn bread. He poured his milk into a bowl, crumbled his corn bread into the milk, and ate with relish. I was surprised—didn't he pour his milk over his corn bread? He looked at me equally stunned. "Pour buttermilk on corn bread?" he asked scornfully.

For a moderate, rational intermediary, we turned to his uncle Joe Elliott, who has been eating corn bread and buttermilk since he was a farm boy. He was amused at our dispute. "There were twenty to feed on our farm," he said, "morning, noon, and night. When the women made the corn bread, they made at least four pans of it. With luck there was some left over when we came home from school.

We would pull out the largest mixing bowl we could find, and one would crumble the corn bread into pieces and the other would pour buttermilk into it or the other way around. We would take it out around the house with spoons for all and lie sprawling out on our stomachs on the ground facing it, all digging into the same bowl, until it was all gone, little more than puppies lapping it out of the bowl. It didn't matter which went in first, corn bread or clabber, we ate it as fast as we could."

gently shaking off any excess flour. The dough is so soft that it will not hold its shape. As you shape each biscuit, place it into an 8-inch round cake pan, pushing the biscuits tightly against each other so that they will rise up rather than spread out. Continue shaping the biscuits in this manner using all the dough.

Brush the biscuits with the melted butter and place on the oven shelf just above the center. Increase the oven temperature to 475°F. and bake 15 to 18 minutes, until lightly browned. Cool a minute or two in the pan. HERBED BUTTERMILK BISCUITS: Stir 2 to 4 tablespoons chopped fresh parsley or mint into the dough just before adding the buttermilk. Shape and bake as usual.

The Perfect Biscuit

The quest for the perfect biscuit is endless for most Southerners. Biscuits have a time-honored place on our tables, and it is hard to imagine a memorable meal without them. The smell of biscuits baking evokes memories of the feel and texture of hot biscuits on a well-polished table, of carrying warm biscuits inside a napkin on your way to school, of coming home later that day to your mother's hot biscuits, making a hole in the center of them and pouring in syrup, a snack to eat while running and chasing friends and dogs on a crisp fall day.

Many years ago I embarked on my own search for the perfect biscuit. I tried recipes from cookbooks and sampled the tried-and-true techniques of old friends. I judged the biscuits, awarding scores of 1 to 10 based on color, fluffiness, moistness, crispness of exteriors, and so on. Shirley's recipe comes as close to perfection as any I've found, but I'm still looking.

You don't rate biscuits like you do ice dancers, with so many points for poise, so many for technical merit, and so many for musical score. A biscuit can't be divided that way—it's a total experience (just think about those homemade ones you remember being presented piled high and piping hot on a plate). Do you want one to melt in your mouth, oozing with butter, or one that is firm enough to sandwich a piece of sausage or pork tenderloin?

The ideal Southern biscuit is feathery light with a light brown crust on the top and a moist interior. It may have slight indentations on the sides where it has bumped into other biscuits as it baked. Although it may be made with lard, butter, or some other fat, it is most often made with shortening and a minimum amount of low gluten flour and baking powder to ensure a texture generally referred to as "fluffy."

Some people like a thick biscuit, some a flat one. Personally, I don't want too big a biscuit, because I enjoy the brown outside as much as the inside. Too thick a biscuit requires too much baking powder to reach an appealing height, and a strong taste of baking powder can ruin a biscuit.

Finally, I should say that to make true Southern biscuits requires something my colleagues and I call a touch of grace—a gift that some people are blessed with.

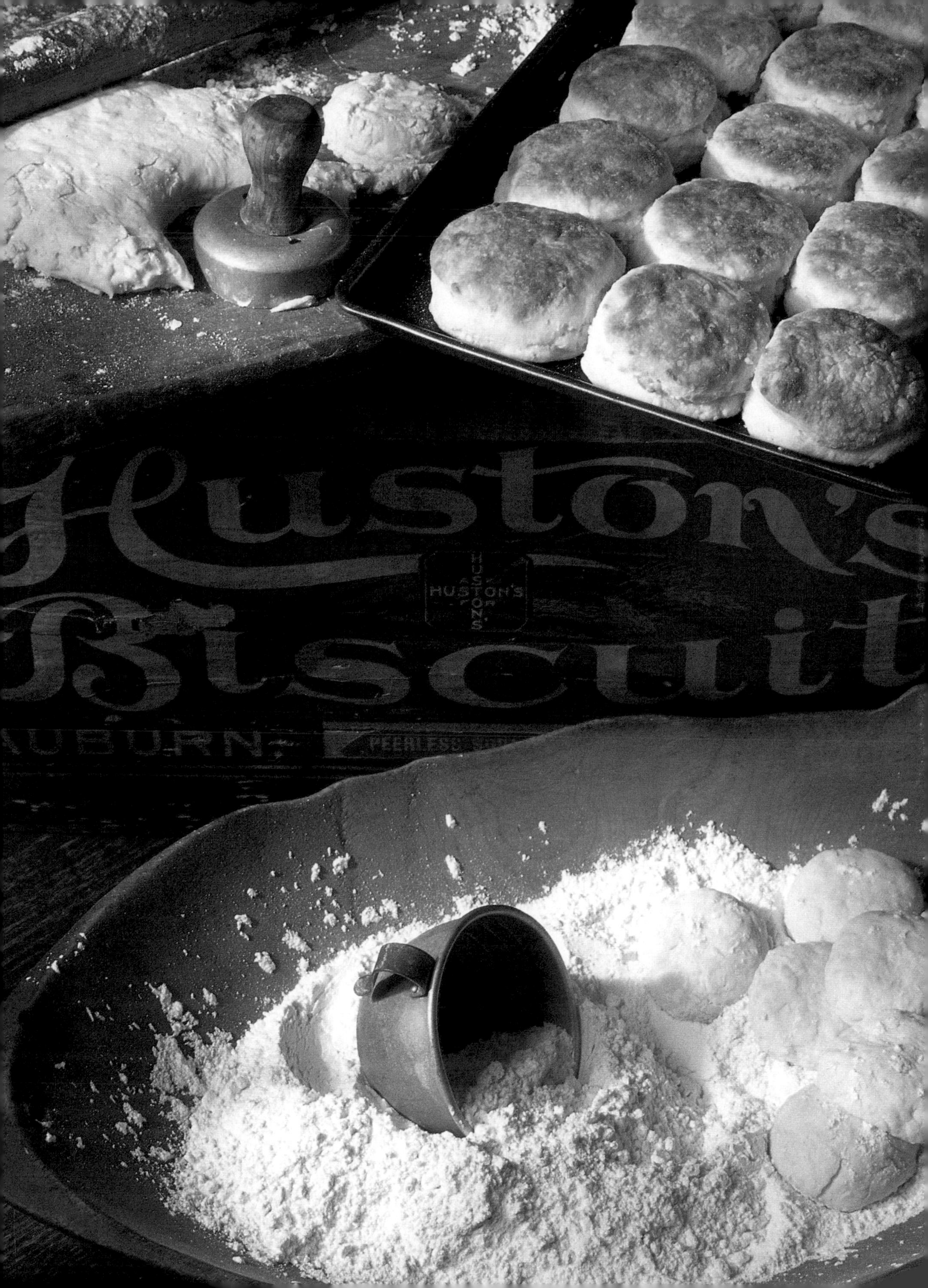
Huston's
HUSTON'S
AUBURN,

TURNIP CASSEROLE
SERVES 8 TO 10

Elizabeth Burris is a student of mine who frequently brings me glorious recipes to try. This one is a real winner and can also be made with rutabagas or carrots.

For a Christmas effect, arrange pimiento strips in the form of a poinsettia on top of the crumbs.

> 8 to 10 white turnips, peeled and sliced
> 1 8-ounce package cream cheese, softened
> ¼ cup sugar (optional)
> ½ cup (1 stick) butter
> Salt
> Freshly ground black pepper
> Buttered breadcrumbs

Preheat the oven to 350°F.

Cook the turnips in boiling salted water for 15 to 20 minutes, or until very tender. Drain and mash. (You should have about 6 cups.) Beat in the softened cream cheese, sugar, and butter. Season to taste with salt and pepper and mix well. Pour into a greased casserole and top with the breadcrumbs. Bake until bubbly hot and lightly browned, about 15 to 20 minutes.

CHEESE GRITS CASSEROLE WITH JALAPEÑO PEPPERS
SERVES 10 TO 12

Perhaps the most popular of all grits dishes, this casserole is sturdy enough to travel, but creates the light impression of a soufflé. The jalapeños may be omitted if you are a classicist, but they do add zing. This goes well to church suppers in a hot casserole wrapped in newspapers for insulation, or in a covered dish, but it's also wonderful for brunch.

> 1 pound sharp cheddar cheese, grated
> ½ cup (1 stick) butter
> ½ teaspoon ground mace
> 1 teaspoon salt
> ¼ teaspoon cayenne pepper
> 2 to 3 garlic cloves, finely chopped
> ¼ cup finely chopped jalapeño peppers (optional)
> 1 cup hot grits, cooked in milk according to package directions
> 6 eggs

Preheat the oven to 350°F.

Butter a 2-quart casserole or 8½ × 11-inch baking dish. Stir the cheese, butter, mace, salt, cayenne pepper, garlic, and jalapeño peppers into the hot grits. Beat the eggs well, then beat them into the grits mixture. Pour into the prepared dish, and bake until set and lightly browned, 30 to 45 minutes. This casserole can be frozen after baking, and reheated in a microwave or oven until heated through.

Poke Sallet

Poke, short for pokeweed, grows abundant-ly in Georgia and most of the southern United States as well, but is not commercially marketed. Some people find its wild and tender taste the most flavorful of the Southern greens. The word poke originated from the Algonquian Indian term "puccoon." Sallet is an old English term, and to us it means a "mess of greens."

I was first introduced to poke one very hot spring day when I set out to dig up my garden at Mt. Pleasant Village. My friend Grace Reeves, whom I barely knew at the time, stood a ways away from me, watching with amusement as I amassed a knee-high pile of weeds. "Nathalie," she said, "what are you doing?" "Getting rid of these weeds," I answered. She nearly snorted. "That's poke," she said, "not a weed."

HOPPING JOHN
SERVES 6 TO 8

This dish is an important "traditional" dish that is served on New Year's Day to guarantee a long life. It combines what is usu-ally on hand—cooked black-eyed peas (which some say are fixed in memory of Confederate soldiers who died in the War Between the States) and cooked rice. Chilled and dressed with a vinaigrette, it's a very special salad.

2 cups dried black-eyed peas, soaked
    overnight and drained
3 slices bacon
1 jalapeño or other hot pepper, chopped
1 red onion, chopped
½ cup celery, chopped (about 2 ribs)
    Salt
    Freshly ground black pepper
8 cups chicken stock
1 cup uncooked rice
3 green onions or scallions, chopped,
3 slices bacon, fried, drained on paper
    towels, and crumbled

Place the peas, bacon, hot pepper, red onion, celery, and salt and pepper to taste into a large pot. Cover with the chicken stock. Bring to the boil, reduce the heat, and cover and simmer until the peas are tender, about 1½ to 2 hours. Add additional water as needed. Drain the peas, reserving the liquid. Discard the bacon. With the reserved liquid (about 3 cups), cook the rice in a small pot, covered, until the liquid is absorbed and the rice is tender, about 20 to 25 minutes. Fluff with a fork. Mix together the peas and rice. Place in a large serving bowl and sprinkle with the chopped green onions and crumbled bacon.

SAUTÉED POKE SALLET
SERVES 4

Just about the time the dogwoods drop their petals, creating a blanket of white pink down the hill behind my home, the poke sallet arrives next to the creek bank and among the other weeds coming up to the mown grass. Poke sallet can only be gathered a few weeks each year; when it gets too large it isn't as good to eat. The littlest plants, with stems like tender asparagus, are best. The leaves may be cooked like turnip greens and collards, or in this modern manner.

> 2 *pounds poke sallet leaves, well washed*
> 2 *tablespoons bacon drippings or butter*
>   *Salt*
>   *Freshly ground black pepper*

Combine the poke sallet with a gallon of cold water in a large pot. Bring to the boil, uncovered, over high heat, then drain immediately . Rinse in cold water and squeeze well. Heat the drippings or butter in a large frying pan until very hot. Add the poke and toss in the fat just until heated through. Season with salt and freshly ground pepper to taste.

TURNIP GREENS SOUP
SERVES 6 TO 8

In late spring or early fall, when a sheeting rain and a light frost that chills your bones can come just a day or two after a scorcher, it's turnip greens time. The broth from the cooked greens is called potlikker because it is so heady, so rich, so full of flavor. We often eat the greens and likker like soup, but the greens are served as a side dish. The broth is boiled down and reduced. Be sure not to cook with salty broth; the fatback supplies ample salt. Today, some may also cook turnip greens only in chicken broth, recapturing a bit of the familiar flavor without the fat.

> 3 *pounds turnip or collard greens,*
>   *thoroughly washed and drained*
> 8 *cups chicken broth or stock*
> ¼ *to* ⅓ *pound fatback (salt pork)*
>   *Salt*
>   *Freshly ground black pepper*
>   *Hot sauce (optional)*

Remove the thick stems from the cleaned greens. Rinse several times in cold water to be sure the greens are free of sandy soil. In a large pot, bring 6 cups broth to the boil. Rinse the fatback, slice or cube it, and add it to the stock. Add the greens. When the broth returns to the boil, lower the heat, cover, and simmer for 2 hours. Remove the greens with a slotted spoon and chop roughly. Season to taste with salt, pepper, and hot sauce, if using. Add the remaining broth to the pot if needed to make 5 cups. Just before serving, return the greens to the broth and reheat.

LEFT: *Tender poke sallet stalks.* RIGHT: *Turnip Greens Soup and corn bread with red peppers makes a homey meal.*

ONE POT CHICKEN AND RICE CASSEROLE
SERVES 4 TO 6

Not only is this an easy recipe for the pot watcher of the family—it's also very tasty, very totable, and very inviting.

1 tablespoon butter
1 3½- to 4-pound fryer, cut into 8 pieces
2 medium onions, sliced ⅛ inch thick
2 garlic cloves, finely chopped
1 1-pound can tomatoes, drained and cubed
1 yellow squash, sliced ⅛ inch thick
½ red bell pepper, coarsely chopped
1½ cups rice
3 cups chicken broth
1 teaspoon salt
½ teaspoon freshly ground black pepper
½ teaspoon paprika
¾ teaspoon turmeric
2 teaspoons chopped fresh thyme

Preheat the oven to 350°F.

Heat the butter in a large pan. Add the chicken, skin side down, and brown over medium-high heat on all sides. Remove the chicken from the pan, and set aside. Add the onions to the pan and sauté for 1 minute. Add the garlic, tomatoes, squash, and red pepper and sauté for 2 minutes. Add the rice and cook 1 more minute. Add the chicken broth, season with salt, pepper, paprika, turmeric, and thyme, and bring the mixture to the boil. Return the chicken to the pan, cover, and bake 30 minutes or until the rice is tender. This can be made ahead and reheated before serving or frozen.

COUNTRY HAM BAKE
SERVES 4

This gooey, cheesy mixture is good for brunch, lunch, or a Sunday supper.

1 cup milk
2 eggs
2 tablespoons butter
4 1½ inch slices stale Italian bread
4 tablespoons peanut oil
1 medium onion, sliced
2 garlic cloves, chopped
½ red bell pepper, sliced
½ green bell pepper, sliced
1 14½-ounce can whole tomatoes, drained
2 tablespoons chopped fresh basil
1 tablespoon chopped fresh oregano
4 slices country ham, soaked in water 1 hour and drained
2 cups grated mozzarella cheese
Freshly ground black pepper

Preheat the oven to 400°F.

In a small bowl, beat together the milk and the eggs. In a large skillet over medium-high heat, melt the butter. Dip the bread slices in the milk and egg mixture and add to the pan. Fry one side until golden, then turn and fry the other side. Place the bread in a greased 9 × 13-inch casserole dish. Add the oil to the skillet and heat until hot. Add the onion, garlic, red and green peppers, and sauté until soft, about 10 minutes. Add the tomatoes, breaking them up with a wooden spoon. Cook the mixture until the tomatoes are heated through and the mixture is thick. Stir in the basil and oregano. Place the ham slices on top of the bread and top with the tomato mixture. Bake for 10 minutes, then sprinkle with the cheese and bake for an additional 10 to 15 minutes, until bubbly. Season with pepper to taste.

Putting Up a Hog

At hog-killing time—around Thanksgiving, when the weather is real cold—kill the hog. Scald and get rid of the hair. Hang up by the heels and take the insides out. Put on a table and cut the hams and shoulders apart. Slit the backbone in half and remove the ribs. Pull out the tenderloins and have one fried and sliced for dinner with biscuits and gravy. Lay out the rest of the hog overnight to get cold and trim it close, saving all fat and scraps to make lard and sausage. Salt the shoulders, ham, ribs, fatback (salt pork), and streak-of-lean bacon from the side; put it in a box for at least six weeks.

Then remove, wash the salt off, and rub the meat with black pepper and cornmeal. Wrap up and hang in a cold place, preferably in a separate storehouse where the ground is dry and dug down some to make it cooler.

Cut the rind into cubes and render (cook over low heat a long time to make lard) in a black wash pot out in the yard. Strain the fat in a country store lard can.

Make sausage out of the lean scraps and some fat; grind upand season. Fry the sausage, put it in jars covered with fat to preserve, put lids on, and upend the jars.

The hog's head can be used for Brunswick stew, pressed meat—headcheese or sausage meat—or it can be salted down to save and boiled in the winter with dried peas.

COUNTRY HAM AND COCA-COLA SAUCE
MAKES 1 HAM

"Baked" country ham is really a misnomer. The ham is first simmered, either in the oven or on top of the stove, then glazed in the oven, hence "baked." The sweet Coca-Cola soaks up the saltiness. If the ham is to be sliced very thinly, it need not be glazed.

> 1 12- to 15-pound uncooked country
>   ham, smoked and cured
> 1 gallon Coca-Cola Classic
> 1 gallon water

Scrub the ham very well, removing any mold. Place in a large vat, cooler, or even the bathtub and soak for 1 to 2 days, changing the water as frequently as possible, preferably every 8 hours. Test the saltiness by slicing off a piece of the ham and frying it; if it is still too salty, change the water again and continue to soak.

Preheat the oven to 325°F.

Place the ham in a roaster, fat side up. Mix enough Coca-Cola and water to come 1½ inches up the side. Alternatively, place the ham in a deep pot with Coca-Cola and water to cover, bring to the boil, reduce the heat, cover, and simmer. Cook for 4 to 6 hours, approximately 20 to 25 minutes per pound, or until the internal temperature reaches 160°F. on a meat thermometer. Baste frequently. Remove the ham to a rack, let it rest at least 10 minutes, then remove the skin and fat.

Brunswick Stew

Brunswick stew is another comfort food rich in folk-associations. Some people feel the recipe evolved naturally when the spoils of the hunt were given to farmhands, who threw them all in a pot with whatever else they had on hand, making enough to feed everyone. It might have contained a squirrel and a haunch of venison, along with a rabbit, all cooked together with what could be picked or dug from the garden. Hot peppers helped to preserve and to season. Though few have access to squirrel or wild rabbit these days, memories of those savory stews abound in family lore.

BRUNSWICK STEW
MAKES 3 GALLONS

According to folk legend, this dish's name refers to Lord Brunswick who, during one visit to the colonies, declined a very elegant dinner in favor of the tasty concoction he found the yard hands stirring together. Both Brunswick, Virginia, and Brunswick, Georgia, claim the dish, and an annual contest alternates between the two states. Having judged the contest, I've seen dozens of recipes, all claiming authenticity. This version substitutes readily available meats for the traditional squirrel or venison.

2 4- to 5-pound chickens
8 pounds boneless beef chuck,
   cut in chunks

8 pounds pork roast, including
   bones, cut in chunks
4 28-ounce cans tomatoes, undrained
4 1-pound can corns, drained
4 large onions, chopped
1 12-ounce bottle ketchup
2 tablespoons cayenne pepper
   (or less to taste)
   Salt
   Freshly ground black pepper

Cut the chickens in quarters and place them in a large heavy kettle or Dutch oven. Cover with water and cook over medium heat until just done, about 45 minutes. When cool enough to handle, remove the chicken from the broth and take out the bones, discarding the skin. Reserve the chicken and cooking liquid separately. Meanwhile, grill the chunks of beef and pork over a charcoal fire until charred all over. Put the chicken, beef, and pork with the tomatoes, corn, onions, and ketchup in a large heavy pot. Add the cayenne, salt and pepper to taste, and enough of the reserved chicken broth to make a stewlike consistency. Cook over low heat 1 to 2 hours to blend and thicken, stirring frequently to prevent sticking and scorching. Add broth as needed. The stew may be made ahead and reheated. It freezes well.

FISH MUDDLE
SERVES 6

Fish muddle is a very old traditional recipe from the islands (called the Outer Banks) of North Carolina as well as the ocean side of Virginia. It emphasizes single vegetables as well as seafood, indicating the use of what was fresh and available to the cash poor. The unusual topping of softly poached eggs adds a real difference. The recipe doubles easily.

1½ pounds large, firm, nonoily
    white fish fillets

½ pound sliced bacon

4 medium onions, thinly sliced
    (1½ pounds)

2 garlic cloves, chopped

4 medium boiling potatoes,
    peeled and thinly sliced

1 28-ounce can Italian plum tomatoes,
    chopped, with their liquid

3 tablespoons chopped fresh parsley,
    divided

1 teaspoon chopped thyme,
    preferably fresh

¾ teaspoon red pepper flakes

4 to 5 cups fish stock or clam juice
    (see Note)
    Salt
    Freshly ground black pepper

6 eggs

4 green onions or scallions, chopped,
    both green and white parts

Cut the fish into 1½-inch cubes. In a large casserole, fry the bacon until crisp; remove the bacon with a slotted spoon, crumble, and set aside. Add the onions to the fat remaining in the casserole and cook over medium heat until soft, about 5 to 7 minutes. Add the garlic and cook briefly. Add the potatoes, tomatoes, 1½ tablespoons parsley, the thyme, red pepper, vinegar, and enough fish stock to cover the mixture. Bring to the boil, cover, and cook until the potatoes are nearly soft, about 20 minutes. Add the fish and enough additional stock to barely cover. Return to the boil, reduce the heat, and simmer for 2 minutes. Season to taste with salt and pepper.

Crack the eggs individually into a saucer and slide onto the top of the soup. Cover and cook until the eggs are lightly poached, uncovering after 1½ minutes and basting with the simmering fish broth. Recover and cook approximately 1½ minutes more. Immediately spoon the eggs into 6 soup bowls. Spoon the fish, potatoes, and liquid over the eggs. Mix together the crumbled bacon, green onions, and remaining parsley. Garnish the soup with the bacon mixture as you serve.

NOTE: To make fish stock, combine 3 to 4 pounds of bones and/or shrimp shells with 6 cups water in a pot. Bring to the boil, reduce the heat, and simmer for 20 minutes. Strain.

OPPOSITE: *A hearty helping of Brunswick Stew.*
ABOVE: *Eggs are gently slipped into Fish Muddle's broth to poach.*

TERRY THOMPSON'S BREAD PUDDING WITH TWO SAUCES
SERVES 10 TO 12

Of all the bread buddings I've tasted, this one I've adapted from Terry Thompson's recipe is the best! The peach sauce calls for frozen peaches because fresh peaches turn brown easily, but you can substitute fresh peaches by slicing and then poaching them before adding the other ingredients. The bourbon sauce is equally wonderful over cream puffs.

1 *pound French bread (about*
  2 baguettes)
2 *cups milk*
2 *cups heavy cream*
3 *tablespoons butter, melted*
3 *eggs, lightly beaten*
2 *cups sugar*
2 *tablespoons vanilla extract*
1 *teaspoon ground cinnamon*
1 *cup raisins or currants, soaked in*
  ½ cup water or bourbon,
  and well drained

PEACH SAUCE
1 *pound frozen peaches*
⅓ *cup confectioners' sugar*
2 *tablespoons orange juice*

MARY HATAWAY'S
BOURBON SAUCE
2 *quarts heavy cream*
1 *cup sugar*
2 *tablespoons vanilla extract*
¼ *cup bourbon*

Preheat the oven to 375°F.

Tear the bread into 1-inch pieces and place them in a very large bowl. Pour in the milk and cream and let the bread soak until saturated, about 30 minutes; then stir. Brush the melted butter over the bottom and sides of a 13 × 9-inch baking dish. Stir the eggs and sugar into the bread mixture. Stir in the vanilla, cinnamon, and drained raisins. Pour the mixture into the prepared baking dish and bake until the pudding is set, about 1 hour.

To make the peach sauce, puree the peaches in a food processor or blender. Add the confectioners' sugar and orange juice and blend. Chill

To make the bourbon sauce, combine the cream, sugar, vanilla, and bourbon in a heavy saucepan; cook until reduced by half. Strain and refrigerate. Serve the pudding warm or at room temperature, topped with either sauce.

NOTE: The baked pudding freezes well.

EASY COBBLER
SERVES 6 TO 8

This deep-dish batter cobbler is a favorite Southern dessert, partly because it is so easy to make. Mothers serve it piping hot from the oven for a light snack, then reheat it for supper when the dish will be scraped clean. It is replete with fruit surrounded by a buttery sweet cake and may be varied by changing the sugar from white to brown and using different fruits. A touch of candied ginger is nice too.

½ *cup (1 stick) butter*
1 *cup all-purpose flour*
1½ *teaspoons baking powder*
½ *teaspoon salt*
1 *cup milk*
1 *cup granulated sugar or light*
  brown sugar, packed
2 *cups peaches, apples, whole*
  strawberries, raspberries, or
  blueberries, fresh or frozen
  (if frozen berries are used, reduce
  the sugar to ⅔ cup)

Preheat the oven to 350°F.

Put the butter in an 8 × 12-inch ovenproof serving dish and place in the oven to melt. In a large bowl, mix together the flour, baking powder, and salt. Stir in the milk and sugar. Pull the hot dish of melted butter out of the oven and pour in the batter, which will bubble around the sides. Spoon the fruit and its juices evenly over the batter. Place the dish back in the oven and bake until the batter is browned and has risen around the fruit, about 30 minutes. Serve warm or at room temperature.

NOTE: The baked cobbler can be frozen.

TRADITIONAL CARROT CAKE
MAKES 1 CAKE

During a stint as dessert chef for a restaurant, I made four carrot cakes a day. I kept trying different recipes to break the monotony, and I still know them all by heart. Thank goodness for food processors. I used to grate the carrots by hand, which was an onerous task for four cakes. This recipe can be doubled.

1½ cups whole wheat flour
⅔ cup all-purpose flour
 2 teaspoons baking soda
 2 teaspoons ground cinnamon
 ½ teaspoon salt
 ½ teaspoon ground nutmeg
 ¼ teaspoon ground ginger
 1 cup granulated sugar
 1 cup brown sugar, firmly packed
 1 cup buttermilk
 ¾ cup vegetable oil
 4 eggs
1½ teaspoons vanilla extract
 1 1-pound bag carrots, peeled and grated

 1 cup chopped pecans or walnuts
 1 cup flaked coconut
 ½ cup raisins or currants

CREAM CHEESE FROSTING
 ½ cup (1 stick) butter, at room temperature
 1 8-ounce package cream cheese, at room temperature
 1 16-ounce package confectioners' sugar
 2 teaspoons grated orange peel (no white attached)
 1 teaspoon vanilla extract
 Whole pecan halves for garnish

Preheat the oven to 350°F.

Sift together the flours, baking soda, cinnamon, salt, nutmeg, and ginger onto a sheet of wax paper. Mix the sugars together in a large bowl, then stir in the buttermilk, oil, eggs, and vanilla. Pour in the flour mixture, carrots, nuts, coconut, and raisins or currants, stirring just until well blended.

Grease and flour three 9-inch round cake pans. Cut rounds of wax paper to fit the bottoms of the pans, grease and flour the rounds, and add them to the pans.

Pour the batter into the cake pans and bake until a wooden toothpick inserted in the center comes out clean, about 30 minutes. Cool in the pans 10 minutes, then loosen the cake layers from the edges of the pans and invert onto wire racks. Peel off the wax paper and cool completely. The cake can be made 1 to 2 days ahead or frozen.

To make the frosting, beat the butter and cream cheese together in a medium bowl until light. Add the confectioners' sugar, orange peel, and vanilla, mixing well. Spread the frosting between the layers and on the top and sides of the cake. Cover, and refrigerate overnight before serving.

Decorate with pecans halves.

The Vegetable Patch

*T*HOSE WHO HAVE NOT HAD THE OPPOR-
tunity to visit and eat in our homes may
not realize the depth of Southerners' pas-
sion for foods from the garden. But once the
Vidalia onions meet summer's tomatoes in a perfect
straight-from-the-garden salad, the Southern table is
a nonending parade of vegetables that goes on until
late fall and then some.

Southern food has long been more vegetable than
meat oriented. In fact, Thomas Jefferson once wrote
that he did not eat meat as an aliment, but a condiment for vegetables. In years gone
by, the focal point of every meal
was a big pot of beans, cooked
long and low on the back of the
stove, with perhaps a bit of pork
thrown in. Maybe they were
cooked this way because the fire
couldn't be tended, as the cook

A storehouse filled to bursting with freshly harvested corn.

was elsewhere, with the children or in the field. Or perhaps Southerners intuited early on that adding water to vegetables and eating every bit of the broth—called potlikker—spooned over corn bread or biscuits or lapped up with a spoon like soup, was (as now is proved by nutritionists) an important way to extract every vitamin. By and large, all our traditional vegetables are cooked in this time-honored fashion.

Everyone seems to have a small plot of land, somewhere, where they can grow their own vegetables. As a young newlywed, I planted a garden surrounded by sunflowers whose roots were Jerusalem artichokes, with garlic sentries guarding the vegetables from snails. We grew all sorts of herbs in an era when herbs were not plentiful in the stores. We had wild watercress (called cressi) that grew on the banks of the stream behind the restaurant, and we had corn that reached the sky, and fresh tomatoes—supplemented by the woman who lived down the road and brought us bushelfuls at a time. We had zucchini, which grew overnight from finger-sized to giant, and watermelon and squash.

Squash, particularly the yellow crookneck variety not commonly found in other regions, is perhaps the best way to seduce a Southern man if you believe the way to a man's heart is his stomach. We stuff it, fry it, use it in soufflés and casseroles, and, finally, put it up in freezer bags to use later on a holiday table.

*A*nd we love our peas. The South isn't particular about what it calls a bean and what it calls a pea; both are legumes. Both are a necessary part of the South's cooking and furnish important protein. Whether fresh or dried, they are usually cooked a very long time; coupled with rice, they form a perfect protein. With the addition of pork or pork fat, they make an even more substantial meal. And when summer draws to a close, the garden's bounty is likely to find its way into the pantry, "put up" to bring a taste of spring to winter tables. Having jars of something homemade on hand is as much a part of Southern life as a cool glass of iced tea on a hot summer day.

Offerings from the summer garden include parslied potatoes, Butter Beans, Creamed Corn, Sautéed Cabbage, Green Snap Beans, Summer Squash, Glazed Carrots, and various condiments.

POLE BEANS
SERVES 6 TO 8

Pole beans are tougher than runner or string beans. They are longer, flatter, and wider. To be tender in the time-honored Southern way, they need to be stringed and then cooked a long time. Of course, you may cook them less if you prefer, but they won't melt in your mouth. My personal theory is that this method was derived to incorporate the fat into the beans as an important source of energy. No vitamins are lost as the broth is eaten, too. White bacon is the affectionate Southern name for salted pork, fatback is the saltiest back fat, and streak-o-lean is from the belly. Of course, ham hocks could be used, too.

2 pounds pole beans
3 cups water
2 cups chicken broth or stock
¼ cup white bacon, fatback, or streak-o-lean, cut up
1 onion, peeled and sliced
Salt
Freshly ground black pepper

Snap off the ends and string the beans. Break them into 1- to 1½-inch pieces. Bring the water and broth to the boil. Add the beans and fatback. Cover, reduce the heat, and simmer 1½ hours. Add the onion and cook, covered, until beans are very tender, another 45 minutes. Season to taste with salt and pepper.

POLE BEANS AND CREAMERS POTATOES: Add 8 small (1-inch) new potatoes and a chopped onion to the pole beans for the last 45 minutes of cooking. Cook until tender but not mushy.

GLAZED CARROTS
SERVES 4

This is also a good way to prepare tender, new baby carrots when they are in season.

1 pound carrots, peeled and sliced ¼
   to ½ inch thick
3 tablespoons butter
2 teaspoons sugar
   Salt
   Freshly ground black pepper
1 to 2 tablespoons chopped fresh mint

Place the carrots in a saucepan with water just to cover. Bring to the boil. Add the butter, cover, reduce the heat, and simmer 15 to 20 minutes. Remove the cover, add the sugar, and boil down until the liquid has evaporated. Season to taste with salt, pepper, and the mint.

SUMMER SQUASH
SERVES 6 TO 8

I often freeze any leftovers of this dish to brighten winter meals.

4 tablespoons (½ stick) butter
1 to 2 onions, sliced
2 pounds yellow crookneck squash or
   zucchini, sliced ¼ to ½ inch thick
½ cup chicken stock
   Salt
   Freshly ground black pepper

Melt 3 tablespoons butter in a large saucepan. Add the onions and sauté over medium heat until soft, 8 to 10 minutes. Add the squash and stock. Cover and cook over medium heat until tender, about 15 to 20 minutes. Drain off the excess liquid. Season to taste with salt and pepper and add the remaining butter if desired.

HOME-STYLE GREEN
BEANS CASSEROLE
SERVES 4 TO 6

When I was a young girl, one of the more popular dishes to take to church revival meetings and covered dish suppers—the casseroles wrapped in newspaper to keep warm—was canned green beans topped with mushroom soup and canned onion rings. We children thought it delicious. I developed this recipe to comfort me the same way today but with fresh ingredients. It's the perfect accompaniment for a Thanksgiving meal and a good make-and-take recipe.

> 7 *tablespoons butter*
> 2 *tablespoons all-purpose flour*
> 1¾ *cups milk, heated to a simmer*
> ½ *cup shredded Swiss cheese*
>   *Salt*
>   *Freshly ground black pepper*
> 1 *cup mushrooms, sliced*
> 1 *pound cooked green beans*
> ½ *cup shredded Swiss or Cheddar*
>   *cheese (optional)*
> 4 *to 5 thinly sliced onions*

Preheat the oven to 350°F.

In a medium-size heavy saucepan, melt 2 tablespoons butter. Add the flour and whisk to combine. Cook 2 to 3 minutes over low heat. Whisk in the hot milk all at once, stirring constantly, until the mixture is thick. Bring quickly to the boil, then remove from the heat and stir in the Swiss cheese. Season to taste with salt and pepper and set aside.

Melt 1 tablespoon butter in a small skillet. Add the mushrooms and sauté over medium heat until softened, 4 to 5 minutes. Mix the green beans and sautéed mushrooms into the cheese sauce. Pour into a baking dish and top with the additional cheese if desired. Mean-

while, melt the remaining 4 tablespoons butter in a large skillet and sauté the sliced onions until they caramelize and are a nice brown color. Top the green bean mixture with the caramelized onions. Bake until heated through, about 15 minutes.

GREEN SNAP BEANS,
OLD STYLE
SERVES 4 TO 6

These beans, cooked in the broth from ham hocks, are cooked in the soul-satisfying manner. Yankees may not appreciate them, but when we crave Southern food, these beans are part of what we crave. They are very soft and tender, and are coated in the rich broth.

> 2 *ham hocks or ¼ cup white bacon,*
>   *streak-o-lean, or fatback, sliced*
>   *(see page 80)*
> 2 *pounds green snap beans, snapped*
>   *into 2-inch pieces*
> 1 *teaspoon sugar*
> 1 *onion, peeled*
>   *Salt*
>   *Freshly ground black pepper*

Place the hocks in a pot with water to cover. Bring to the boil and cook for 30 minutes. Remove the ham hocks from the pot and add the green beans. Sprinkle the sugar over the beans. Put the ham hocks on top of the beans and add the whole onion to the pot, also on top of the beans. Bring to the boil. Do not stir or shake—you want the ham to stay on top and flavor the beans. Reduce the heat and simmer until very tender, about 1 to 1½ hours. Season to taste with salt and pepper. You may remove the ham from the bones and serve it with the beans.

Field Peas

One year, in a small market town in South Georgia, I came across a rare find—a refrigerator case of shelled green white acres, lady peas, and other field peas in tiny plastic bags. I bought all they had, borrowing money to purchase five small bags, as shelled peas cost the earth. I froze them and saved them for two special occasions. One occasion was a dinner party honoring my friend Dudley Clendenin's parents at which Calvin Trillin and Pat Conroy held forth at separate tables. The other event was a meal for renowned Italian cooks Victor and Marcella Hazan. I wanted to serve the best I had—in that case, the peas. In both instances it was the peas that got the raves.

There are those who might think, "What! They didn't ooh and ahh about the perfectly poached fish or the puff pastry or the impressively difficult dishes?" No, they didn't go on about them. I mean, they were polite and said they liked them very much; but the peas were what enchanted them.

BUTTER PEAS OR BUTTER BEANS
SERVES 4 TO 6

Lima beans are called butter peas by some, butter beans by others. I personally think of butter peas as the smallest, sweetest lima beans. I love their delicacy and moistness.

> 3 cups water
> 4 cups shelled fresh butter peas or
>   butter beans
> ¼ cup (½ stick) butter
> Salt
> Freshly ground black pepper

Bring the water to the boil in a saucepan. Add the peas or beans and the butter. Reduce the heat, cover, and simmer until the peas are tender but not mushy, about 20 to 30 minutes. Remove the peas with a slotted spoon and place in a serving bowl; keep warm. Boil the liquid for approximately 5 to 10 minutes until somewhat reduced. Season to taste with salt and pepper and pour over the peas.

WHITE ACRE PEAS
SERVES 4

These tiny field peas are a well-loved Southern vegetable, a miracle of summer when freshly snapped—but, ah, so hard to find fresh. I have found the frozen very acceptable and preferable to the canned.

> 1 16-ounce package frozen white
>   acre peas
> 2 dried hot red peppers
> 2 slices bacon, cut in ½-inch pieces
> 3 to 4 cups chicken stock
> Salt
> Freshly ground black pepper
> ½ teaspoon red pepper flakes

Combine the peas, dried red peppers, and bacon with the stock to cover in a saucepan or Dutch oven. Bring to the boil, then cover and reduce the heat. Simmer until the beans are soft but not mushy, about 30 to 45 minutes, adding more liquid if necessary. Season to taste with salt, pepper, and red pepper flakes.

Salt Pork

Pork as a seasoning has long been crucial to the South. Historically, it was put up in the fall, salted down to be used all year long, usually parceled out in vegetable dishes, and the lard rendered down for frying. Down the road from where I lived at the Hub in Covington, Georgia, some neighbors put up hogs every year until just a few years ago.

Pork fat is a standard ingredient in Southern cooking, used both to flavor and preserve foods. It can be fresh or cured. Fat from the back of the animal is called fatback, and it contains no meat at all. Fat that is ribboned with meat, like bacon, is called streak-of-lean or streak-o-lean. When you can't find fatback, any salt pork will do. The most common salt porks now are white bacon, fatback, streak-of-lean, bacon (from the belly), hog jowl, and country ham. You can reuse salt pork in your vegetable dishes— refreeze or refrigerate it.

About once a year I give in to temptation and thinly slice some salt pork (boiled or not), heat up a frying pan, and fry it like bacon. Then I fry two pieces of bread in the fat until brown and crisp. With the remaining fat, some flour and milk, I make a cream gravy and pour it over the bread. I consume this cholesterol-laden wonder with a plate of country vegetables, sliced tomatoes and cucumbers on the side, and I wind up very happy. I know it's not healthy. I know it's sinful. I gave up potato chips except for car trips all year long, so once a year I can have my fried white bacon. It is crunchy crisp on the outside and meltingly tender on the inside as only pure fat can be.

$Seeds$

When the Vidalia spring onions meet the very first ripe tomatoes at the stands, I know it is time to head for Patrick's Seed and Feed Store in Covington, Georgia, to look at the array of bean and pea seeds.

Patrick's seems more crowded on a rainy day, perhaps because it is impossible to work outside in a pelting spring rain. The seeds occupy 20 feet of tables. I pore over the pea and corn seeds; their names dazzle me. I imagine eating tender flavorful ears of Silver Queen, fresh from the garden, with butter melting down and around the rounded ear, and I want to gather all the seeds in my arms and rush home and turn my fantasies into reality.

But it is the field peas that really inspire reveries. It will be months before any pink-eyed crowders or striped bush limas are ready to snap. I'm dependent on the goodwill of others for my lady peas and on McKenzie's frozen foods for white acre peas. Although I can buy butter beans and baby limas, I never see butter peas for sale. Because I don't have a place to grow any beans or peas, I am dependent on those people who set up open trucks with brown bags on the back and deal only in cash or on friends; I watch the purchases of these seeds carefully, hoping someone I know will turn up at the weigh-in scales. I leave with packages in my pockets that will never be planted, but give me hope of spring.

SUMMER SOUTHERN CHOWDER
SERVES 6 TO 8

There is a magic time in late spring when the tomatoes are ripe, the corn sweet, and the okra tiny. With luck even a few Vidalia onions are around. When that happens you can't go wrong with this light soup, which is delightful for a light lunch as a starter.

Southerners call extracting every bit of flavor from an ear of corn "milking" it—slicing, then scraping it—as in this recipe.

1 tablespoon butter
1 tablespoon olive oil
1 large onion, sliced
2 garlic cloves, finely chopped
4 cups chicken stock
2 ears fresh corn
½ pound fresh okra, caps removed, sliced ¼ to ½ inch thick
2 large fresh tomatoes, peeled (see Note), seeded, and chopped, or 1 16-ounce can Italian tomatoes, drained, seeded, and chopped
Salt
Freshly ground black pepper
Garlic pepper oil (see Note)
2 hot green peppers, finely chopped, for garnish

Heat the butter and oil together in a large saucepan. Add the onion and sauté until soft and translucent, 5 to 6 minutes. Add the garlic and cook briefly. Pour in the chicken stock and bring to a simmer.

Slice the kernels from each ear of corn, then scrape the ears with the back of the knife blade to remove the remaining corn and its milk. Add the okra, tomatoes, corn, and the corn milk to the stock. Bring to the boil, reduce the heat, and cook 3 to 5 minutes, uncovered. Season to taste with salt and pepper.

To serve, ladle the soup into serving bowls, top with a splash of garlic pepper oil, and sprinkle with hot peppers, if desired.

NOTE: To peel the tomatoes, bring a pan of water to the boil. Cut a cross into the tomato skin at the blossom end. Dunk the tomatoes in the boiling water for 10 to 15 seconds, then run under cold water. Peel, starting at the cross.

To make the garlic pepper oil, mix together 1 cup olive oil, 3 chopped garlic cloves, and ½ teaspoon hot pepper flakes in a jar. Let sit overnight. The oil keeps indefinitely in the refrigerator.

QUICK PEPPER MÉLANGE
SERVES 4

Just when everything is beautiful in our gardens and the Vidalia green (spring) onions are perfect, it "comes up" a spring hot spell to rival August. The microwave is the only answer for a cool house.

2 large red peppers, seeded, stemmed, and cut in thin strips
2 large green peppers, seeded, stemmed, and cut in thin strips
4 large Vidalia green spring onions, trimmed and sliced ¼ inch thick
½ cup water
2 tablespoons Worcestershire sauce
Salt
Freshly ground black pepper

Place the peppers and onions in a 2-quart microwave casserole dish. Add the water and the Worcestershire sauce, and mix well. Cook on high for 3 minutes, then stir, and continue cooking on high for an additional 2 minutes. Salt and pepper to taste and serve hot or at room temperature.

COCONUT SQUASH

SERVES 8 TO 10

I am hopelessly nearsighted and once, when I was in a rush and distracted by the phone, I looked into the freezer and grabbed coconut rather than breadcrumbs. I didn't discover my mistake until I tasted the finished dish. It was great, so I served it and keep serving it. It's especially good for holiday meals.

    10 small to medium summer squash
            (2½ to 3 pounds)
     6 tablespoons (¾ stick) butter
     2 onions, chopped
    ⅓ cup flaked, sweetened coconut
     2 tablespoons chopped fresh thyme
            (optional)
    ½ cup freshly grated imported
            Parmesan cheese
    ½ cup grated Swiss cheese
        Salt
        Freshly ground black pepper

Cut the squash in half lengthwise. Spoon out the pulp, making a boat of each half. Place the boats in boiling water to cover and cook about 10 minutes, or until just tender. Chop the pulp roughly. Meanwhile, melt 5 tablespoons butter in a sauté pan. Add the onions and cook until soft, 8 to 10 minutes. Add the squash pulp and cook briefly. Add the coconut and thyme and cool slightly. Stir in the cheeses, then season to taste with salt and pepper. Drain the boats and stuff with the filling. (The recipe may be made 1 to 2 days in advance to this point.) Place in a buttered ovenproof serving dish. Dot with the remaining tablespoon butter. When ready to serve, heat in a 350°F. oven until the cheese is melted and the squash is heated through, about 15 minutes. The squash can also be reheated in the microwave.

BUTTER BEAN AND CORN SALAD

SERVES 6 TO 8

The ways to combine butter beans and corn are endless. This recipe came about as a way to use up leftovers. I wasn't sure I'd like this combination of garden vegetables, but to my amazement I loved it! It's very flavorful and sings of the best of the garden.

     1 pound fresh shelled petite butter
            beans (butter peas) or 1 1-pound
            package frozen butter beans
     6 ears fresh white Silver Queen
            corn, kernels scraped from the cob
            (about 1 pound), or 1 1-pound
            package frozen white shoepeg corn
     6 scallions, chopped, both white
            and green parts
    10 slices bacon, fried and crumbled
    ¾ cup mayonnaise
     4 tablespoons white wine vinegar
     3 to 4 tablespoons freshly chopped
            thyme, tarragon, or dill
        Salt
        Freshly ground black pepper

Quickly blanch the butter beans and corn in boiling water until crisp-tender, about 5 minutes. Drain the beans and corn and run cold water over them to stop cooking and refresh them. Drain thoroughly.

Combine the butter beans, corn, scallions, bacon, mayonnaise, vinegar, herbs, and salt and pepper to taste. Toss to coat. Refrigerate at least 2 to 4 hours for the flavors to marry.

ABOVE: *Wedges of Grilled Cabbage.* OPPOSITE: *Okra frying in the time-honored fashion in a cast-iron skillet.*

GRILLED CABBAGE
SERVES 4

I frequently grill several vegetables at one time, serving them at one meal. Cabbage takes especially well to this treatment. It's very unusual, so it's a conversation piece as well.

>1 small head cabbage (1½ to 2 pounds)
>2 to 3 tablespoons olive oil
>   Salt
>   Freshly ground black pepper
>   Hot pepper vinegar

Remove any wilted outer leaves from the cabbage and cut it into quarters. Cook the cabbage in a steamer, microwave, or boiling water for several minutes, just until it begins to soften. Cool the cabbage and pat dry. Brush all the surfaces with olive oil and place on a hot grill. Cook about 10 minutes per side, checking to see that it does not burn. Season to taste with salt and pepper, and sprinkle with vinegar to serve.

DEEP-FRIED OKRA
SERVES 6

Margaret Lupo of Mary Mac's Tearoom in Atlanta is the queen of fried okra. Frying okra is truly an art form with her, the secret being the cracker crumbs, which give the okra a nice, thick, crisp exterior. The hardest part of frying okra is getting it to the table for a meal; whenever I make it, people smell it cooking and hang around the kitchen, snitching pieces!

>2 pounds okra, well rinsed
>1 egg, beaten
>2 tablespoons water
>2 cups buttermilk
>4 teaspoons salt
>2 cups all-purpose flour
>2 cups cracker meal or saltines crushed
>   to the consistency of cornmeal
>   Freshly ground black pepper
>4 cups vegetable oil

Cut the stem ends off the cleaned okra and slice ¼ inch thick. In a large bowl, mix together the egg, water, buttermilk, and 2 teaspoons salt. Add the okra to the mixture. Mix together the flour, cracker meal, the remaining 2 teaspoons salt, and the pepper in another bowl. Remove the okra from the buttermilk with a slotted spoon and add by spoonfuls to the flour. Toss lightly to coat and remove to a cake rack to shake off the excess flour. Meanwhile, heat the oil in an electric skillet or deep-frying pan to 350°F. Add the okra by large spoonfuls and fry until golden brown, turning as necessary. Remove with a slotted spoon to a paper towel to drain. Keep warm while you fry the remaining okra. Serve hot.

CREAMED OR FRIED CORN
SERVES 6 TO 8

What is better to eat than fresh-picked corn, cut off the cob and cooked in drippings? Whether you call it creamed or fried, it is an incredible taste experience and one of the most beloved Southern recipes.

10 ears fresh corn
3 slices country-style or regular bacon
1 cup water
6 tablespoons (¾ stick) butter
Salt
Freshly ground black pepper

Stand an ear of corn on its end in a shallow bowl or pan. Slice the tips of the corn kernels from the cob with a sharp knife, then scrape the cob with the back of the knife to remove the remaining kernels and "milk." Repeat with remaining ears of corn.

In a 10-inch iron skillet or heavy frying pan, cook the bacon until crisp; transfer the bacon to paper towels, leaving the drippings in the pan. Add the corn and its liquid to the pan and add the water. Bring to the boil, then add the butter and reduce the heat to a slow simmer. Simmer for 30 minutes, stirring occasionally. Season to taste with salt and pepper. Crumble the bacon and use it as a garnish if desired.

FRESH CROWDER PEAS
WITH SNAPS
SERVES 4 TO 6

As with many field peas, there are several varieties of crowder peas, and I love them all. They are a nuisance to shell, however, best done in front of a TV set or sitting around on the porch gossiping with friends; so I search for markets that sell them shelled.

2½ pounds fresh crowders or lady peas
     (1½ pounds shelled)
3 ounces fatback (salt pork) in 1 piece
4 cups water
1 small dried hot red pepper (optional)

Shell the peas, discarding those with worm holes. If you have any pods that are too tiny to shell, leave them whole or snap them in half.

Slice into the fatback in 4 places, leaving the rind intact, and place in a heavy pan with the peas and snaps, water, and hot pepper, if using. Cover and bring the mixture to the boil, then reduce the heat and simmer until the fat is soft, about an hour.

TURNIP GREENS WITH
WHITE TURNIPS
SERVES 4 TO 6

Turnip greens are not just discarded turnip tops. In fact, some new hybrid varieties, sold fresh and frozen, produce only greens. In some poor rural areas, they can be found along the roadside, there for the picking.

3 cups water
2 cups chicken stock
¼ to ½ pound fatback or streak-o-lean
     (page 80)
3 pounds turnip greens, cleaned and
     stemmed
1 pound white turnips, peeled and diced
Salt
Sugar

Bring the water and stock with the fatback to the boil in a large pot. Add the greens, cover, and simmer for 1 hour. Remove the greens with a slotted spoon, chop, and return to the broth with the diced turnips. Cover and cook up to 1 hour, until the turnips are soft. Add salt and sugar to taste.

Vidalia Onions

It used to be that Vidalias were strictly a springtime indulgence, as their brief season lasts only from April until June. But today, more and more growers are keeping Vidalias in cold storage with great success, extending the time of year they are available. I am suspicious about the so-called Vidalias sold loose in the grocery store, however, and recommend buying well-marked twenty-five pound sacks. When buying Vidalias in bulk, a practical but inelegant way to keep the moist onions from rubbing together and rotting as they exude their famous sweet moisture is to store them in clean but used panty hose. An onion is placed in the hose, tumbling down to the bottom, followed by the loose knotting of the panty hose. Another onion is added, then another knot. This requires some extraordinary gyrations as the panty hose becomes fuller and fuller of onions.

Rotten ones do occur over the long winter, however, and they are easily enough separated from the remainder. To access the onions, just snip off the onions with good kitchen scissors as needed, working from the bottom and discarding the hose.

TOMATO CONSERVE
MAKES 1 QUART

I speak often about my former mother-in-law and father-in-law, Celeste and Jimmy Dupree. This deep rich red mass is one of the things I look for on the dinner table when Celeste makes green beans, fried green tomatoes, black-eyed peas, or butter beans.

She and Jimmy would wait until they had a gracious plenty of ripe tomatoes on their vines. There seemed to be mountains of tomatoes they readied for the huge pot. As the tomatoes cooked down their wonderful aroma filled the house, and Jimmy and Celeste watched the pot vigilantly. Then they added the sugar and vinegar, testing and tasting. A recipe for tomato conserve is not an exact thing. It takes a little playing with to get just the right sweetness and just the right thickness—but is a pleasure to eat.

8 pounds fresh tomatoes, skinned and quartered, or 8 1-pound cans of tomatoes with juice
2 cups apple cider vinegar
1 to 1½ cups sugar
Salt
Freshly ground black pepper

Combine the tomatoes, vinegar, and 1 cup sugar with salt and pepper to taste in a heavy saucepan. Simmer until the mixture is thick enough to cling to a spoon, about 1½ hours. Taste and, if desired, add some of the remaining sugar to make it sweeter. This will keep in the refrigerator for a couple of weeks. It can also be frozen.

SLICED TOMATO AND CORN PLATTER
SERVES 3 TO 4

This easy, do-ahead summer salad made with red wine vinegar is timeless. Mild balsamic vinegar gives the dressing a mellow flavor, but if you don't have any on hand, use a total of 3 tablespoons red wine vinegar.

> 2 *large ripe tomatoes, peeled and sliced*
> 1 *ear sweet white corn, cooked and*
>   *kernels cut off the cob*
> 1 *to 2 green onions or scallions,*
>   *thinly sliced*
>
> DRESSING
> 2 *tablespoons red wine vinegar*
> 2 *tablespoons balsamic vinegar*
> ½ *cup olive oil*
> 2 *to 3 tablespoons finely chopped*
>   *fresh basil*
>   *Salt*
>   *Freshly ground black pepper*

Arrange the tomatoes on a platter. Sprinkle with the corn and sliced green onions.

To make the dressing, whisk together the red wine vinegar, the balsamic vinegar, oil, basil, and salt and pepper to taste in a small mixing bowl. Pour over the salad.

SLICED TOMATO AND ONION SALAD; Substitute 1 large Vidalia or green Vidalia onion, thinly sliced, for the corn and onions, and sprinkle the dressed salad with ¼ cup chopped mint.

Fresh cooked corn kernels, stripped from the cob, make a quick and colorful salad with tomatoes, green onions, and herbs.

CUCUMBER-AVOCADO-TOMATO-VIDALIA GREEN ONION SALAD
SERVES 6

Part of the beauty of this salad is the wedge and crescent shapes of the vegetables. It's unusual and very good!

> 1 large firm ripe tomato, cut into
>   8 wedges
> 1 Vidalia onion, halved and cut into
>   ¼-inch-thick slices
> 1 large cucumber, peeled, halved,
>   seeded, and sliced
> 1 ripe avocado, halved, seeded, peeled,
>   and cut into ¼-inch-thick slices
> ¾ cup Greek olives, pitted and halved
>
> DRESSING
> 6 tablespoons olive oil
> 2 tablespoons red wine vinegar
>   Juice of 1 lemon
>   Juice of ½ orange
> 1 garlic clove, finely chopped
>   Pinch sugar
>   Salt
>   Freshly ground black pepper

Combine the tomato, onion, cucumber, avocado, and olives in a large salad bowl. Whisk together the dressing ingredients and pour over the salad. Toss, and serve at once.

EDNA LEWIS'S COOKED WATERCRESS
SERVES 10 TO 15

Watercress, also called cressi, is frequently found growing wild next to Southern streams. Edna Lewis is a glorious Southern cook who picks watercress wild at her family's home in Virginia. She cooked this incredibly delicious dish for my "New Southern Cooking" Christmas special.

> 1¼ to 1½ pounds smoked pork
> 10 bunches watercress, preferably wild

Bring 4 to 6 cups of water to a boil in a large pot. Cut the pork into pieces and drop them into the boiling water. Simmer about 1 hour until completely tender. Wash the watercress carefully, cutting off the root and some of the tough stem; add it to the pot and simmer 45 minutes. Discard the meat and serve the watercress with its cooking liquid.

DIXIE RELISH
MAKES 12 PINTS

This pretty condiment, similar to chow-chow, can be served either as an accompaniment to meats and vegetables or on its own as a salad.

A number of peppers are indigenous to our area. Although the jalapeño peppers are most familiar, I like the little peppers we call finger peppers, the long cowhorns, and those used in Tabasco pepper sauce. They vary in mildness, with the rule of thumb being the smaller the pepper the hotter. I prefer the peppers left on the vine until they are fiery red, like the Tabascos that are made into hot sauce in vast copper cauldrons in Louisiana, where the landscape is filled with waist-high plants as far as the eye can see.

1 green cabbage, finely chopped

1 red cabbage, finely chopped

6 red bell peppers, finely chopped

6 green bell peppers, finely chopped

10 hot finger peppers, finely chopped

6 Vidalia onions, finely chopped

1 bunch green onions or scallions, sliced

6 garlic cloves, finely chopped

½ cup salt

4 cups sugar

1 quart apple cider vinegar

2 tablespoons ground ginger

2 tablespoons dry mustard

2 tablespoons turmeric

1 tablespoon celery seed

1 teaspoon peppercorns

Mix together the green and red cabbage, the red and green peppers, the finger peppers, onions, green onions, and garlic. Toss with the salt and drain in a large colander for 3 hours. Transfer the vegetables to a large stockpot and add the sugar, vinegar, ginger, mustard, turmeric, celery seed, and peppercorns. Bring to the boil and cook on high for 3 to 4 minutes. Ladle into hot sterilized pint jars and seal.

HORSERADISH JELLY
MAKES 3 ½ PINTS

There are those who won't eat a beef steak without horseradish jelly.

3¼ cups sugar

¾ cup freshly grated horseradish

2 jalapeño peppers, finely chopped

1 red onion, finely chopped

½ cup apple cider vinegar

4 ounces liquid pectin

In a large pan, mix together the sugar, horseradish, peppers, onion, and vinegar and cook over low heat until the sugar dissolves. Increase the heat to high and bring to the boil. Immediately stir in the pectin and bring back to a rolling boil. Remove from the heat and skim off the foam on top. Ladle into hot sterilized jars and seal. Store in a cool dark place.

HOT PICKLED OKRA
MAKES 4 PINTS

This spicy variety of pickled okra is a real mouth and eye-opener!

3½ pounds okra

1 quart white vinegar

2 tablespoons salt

2 tablespoons black peppercorns, slightly crushed

2 teaspoons red pepper flakes

1 tablespoon dill seed

1 teaspoon dry mustard

2 garlic cloves, sliced

1 medium onion, sliced

4 whole cloves

1 teaspoon Tabasco sauce

Wash and drain the okra. Place in ice water and soak for 2 hours to insure crispness. In a large pot, mix together the vinegar, salt, peppercorns, red pepper flakes, dill seed, mustard, garlic, onion, cloves, and Tabasco. Bring to the boil, reduce the heat to a simmer, and cook gently for 10 minutes. Pack the okra in hot sterilized jars and fill with brine to within ¼ inch of the top. Wipe the rims dry and put on the lids. Set aside to seal. Store in a cool dark place. Refrigerate at least 1 day before serving.

COLORFUL CORN RELISH
MAKES 3 PINTS

This is a delightfully different relish, perfect for greens, beans, and anything in between. Not only is the flavor bright, the color will excite your eye as well. Instead of salsa, try this with chips or as a topping for tacos or fajitas. You'll be pleasantly surprised.

> ¼ cup sugar
> 1 teaspoon salt
> 6 ears fresh corn, kernels cut
>   from the cob (about 4 cups)
> 2 tablespoons butter or olive oil
> 1 to 2 jalapeño peppers, finely chopped
> 1 green bell pepper, chopped
> 1 red bell pepper, chopped
> 1 red onion, chopped
> 1 tablespoon celery seed
> 2 teaspoons mustard seed
> 1 teaspoon coarsely ground black pepper
> ¾ cup apple cider vinegar

In a large bowl, sprinkle the sugar and salt over the corn. In a large skillet, heat the butter or olive oil and quickly sauté the peppers and onion until softened, 3 to 5 minutes. Add the corn mixture to the skillet and cook for just 2 to 3 minutes. Add the celery seed, mustard seed, pepper, and vinegar and bring to the boil. Cool the mixture and pack in sterilized pint jars and store in the refrigerator.

HOT PEPPER JELLY
MAKES ABOUT 8 CUPS

This jelly is a staple in Southern homes, ready to be served with crackers and cream cheese at a moment's notice. It combines the Southern yen for sweetness with the fire of the local peppers. Hotness varies according to the pepper, whether the better known Tabasco and jalapeño peppers or the Georgia cowhorns and finger peppers. Remember, the smaller the pepper, the hotter it will be, and every pepper on a bush can vary in heat.

½ cup seeded and coarsely chopped hot red pepper

½ cup seeded and coarsely chopped hot green pepper

1 cup chopped onion

1½ cups apple cider vinegar

5 cups sugar

2 pouches liquid pectin

Place the hot peppers, onion, and cider vinegar in a food processor or blender. Process until very finely chopped and combine with the sugar in a heavy nonaluminum pot. Bring to the boil and boil for 1 minute, then remove from the heat and stir in the pectin. Return to the heat and boil 1 minute longer. Let the jelly sit for 5 minutes, and then skim off any foam with a slotted spoon. Ladle into sterilized jars and seal. Turn the jars upside down occasionally to keep the peppers mixed until the jelly is cool and set.

ABOVE AND OPPOSITE: *Hot Pepper Jelly is a Southern pantry staple.*

93

PICKLED BEETS
MAKES 7 TO 8 PINTS

The amount of beets in this recipe is flexible. In fact, the original recipe did not include beets except in the simple instructions: "Make pickling solution, add beets, and fill jars, continue until finished." The brine was made ahead, and beets were added as they became ready to pickle over the course of several days.

3 to 6 pounds beets
1 teaspoon whole cloves
1 teaspoon whole allspice
2 cups sugar
2 cups water
2 cups vinegar
4 cinnamon sticks
1 tablespoon Fruit-Fresh

Trim off as much of the beet roots and stems as possible without cutting into the beets, which would cause the color to run, and place in a large pot of cold water. Bring to the boil and simmer 45 minutes to 1 hour, or until a knife or skewer can easily be inserted into the center. They should be firm but not resistant. Set aside to cool. When the beets are cool, peel them and cut into chunks.

Tie the cloves and allspice in a cheesecloth bag. Combine the sugar, water, vinegar, cinnamon, and spice bag in a large pot. Slowly bring to the boil, lower the heat, and simmer, uncovered, for 30 minutes.

Add the beets and bring to the boil. Discard the spice bag and the cinnamon sticks. Stir in the Fruit-Fresh. Spoon the beets into sterilized canning jars and add liquid to within ½ inch of the top. Seal. Set aside for at least a week to let the flavors develop. (But they can be eaten right away if you must.)

RUBY LANDS'S CRUNCHY CUCUMBER STICKS
MAKES 7 PINTS

Ric Lands's mother has had this recipe a long time, originally shared by a neighbor now eighty some odd years old. The sticks, which almost have the texture of a pickled rind, are best served cold, and they are extraordinarily refreshing. Lime and alum are available at local Southern grocery stores wherever canning supplies are sold. The cucumbers can be very old—those left on the vine until they are yellow.

7 pounds very large cucumbers
2½ cups lime
¼ pound alum
5 tablespoons mixed pickling
    spices (see Note)
1 tablespoon pickling salt
2 quarts apple cider vinegar
5 pounds sugar

Peel and seed the cucumbers. Be sure to cut off all the seed hollows, otherwise the pickles will be soft. Cut the cucumbers into ½-inch-thick sticks as long as your canning jars are tall. Mix the lime and 2 gallons water. Soak the cucumbers in the lime water for 24 hours, weighing the cucumbers down with a towel to make sure they stay under the liquid. Remove the cucumbers from the lime water and rinse well.

Mix the alum and 2 gallons water. Soak the cucumbers in the alum water for 12 hours. Again, weigh down the cucumbers. Remove the cucumbers from the alum water, rinse well, and soak in clear water for 6 hours. Drain well.

Tie up the pickling spices in a cheesecloth bag or tea ball and combine in a saucepan with the pickling salt, vinegar, sugar, and 1 quart water. Bring the brine to the boil, pour

Put-ups

Putting up food for later times, putting up food to be given away, putting up food just to have, is an important tradition in the South. When someone drops by, why you can run to the jam closet, and pick out a jar for them to take home.

Putting up was originally an economic necessity, but it yielded some luxuries as well, including the South's prized hams and sturgeon roe caviar. Even now, put-up condiments are part of the life of small towns. When you visit small Southern towns you will always find a jar of vinegar packed with hot peppers sitting on the oilcloth-covered tables of the local diner. It used to be you'd see those same jars on every home table as well—ready for dousing the turnip greens or collards.

it over the pickles, and let stand for 4 hours. Bring the pickles to a boil and simmer until the pickles are clear, about 30 minutes. Discard the pickling spices.

Pack the pickles upright in sterilized canning jars. Pour in the pickling liquid to within ½ inch of the top. Seal with the two-part lids. Process in a water bath: Put the jars on a rack in a large pot with enough boiling water to cover. Simmer for 10 minutes. Remove the jars from the pot and let stand until cool. As they cool, the tops will "pop" inward, showing they are properly sealed. The sealed pickles will last on the shelf up to a year.

NOTE: Mixed pickling spices will make very hot pickles. I usually pick out as much of the red pepper as possible and some of the black peppercorns as well.

BREAD AND BUTTER PICKLES
MAKES 8 PINTS

When that time of summer arrives when the cucumber plants won't stop bearing, it is time to pickle. Come fall and winter, and the next summer, they bring pleasure that far outweighs the effort.

12 medium cucumbers, unpeeled, sliced ¼ inch thick
4 Vidalia onions, sliced
1 red bell pepper, sliced
½ cup kosher salt
6 cups water
1 quart white vinegar
3 cups sugar
1 tablespoon turmeric
1 tablespoon dry mustard
1 teaspoon mustard seed
1 teaspoon celery seed
1 teaspoon whole black peppercorns
1 teaspoon whole coriander seed

Put the cucumber slices, onion, and red bell pepper in a large bowl. Toss lightly to mix. Layer the vegetables and the salt in a colander. Let stand at room temperature for 3 to 5 hours, then rinse and drain thoroughly.

In a large pan, combine the water, vinegar, sugar, turmeric, mustard, mustard seed, celery seed, peppercorns, and coriander. Bring to the boil and then reduce heat to simmer, cooking gently for 20 minutes. Add the drained vegetables and cook slowly for 10 minutes. Ladle into hot sterilized jars and seal. Store in a cool, dry place.

Southern Hospitality

THE SOUTH IS RENOWNED THROUGHOUT THE world for the bounty of its tables and the generosity of its hosts. Southerners say "we don't know a stranger," meaning everyone is welcome, and this attitude goes back to the time of the Washingtons.

One of my earliest memories is of Mount Vernon, George Washington's home on the banks of the Potomac, not far from where I grew up. I often think that it was there as a young girl, learning about the Washingtons, that I first came to understand the Southern notion of entertaining.

Martha entertained so frequently that the story goes she served a ham a day and had enough guests to eat it all—much to the annoyance of the next president's wife, Abigail Adams, who didn't feel able to entertain so lavishly. George took great pride in his garden and his

LEFT: *Tomato–Red Pepper Soup served in heirloom Wedgwood bowls.* RIGHT: *Peach and Blueberry Soup.*

dairy, devoutly ensuring there would always be a feeling of bounty on the table (although he was known to fall asleep over a glass of Madeira while guests were still there!).

The Washingtons along with Thomas Jefferson instilled in me the idea that entertaining should be easy and comfortable. I'm delighted when friends call to say they are in my neighborhood and stop by for lunch. And some of my most memorable meals have been for the times when I miss my friends—after traveling or being particularly lonely—and just call them to say "I'm starting supper, come on over." Other times I pull out all the stops, spending days in preparation so that my guests arrive to find a magnificent spread of unexpected treats awaiting them, and their hostess as eager to join in as they are.

That is perhaps a secret of Southern Hospitality—the food contributes elegance and a certain snap and sparkle without placing an enormous burden on the hosts, leaving them free to spend time with their guests. Vidalia Onion Tart, for instance, may be made ahead and frozen. The Duck and Fennel Salad's components can be cooked and ready to be combined in a trice.

I do have some foods I love to serve just because they impress. My Grits with Cream and Cheese as well as Mississippi Caviar do just that— they make people who think they "know it all" about grits and black-eyed peas eat their words. Buttermilk is something else people scorn ignorantly, but the Buttermilk Pie is so good it will never be forgotten. And new twists on old favorites—like the Peach Raspberry Pecan Shortcake and the Blueberry Tart—are as exciting as their ancestors in a land where hospitality has traditionally been elevated to an art.

TOMATO–RED PEPPER SOUP

SERVES 4 TO 6

This soup has a remarkable fullness and richness of flavor, thanks to the red peppers and cream, and it doesn't take long to make.

2 tablespoons peanut oil

1 medium onion, chopped

2 large garlic cloves, crushed with salt

4 red bell peppers, roasted, peeled, and seeded (see Note)

1 28-ounce can plum tomatoes

1 cup chicken broth or stock, fresh or canned

½ cup heavy cream

Salt

Freshly ground black pepper

3 to 4 tablespoons finely chopped fresh basil

Heat the oil in a heavy saucepan. Add the onion and garlic and sauté until soft and translucent, about 5 minutes. Add the peppers, tomatoes with their liquid, and the stock; simmer 10 to 15 minutes. Puree the solids in batches in a blender or food processor, then return to the pan and add the cream, salt, pepper, and basil. The soup may be served hot or cold.

NOTE: This soup may be made several days in advance and kept covered and refrigerated. To roast the peppers, place them on a charcoal grill or under the broiler; turn until charred all over. Remove and place in a plastic bag to steam. When cool, rub off the charred skin and seeds.

PEACH AND BLUEBERRY SOUP

SERVES 8 TO 10

This cooling fresh fruit soup with mint garnish makes an attractive presentation that captures the colors of the South and its soft femininity. Add the confectioners' sugar to taste, depending on the sweetness in the fruit.

8 cups sliced fresh peeled peaches or 2 1-pound packages frozen peaches

½ cup orange juice

½ cup pineapple juice

¼ cup lime juice

½ cup plain yogurt

½ cup heavy cream

Confectioners' sugar to taste

½ to 1 teaspoon grated fresh ginger

½ cup fresh blueberries

Fresh mint sprigs, for garnish

Combine the peach slices in a food processor or blender with the orange, pineapple, and lime juices, yogurt, and cream. Process or blend at high speed until the mixture is smooth. Add the confectioners' sugar and ginger to taste and chill. Just before serving, gently add the blueberries. Garnish with fresh mint and a dollop of yogurt if desired.

VIDALIA ONION TART
SERVES 8 TO 10

Sweet Vidalia onions from Georgia are especially nice in this rich tart, which makes a wonderful appetizer or accompaniment for soup. A tart pan with fluted edges and removable bottom is best for this recipe, but a glass pie pan works well, too. Baking "blind" is a classic term used for partially prebaking a pie crust, usually for custards or delicate fillings such as this. The baked tart may be frozen.

1 recipe Basic Piecrust (page 192)
2 large Vidalia onions, thinly sliced (about 2 cups)
2 cups grated sharp Cheddar cheese
½ teaspoon salt
¼ cup heavy cream

Preheat the oven to 400°F.

Roll out the pastry ⅛ to ¼ inch thick and line a 9-inch tart pan. Cover with crumpled wax paper and fill with rice, beans, or pie

CHEESE GRITS SOUFFLÉ
SERVES 10 TO 12

Because this light soufflé should be served immediately, but can be combined ahead of time without much deflating, I serve it as a starter for special occasions. If you use a deeper, narrower casserole, increase the cooking time by 5 to 10 minutes.

> 1 cup grits, cooked in milk according to package directions
> 1 pound sharp Cheddar cheese, grated
> ½ cup (1 stick) butter
> ½ teaspoon mace
> 1 teaspoon salt
> ¼ teaspoon cayenne pepper
> 6 large eggs, separated

Preheat the oven to 350°F. Generously butter an 8½ × 13-inch ovenproof serving dish.

Place the hot grits in a mixing bowl and stir in the cheese, butter, mace, salt, and cayenne pepper. Cool slightly. In a small bowl, lightly beat the egg yolks. Stir a little of the grits into the yolks to heat them slightly, then add to the grits mixture and combine thoroughly. Beat the egg whites until soft peaks form and fold into the cheese grits. Pour into the prepared pan. (The soufflé may be made several hours ahead to this point.) Bake the soufflé until it is puffed and lightly browned, 40 to 45 minutes. Serve immediately.

LEFT: *The savory Vidalia Onion Tart.*
ABOVE: *Cheese Grits Soufflé.*

weights to weigh down the bottom and sides. Bake the crust "blind" until it loses its translucent quality, about 10 minutes, and remove from the oven. Remove the weights and liner.

Arrange half the onions in the pie shell and top with half the cheese. Add a second layer of onions and cheese, sprinkle with salt, and drizzle with the cream. Bake 25 minutes, or until the cheese is lightly browned. Remove from the oven and place on a wire rack to cool slightly. Cut into wedges and serve.

GRITS WITH CREAM AND CHEESE
SERVES 4

This really luscious, creamy, cheesy dish is an incredibly delicious accompaniment to a roast or an elegant meal.

1 cup heavy cream mixed with 2 cups milk
¾ cup quick grits
2 tablespoons (¼ stick) butter
Salt
Freshly ground white pepper
1 cup freshly grated imported Parmesan cheese

In a heavy saucepan, bring the milk and cream to a simmer. Add the grits to the liquids, stirring, and return to a boil. Reduce the heat, cover, and cook for 7 minutes, stirring occasionally, to ensure that it doesn't burn. If the grits begins to separate and turns lumpy, add a bit of water to keep it creamy. Remove from the heat, add the butter and salt and pepper to taste, then stir in the cheese. This can be made ahead and reheated over low heat or in a microwave.

CORN BREAD WITH RED PEPPERS AND ROSEMARY
MAKES ONE 8- TO 10-INCH CORN BREAD

Corn bread is a perennial Southern favorite. We love it simply spread with butter or for dipping in the "potlikker" of traditional Southern cooked greens. But for a special occasion, we want it to have some "shine"—which the addition of peppers certainly provides. This colorful corn bread is best made fresh, but leftovers freeze well, reheat fine, and shouldn't be wasted.

¼ cup vegetable oil
2 cups cornmeal mix (see Note)
1½ cups milk or buttermilk
2 egg whites or 1 whole egg
1 to 2 tablespoons finely chopped fresh rosemary
2 roasted and peeled red peppers (page 99), cut or torn into strips

Preheat the oven to 425°F.

Grease an 8- or 10-inch cast-iron or oven-proof nonstick skillet or an 8 × 8 × 2-inch baking pan. Add the vegetable oil to the skillet or pan and place in the hot oven. With a whisk, mix together the cornmeal mix, milk, and egg whites, and whisk until smooth. Fold in the rosemary and red pepper strips. Remove the hot pan from the oven and pour the heated oil into the batter. Give a quick mix, then pour the batter into the hot pan. Bake 25 to 30 minutes, until crispy brown. Remove from the oven. Invert a serving dish over the pan, then flip the pan over. Serve hot.

NOTE: To make cornmeal mix, combine 1 cup cornmeal, 1 cup all-purpose flour, ½ teaspoon salt, and 4 teaspoons baking powder. Store in a tightly covered container for up to 6 months.

ZUCCHINI AND SWEET POTATOES
SERVES 4

The caramel crustiness of sautéed sweet potatoes couples beautifully and deliciously with sautéed zucchini. This can be made in just 10 minutes, but if needed it may be made ahead and reheated.

2 tablespoons butter
1 large sweet potato (about ¾ pound), peeled and sliced ¼ inch thick

1 *large zucchini (about ¾ pound),*
sliced ¼ inch thick
2 *teaspoons chopped fresh thyme*
Salt
Freshly ground black pepper

In a medium sauté pan over medium heat, melt the butter until it sizzles and sings. Add the sweet potato slices and sauté until lightly caramelized on one side, about 5 minutes. Add the zucchini and continue sautéing until both are browned nicely on both sides, about 5 minutes longer. Season to taste with the thyme, salt, and pepper.

LEMON WINTER SQUASH
SERVES 4 TO 6

Nicely different, this casserole brings a lovely color to the table.

3½ *pounds winter squash such as*
Hubbard, Kabocha, or acorn
Grated peel of 1 lemon
(no white attached)
1 *tablespoon fresh lemon juice*
½ *teaspoon grated nutmeg*
2 *heaping tablespoons chopped*
fresh parsley
½ *cup freshly grated imported*
Parmesan cheese
Salt
Freshly ground black pepper

Preheat the oven to 350°F.

Bring a large pot of salted water to the boil. Quarter the squash, add to the pot, and cook 20 minutes, or until very tender. Drain, cool, then scoop out the pulp. Whirl in a food processor or beat with a mixer until fluffy and smooth. Add the lemon peel, lemon juice, nutmeg, parsley, and Parmesan cheese and blend. Season to taste with salt and pepper. Pour the squash puree into a greased 2-quart casserole and bake, uncovered, for 20 minutes, until heated through and lightly browned.

CABBAGE SALAD
SERVES 4 TO 6

This is a great totable dish since it has no eggs and will keep several days refrigerated and several hours unrefrigerated. It would also be decorative on a Christmas buffet with the red and green pepper flecks.

¼ *cup vegetable oil*
½ *cup red wine vinegar or rice vinegar*
1 *teaspoon salt*
¼ *teaspoon freshly ground black pepper*
1 *teaspoon dry mustard*
1 *teaspoon benne (sesame) seeds*
3 *cups thinly sliced cabbage*
1 *carrot, grated*
¼ *cup chopped green bell pepper*
¼ *cup chopped red bell pepper*
2 *tablespoons chopped onion*

In a small mixing bowl, combine the oil, vinegar, salt, pepper, dry mustard, and benne seeds.

Combine the cabbage, carrot, green and red pepper, and the onion in a large salad bowl. Pour the vinaigrette over the cabbage mixture and mix well. Cover the salad and chill thoroughly.

ROASTED RED BELL PEPPER SALAD
SERVES 4 TO 6

By now you may have gathered I have a strong affection for roasted red and green bell peppers, particularly when they have ripened on the plant. They are sweeter and fuller in flavor—almost a different vegetable—and can also be purchased already roasted and peeled in jars and cans. Most of those are more than adequate substitutes for fresh, and they are less expensive. I always try to keep some on hand. Pimientos are pointed bell peppers and come canned and jarred as well, but they are not usually quite as good as fresh.

5 red bell peppers, roasted and seeded (page 99)
¾ to 1 cup vinaigrette (page 110) or
¾ to 1 cup balsamic vinegar

Tear or slice the peppers into finger-size strips. Toss in vinaigrette. May be made ahead several days.

BEEF TENDERLOIN WITH OYSTERS ROCKEFELLER SAUCE
SERVES 6 TO 8

Beef and oysters have been paired for centuries in the South. This festive dish offers an exciting combination of tastes and textures and it is good hot or cold. Trim the beef carefully of all fat, or have your butcher do it; it usually is about a third of the total weight. Any leftover sauce would dress up a dish of scrambled eggs.

1 4- to 5-pound beef tenderloin, trimmed to 3 to 3½ pounds
Peanut oil
2 garlic cloves, mashed to a paste with salt

OYSTERS ROCKEFELLER SAUCE
¼ cup (½ stick) butter
1 small onion, finely chopped or diced
2 garlic cloves, finely chopped
3 cups heavy cream
1 pint oysters, drained, reserving ½ cup juice
1½ teaspoons Creole seafood seasoning
2 teaspoons Worcestershire sauce
Salt
Freshly ground black pepper
1 10-ounce package frozen spinach, thawed and drained well

Preheat the oven to 400°F.

Place the meat on a baking sheet and rub with the peanut oil and garlic. Place in the oven and roast to an internal temperature of 110°F., about 30 to 45 minutes. (The beef can be cooked ahead and reheated, wrapped in foil, in the oven.)

While the beef is roasting, melt the butter in a large heavy saucepan. Add the onion and

garlic and sauté until soft, about 5 to 7 minutes. Add the cream and the ½ cup reserved oyster juice, and bring to the boil. Cook over high heat 5 to 10 minutes, until reduced by almost half, then add the Creole seasoning, Worcestershire, and salt and pepper to taste.

In a blender or food processor, puree the spinach with half the sauce. Add the spinach mixture to the sauce remaining in the saucepan. Bring a shallow pan of water to a simmer. Add the oysters and poach just until the edges curl, 2 to 3 minutes. Drain and add to the sauce.

Slice the tenderloin if desired. Pour some of the sauce over the tenderloin and pass the rest separately.

NOTE: The sauce may be made up to a day ahead and kept refrigerated. Reheat gently before serving with the beef.

LEFT AND ABOVE: *Beef Tenderloin, served with a colorful salad of roasted red peppers, on the deck outside my home.*

SHRIMP COUNTRY CAPTAIN

SERVES 4 TO 6

Country Captain (page 122) is a famous chicken dish, one that my stepfather, who worked in the White House in the 1940s, said Franklin D. Roosevelt sought out when he came to Warm Springs, Georgia. Generally the chicken is left on the bone, which is very tasty to eat but can be messy. This version substitutes shrimp for the chicken, giving the dish a new twist and making it better suited to entertaining.

> 2 *tablespoons butter*
> 2 *tablespoons vegetable oil*
> 2 *red or green bell peppers, cut in*
>   *½-inch dice*
> 2 *medium onions, cut in ½-inch dice*
> 2 to 3 *garlic cloves, finely chopped*
> 2 *tablespoons curry powder*
> 1 *teaspoon mace*
> 2 *teaspoons chopped fresh thyme*
> 1 *28-ounce can tomatoes, roughly*
>   *chopped, with juice*
> ½ *cup raisins or currants*
> 1 *pound medium to large shrimp,*
>   *shelled and deveined*
> ½ *cup (4 ounces) slivered almonds,*
>   *toasted*
>   *Salt*
> 1 *teaspoon sugar or to taste*
> 4 to 6 *cups cooked rice*

Heat the butter and oil in a large frying pan until sizzling and singing. Add the peppers, onions, garlic, curry powder, mace, and thyme. Cook over medium to low heat until the onions are soft but not brown, 5 to 8 minutes. Add the tomatoes and their juice, bring to the boil, reduce the heat, and simmer 10 minutes. Add the raisins and cook another 10 minutes. Add the shrimp and cook 2 to 3 minutes until they turn pink. Add the toasted almonds and salt and sugar to taste. Serve over the hot rice.

GRILLED OR SMOKED PORK CHOPS ON MISSISSIPPI CAVIAR

SERVES 4

This is a very modern dish, and very pretty. I love the contrast of the Mississippi Caviar and the chops. If you can buy smoked chops, or prefer to smoke them yourself, they are equally pleasing in this dish.

> MARINADE
> 2 *tablespoons vegetable oil*
> 2 *tablespoons red wine vinegar*
> 2 *tablespoons lemon juice*
> 1 *teaspoon soy sauce*
> 1 to 2 *teaspoons fresh chopped thyme*
>   *Salt*
>   *Freshly ground black pepper*
>
> 4 *large center cut pork loin chops,*
>   *fresh or smoked*
> 1 *recipe Mississippi Caviar*
>   *(page 3)*

In a mixing bowl, combine the oil, vinegar, lemon juice, soy sauce, thyme, and salt and pepper to taste. Add the pork chops and refrigerate 1 to 2 hours or overnight.

Prepare the grill. Drain the chops and grill them until browned, 8 to 10 minutes per side, depending on the thickness of the chops. If using smoked chops, remove when browned and heated through. Arrange ½ cup Mississippi Caviar on each of 4 plates, top with a grilled chop, and serve immediately.

FAST FRIED CORNISH HENS OR CHICKEN WITH ELIZABETH TILDEN'S CREAM GRAVY

HEN SERVES 3 TO 4 OR CHICKEN 4 TO 6

These crusty little fried hens are tender and juicy and very flavorful, with curry powder or cayenne adding a subtle aftertaste. One of the virtues of game hens is that they fry so fast you can get dinner on the table in half an hour if your peas are done ahead! One Rock Cornish hen is a generous portion for one, but with a lot of side dishes will serve 2.

> 2 *Rock Cornish hens or 1 2½-pound chicken (see Note)*
> 1½ *cups buttermilk*
> 3 *to 5 cups vegetable shortening or oil*
> 1 *to 2 cups all-purpose flour*
> *Salt*
> *Freshly ground black pepper*
> 1 *teaspoon curry powder or ½ teaspoon cayenne pepper*

ELIZABETH TILDEN'S CREAM GRAVY

> ½ *cup all-purpose flour*
> 2½ *cups hot chicken broth*
> *Salt*
> *Freshly ground black pepper*
> ⅓ *cup heavy cream*

Split the Rock Cornish hens or cut the chicken into 8 serving pieces. Place the fowl in a bowl with enough buttermilk to cover and set aside for 15 to 30 minutes. Meanwhile, place enough shortening in a 12-inch skillet to reach two-thirds of the way up the pan (it should come at least halfway up the sides of the fowl when frying). Heat the shortening to 365°F., until it sizzles when flour is sprinkled on it.

Mix together the flour, salt and black pepper to taste, then add the curry powder or the cayenne pepper. Remove the fowl from the buttermilk, place it on a baking sheet, and liberally season both sides with additional salt and black pepper. Roll the fowl in the seasoned flour mixture, coating well.

Place the pieces in the hot oil, skin side down, barely touching. If the pieces will be too crowded, use a second skillet or cook in 2 batches. Cover the pan and fry 5 to 7 minutes for Rock Cornish hens and 10 to 15 minutes for chicken, depending on the size, checking once after 5 minutes to be sure the skin is not browning too fast. Turn the fowl and cook, uncovered, another 5 to 7 minutes for the Rock Cornish hens and 10 to 12 minutes for chicken. Drain on paper towels.

To make the cream gravy, pour off the fat from the pan in which the fowl has been fried and reserve. Scrape the bottom of the pan to loose the browned pieces and return 6 tablespoons reserved fat to the pan. Whisk in the flour and cook over high heat, whisking constantly, for about 2 minutes. Slowly whisk in the hot broth. Boil and whisk continually until the liquid is reduced and the sauce is the consistency of a medium cream sauce, about 3 minutes. Season to taste with salt and LOTS of black pepper. Add the cream and whisk until warmed and the desired consistency. Correct the seasonings and pass in a gravy boat with the fried fowl.

NOTE: It is hard to find a 2½-pound chicken anymore—the ideal size for frying, as it fills up one pan tidily. A 3½-pound chicken is more readily available, but it takes longer to cook. Use two pans of fat for frying or, fry half the pieces, drain out the fat, remove any burned or hard bits, then reheat the fat, and fry the remaining chicken pieces.

Split quail and/or their legs also work quite nicely in this recipe.

CITRUS ROAST PORK
SERVES 4 TO 6

The flavorful combination of citrus and pork is so good it's become a tradition in my family as well as in the South. Roasts are easy to prepare and "stretch" to serve more people, depending on how thinly you slice. To serve a crowd, get a whole boned loin and double the marinade. The cooking time won't vary much because the loin is the same thickness no matter how long it is.

MARINADE

Juice and finely chopped peel of 1 lemon (no white attached)

Juice and finely chopped peel of 1 lime (no white attached)

Juice and finely chopped peel of 1 orange (no white attached)

4 garlic cloves, chopped or mashed

1 3- to 4-pound boneless loin of pork

1 to 1½ teaspoons red pepper flakes

1 to 1½ teaspoons chopped rosemary

SAUCE

Juice of 1 lemon
Juice of 1 lime
Juice of 2 oranges
1 tablespoon all-purpose flour
1 tablespoon butter, softened
½ cup roasted peanuts, finely chopped

To make the marinade, combine the lemon, lime, and orange juices and peels and the garlic; pour over the pork. Marinate 3 to 4 hours or overnight, covered or in a large plastic bag.

Preheat the oven to 400°F.

Remove the roast from the marinade and reserve the marinade for the sauce. Pat the roast dry and rub with the red pepper and rosemary. Place in a shallow baking dish and roast to an internal temperature of 145°F. to 150°F. on a meat thermometer, about 35 to 45 minutes. Transfer to a platter and keep warm.

To make the sauce, combine the reserved marinade, the pan juices, and the lemon, lime, and orange juices in a medium saucepan and bring to the boil. In a small bowl, combine the flour and the softened butter. Whisk the butter and flour mixture into the sauce a little at a time, until it reaches the desired consistency. Add the chopped peanuts.

Slice the pork and serve with the sauce.

BOURBON STEAK
SERVES 2

Whether served with "ice and branch water" or in this tasty sauce for steak, bourbon is always a welcome visitor at the Southern table.

2 tablespoons chopped fresh thyme
2 teaspoons chopped fresh basil
2 teaspoons freshly ground black pepper
2 teaspoons chopped fresh rosemary

1½ teaspoons cornstarch
1 tablespoon water
6 tablespoons (¾ stick) unsalted butter, divided
1½ tablespoons finely chopped shallots
2 teaspoons finely chopped garlic
⅓ cup beef stock or broth
⅓ cup bourbon
2 10-ounce sirloin strip steaks
Salt
1 tablespoon chopped green onion, for garnish

Mix together the thyme, basil, black pepper, and rosemary. In a small cup, combine the cornstarch with 1 tablespoon water and mix well. In a small saucepan, melt 2 tablespoons butter over low heat. Add the shallots, garlic, and the herb mixture and cook until soft, 3 to 4 minutes. Add the beef stock and slowly bring to a simmer. Add 1½ tablespoons cornstarch mixture and whisk until thickened. Bring nearly to the boil, then remove from the heat. Whisk in 2 tablespoons butter. Taste, and add salt if necessary. Set aside.

When ready to serve, heat the remaining 2 tablespoons butter in a sauté pan over medium-high heat. Add the steaks, brown on one side, then turn and brown on the other side, and cook to the desired doneness (about 3 minutes per side for really rare). Remove the pan from the heat and remove the steaks. Add the bourbon to the pan, deglaze over high heat, stirring and scraping the pan. Stir the bourbon into the herb sauce mixture.

Slice each steak ½ inch thick and arrange on a plate topped with some of the bourbon sauce and a sprinkle of green onions.

Temperate fall weather is the perfect time for an al fresco dinner featuring a tangy pork roast.

CHICKEN BREASTS WITH POTATOES, ROSEMARY, AND GARLIC
SERVES 4

Surrounded with vegetables, this lusty chicken dish is great for a cold winter's night or a spring evening when a chill is in the air. You may keep the chicken skin on for a healthy peasant dish, or skin them if you want something a bit more refined.

2 to 4 tablespoons olive oil
1 or 2 potatoes, cut in wedges
2 tablespoons chopped fresh rosemary
1 or 2 garlic cloves, chopped
4 chicken breasts, boned and skinned
1 onion, sliced
2 red bell peppers, roasted, peeled, and seeded (page 99)
¼ cup sherry vinegar, red wine vinegar, or balsamic vinegar
1 or 2 tablespoons chopped fresh thyme and/or parsley (optional)

Preheat the oven to 400°F.

Heat 1 or 2 tablespoons of the olive oil in an ovenproof skillet. Add the potato wedges, and sauté until brown, about 5 minutes. Place the skillet in the oven, and bake the potatoes until crisp. Stir in the rosemary and garlic.

Heat a grill or the broiler. Grill or broil the chicken 3 to 4 minutes on each side, or until cooked through. Heat the remaining oil in a large frying pan until it sings. Add the onion, and cook until soft, about 5 minutes. Puree the peppers and vinegar in a food processor or blender until smooth. Add the puree and chicken to the frying pan, and reheat together, about 5 minutes. Place the chicken on a platter, and surround it with the potatoes and sauce. Sprinkle with the herbs if desired.

DUCK AND FENNEL SALAD
SERVES 4

One of the pleasures of my restaurant garden was an abundant supply of fennel. A variety once grew wild here and can still be found volunteering in some places. The richness of the duck is cut by the crispness of the fennel, apple, and peppers. I serve it in a glass bowl to show the layers.

1 4½- to 5-pound duck
1 to 2 garlic cloves, finely chopped
1 medium onion, coarsely chopped
1 to 2 fennel bulbs (1½ pounds), thinly sliced
2 medium apples (1 to 1½ pounds), thinly sliced (red or green)
2 red bell peppers, roasted, peeled, seeded, and sliced (page 99)

VINAIGRETTE
¼ cup red wine vinegar or sherry vinegar
1 teaspoon Dijon mustard
½ cup vegetable oil
Salt
Freshly ground black pepper

Preheat the oven to 400°F.

Wash the duck well and pat dry. Place the garlic and onion in the cavity, place the duck in a baking dish, and roast until the internal temperature reaches 170°F., about 45 to 50 minutes, discarding the fat periodically. Remove from the oven and let cool.

When the duck has cooled, slice the meat off the bones. Arrange with the fennel, apples, peppers, and duck in layers, ending with the duck.

To make the vinaigrette, mix the vinegar and mustard in a small bowl. Whisk in the oil in a slow, steady stream. Season to taste with salt and pepper. Pour enough vinaigrette over the salad to coat evenly.

QUAIL PIE
SERVES 4 TO 6

There is tremendous drama to a game pie, always hinting at what delicacy is hidden under the blanket of dough. Ours is not only beautiful, its crust is flaky and very special, due perhaps to Denice, one of my assistants, who developed the recipe.

8 quail
3 tablespoons butter
1 large onion, peeled and chopped
¾ pound mushrooms, cleaned and thinly sliced
1 tablespoon all-purpose flour

SAUCE
2 tablespoons butter
2 tablespoons all-purpose flour
1 cup heavy cream
½ cup chicken stock
½ cup dry sherry
1 tablespoon chopped fresh thyme
Freshly ground black pepper
Ground nutmeg

1 pound frozen chopped spinach, thawed and drained well
2 recipes Basic Piecrust (page 192)

GLAZE
1 egg beaten with 1 tablespoon water

Preheat the oven to 400°F.

Cut the legs from the quail and reserve for another use. Place the quail bodies in a large saucepan and cover with cold water. Bring to the boil over medium-high heat, then reduce the heat to a simmer and poach for 20 to 25 minutes. Drain the quail and set aside to cool. Remove the breasts from the bones.

In a medium frying pan, melt the butter. Add the onion and sauté over medium heat until soft, about 5 to 7 minutes. Add the mushrooms and cook for 1 minute longer. Stir in the flour and set the mixture aside.

To make the sauce, melt 2 tablespoons butter. Add the flour and stir over low heat until golden, about 3 to 4 minutes. Add the cream, stock, and sherry and bring to the boil. Cook, stirring constantly, until thickened. Season with thyme, pepper, and nutmeg.

In a medium bowl, combine a third of the sauce with the thawed and drained spinach. Season with pepper.

Roll out the pastry into 2 rounds ⅛ inch thick. Line a 9-inch pie plate with one round and spoon the spinach mixture evenly over the bottom. Next layer the mushroom mixture, then the quail breasts; top with the remaining sauce. Brush the outer edge of the bottom crust lightly with water. Place the second (top) crust over the pie and seal the edges with a fork. Brush with the egg glaze and cut three slits in the crust to release steam. Bake on the bottom rack of the oven for 30 minutes, until golden brown and bubbly.

NOTE: The pie may be made ahead and reheated.

PEACH OR RASPBERRY PECAN SHORTCAKE
SERVES 6

Shortcake is a Southern classic, split and filled with whipped cream and peaches and/or raspberries, depending on the season. I love them combined, but both are seasonal. Pecan meal gives our shortcakes a different flavor and they melt in your mouth.

SHORTCAKES
2 cups all-purpose flour
2 tablespoons sugar
½ teaspoon salt
1 tablespoon baking powder
4 tablespoons (½ stick) butter, chilled
½ cup pecan meal or very finely ground pecans
1 cup heavy cream
1½ cups heavy cream, whipped and flavored with 2 to 3 tablespoons bourbon

1 pint raspberries or 2 to 3 cups sliced peaches, or a combination

Preheat the oven to 450°F.

Lightly grease a baking sheet and set aside. Combine the flour, sugar, salt, and baking powder in a mixing bowl. Cut in the chilled butter until the size of small peas. Add the pecan meal and combine, then gently mix in the cream just until blended. Pat the dough into a round about ¾ inch thick. Use a floured 3-inch cutter to make 6 rounds and place them ½ inch apart on the greased baking sheet. Bake 13 to 15 minutes, until puffed and lightly browned. Cool on a rack. When the shortcakes have cooled slightly, split them. Spoon a generous amount of whipped cream onto each shortcake, then top with the berries and/or a few peach slices. Cover with the biscuit tops and serve immediately.

Homey shortcakes become elegant fare served on fine china in a formal setting.

CHOCOLATE PECAN TARTS
SERVES 4

Candles and flowers and a roaring fire have their places in seduction. But perhaps the best seduction is this rich chocolate and pecan filling in its delicately thin crust.

The fabulous shortcrust pastry in these tarts sturdily holds the chocolaty, caramel-y, pecan filling, but melts in your mouth with a hint of cinnamon.

CRUST
1¼ *cups all-purpose flour*
¼ *cup sugar*
¼ *teaspoon ground cinnamon*
⅓ *cup (⅔ stick) butter, softened*

FILLING
⅓ *cup dark corn syrup*
¼ *cup sugar*
¼ *cup (½ stick) butter*
¼ *cup semisweet chocolate chips*
2 *large eggs*
1 *cup coarsely chopped pecans*
2 *tablespoons all-purpose flour*
½ *teaspoon vanilla extract*

Dark or white chocolate curls,
   optional (page 180)
Pecan halves (optional)
Confectioners' sugar (optional)

Preheat the oven to 350°F.

In a medium bowl, combine the flour, ¼ cup sugar, and the cinnamon. With 2 knives, cut in the softened butter until coarse crumbs form. Divide the mixture among four ½-inch-deep by 3½-inches-round fluted tart pans with removable bottoms; press evenly onto the bottoms and sides of the pans. Set aside.

Stir the corn syrup and the ¼ cup sugar together in a small saucepan over medium heat until the sugar dissolves and the mixture boils. Remove from the heat and stir in the butter

and chocolate chips until melted and smooth; set aside to cool slightly. With a whisk or fork, beat the eggs in a large bowl until frothy; add the chocolate mixture in a slow, steady stream, beating constantly. Stir in the chopped pecans, flour, and vanilla.

Pour the filling into the prepared tart shells and bake until the filling is set in the center and slightly puffed, 25 to 30 minutes. Cool in the pans on wire racks. Remove the sides of the tart pans and release the tarts. Serve decorated with chocolate curls and pecans or a sprinkling of confectioners' sugar.

CHOCOLATE CHESS PIE
SERVES 10 TO 12

Chess is a well-known Southern pie, usually made with lemon. This lovely variation was adapted by Margaret Ann from one of the first books I cooked from, *River Road Recipes*, by the Junior League of Baton Rouge, 1959.

1 *cup sugar*
4 *eggs*
6 *tablespoons butter, melted*
¾ *cup heavy cream*
4 *ounces semisweet chocolate*
   chips, melted
1 *prebaked Basic Piecrust (page 192)*
2 *tablespoons confectioners' sugar*
1 *teaspoon vanilla extract*

Preheat the oven to 325°F.

In a mixing bowl, beat the sugar and the eggs together until light and fluffy. Beat in the butter, ½ cup cream, and the melted chocolate. Pour the mixture into the prebaked piecrust. Bake until set, 30 to 35 minutes. Cool on a wire rack, then chill. Just before serving, whip the remaining cream with the confectioners' sugar and vanilla. Top the pie with the cream.

ELEGANT BUTTERMILK PIE
SERVES 8

This tender buttermilk custard pie is amazing! It's as delicious as cream pies can be, and so tender it reminds me of a baby's sweet smile.

   1 *recipe Basic Piecrust (page 192)*
   ½ *cup (1 stick) butter, melted*
   3 *eggs*
   ¾ *cup buttermilk*
   ½ *teaspoon vanilla extract*
   2 *tablespoons all-purpose flour*
   1¾ *cups sugar*
   ½ *teaspoon salt*

Preheat the oven to 350°F.

Flour a board or wax paper. Using a floured or stockinged rolling pin, roll the pastry out ⅛ inch thick or less and at least 1½ to 2 inches larger than your pan. Fold the round in quarters. Place the pastry in a 9-inch pie pan and unfold. Trim the pastry 1 inch larger than the pie pan. Folding the overhanging pastry under itself, either press the tines of a fork around the edge to form a pattern or use your thumbs to flute the dough all around. Place the shell in the freezer or the refrigerator for 30 minutes before baking.

In a medium mixing bowl, mix the butter and eggs together until well combined. Add the buttermilk and vanilla, and mix well. Combine the flour, sugar, and salt, and stir into the liquid. Pour the filling into the unbaked pie crust and bake until set and lightly browned, 40 to 45 minutes. Let cool to room temperature on a rack. Serve warm, at room temperature, or chilled.

BLUEBERRY PEACH TART
SERVES 4 TO 6

This tart epitomizes summertime! When the first blueberries hit the bushes, put them on top of this special peach butter for a very special dessert. The peach butter can be kept in the refrigerator because the lemon juice acts as a preservative.

PEACH BUTTER
   1 *7-ounce package dried peaches*
   ½ *cup water*
      Juice and finely grated peel of 3
        lemons (no white attached)
   ½ *cup sugar*
   ½ *cup (1 stick) butter*
   6 *egg yolks*

   ¾ *cup heavy cream*
   1 *prebaked Basic Piecrust (page 192)*
   1 *pint fresh blueberries*

Place the peaches and water in a heavy saucepan and bring to a simmer. Cook 8 to 10 minutes to plump and soften the peaches; most or all of the liquid will be absorbed. Puree the peaches in a blender or food processor until fairly smooth. Return the mixture to the saucepan, and add the lemon juice and peel, the sugar, butter, and egg yolks. Cook gently over medium heat until the mixture is very thick, stirring or whisking constantly. Bring just to the boil, remove from the heat, and cool.

Whip the cream and fold it into the peach butter. Spoon the peach mixture into the prebaked tart shell and top with the blueberries. Chill until ready to serve.

Sunday Family Dinner

FEW WOULD GIVE UP THE LUXURY OF BRUNCH or the ease of a simple supper, but most would agree that Sunday dinner is the star of family meals. For many years "dinner" referred to the noontime meal, a holdover from the days when farm and small town families returned home from work for their main meal at midday; supper consisted mainly of leftovers. Today I use dinner to describe weekday evening meals, but when Sunday is attached it melds into one word, "Sundaydinner," that means something very special indeed.

They are often communal affairs, with family and friends hanging around the kitchen talking to the bread baker, watching the roast chicken being carved, and picking at the corn bread. The slanting sun of late afternoon finds everyone sitting around the table—with perhaps a card table or two added for the overflow—the

LEFT: Ray's Chicken-n-Dumplings are served on beloved family china.
RIGHT: Margaret Ann's "Burnt Sugar" Caramel Cake.

white tablecloth laid, the special china and crystal out, and a blessing made before the reach for favorite foods begins.

I am known for my "church hunger," a malady caused by years of Sunday afternoon family dinners. No matter that sausage and apples, or fried green tomatoes and eggs, or even Easter eggs might reside in my stomach—the quiet time of listening to the offertory, rather than helping me contemplate my soul, gives me too much time to think of the dinner waiting for me at home. Angel biscuits, quite appropriately, flit through my mind. Spoonbread is another light and airy creation, and my particular thoughts dwell on ham-and-greens spoonbread.

I can hardly fend off thoughts of chicken and dumplings in one of Ma-Ma's delicate bowls, a steaming casserole of Country Captain, redolent of curry and tomatoes, or Sunday-best roast chicken surrounded with vegetables. On the other hand, beef pot roast in a barbecue sauce could already be in the oven, ready to come out the instant I hit the door. A vegetable soup topped with thyme from my garden might be there to keep us going if the wait is longer, for a turkey perhaps. Dessert will be a caramel cake, or peach cobbler, its soft cakelike exterior surrounding tender little dots of fruit, the end pieces crisp and buttery.

The tradition of coming home for lunch during the week has gone now, and it is only in rural areas that dinner is served on a day other than Sunday. But the importance of these weekly get-togethers is greater than ever. To my way of thinking, the family that eats together stays together and lives longer. The hurry-up-and-eat syndrome doesn't sit well with current notions of how people thrive; sitting and talking over a Sunday pot roast builds as much understanding and companionship as watching a ball game. (With the possible exception of the Atlanta Braves.)

Even though my mother lives an hour away she and I still get together for a noon meal on Sundays, and now it is I who does the cooking. With the use of a microwave and freezer, we can assemble many of the same ingredients we had when the whole family got together for the noon meal and capture the spirit of those noisy, loving, and delicious gatherings of the past.

SUMMER VEGETABLE SOUP
SERVES 8 TO 10

If a patch of land is available, a Southerner will usually find a way to have a home garden, producing corn, zucchini, pole beans, butter peas, and field peas. And oh, my, we grow wonderful tomatoes! Make this soup in the summer when all the vegetables are in season, then freeze it to eat all year round.

   2 tablespoons butter
   4 garlic cloves, very finely chopped
   2 onions, chopped
   2 zucchini, sliced ¼ inch thick
   1 cup green beans, cut into 2-inch pieces
   1 cup shelled butter beans (lima beans)
   1 cup peeled new potatoes or larger
        potatoes, cut into 2-inch chunks
   1 cup shelled field peas
1½ cups peeled, chopped tomatoes or 1
        cup canned tomatoes, with juice
   6 to 8 cups chicken stock
       Salt
       Freshly ground black pepper
   2 tablespoons chopped fresh basil
   2 teaspoons chopped fresh thyme or
       ½ teaspoon dried thyme
   1 cup freshly grated imported
       Parmesan cheese

Heat the butter in a large stockpot or kettle. Add the garlic and onions, and cook over medium heat until they are soft, 5 to 7 minutes. Add the zucchini, green beans, butter beans, potatoes, field peas, tomatoes and their juice, and 6 cups stock; cover and bring to the boil. Reduce the heat and cook until the vegetables are soft, about 30 minutes, adding more stock if necessary. Season to taste with salt and pepper. Add the basil and thyme and heat for a minute or two. Ladle into bowls and sprinkle each serving with Parmesan cheese.

Memorable Meals

I never think of Southern vegetables without thinking of David's grandmother, Ma-Ma Dupree. Ma-Ma Dupree was in her late seventies when I met her in the old family homestead in Americus, Georgia. David and I were engaged, and she made us a wonderful Sunday dinner served, according to custom, at noontime.

There were at least a dozen vegetables spread out on the table, accompanied by some wonderful pickles and relishes and two or three meats in beautiful but unmatched china dishes from different eras of her life. After lunch she threw a large, snowy white tablecloth and a quilt over the feast, leaving it on the table. We sat around and snoozed and talked and listened to the lazy ceiling fan until it was time for supper, when we sat down and continued where we had left off.

COUNTRY CAPTAIN
SERVES 6 TO 8

It's fascinating to me to see the way this recipe is similar to the one in *A Virginia Housewife* for curried chicken, particularly since most Southerners will tell you it's a regional specialty.

1 5-pound chicken
⅓ to ½ cup all-purpose flour
½ teaspoon Hungarian paprika
¼ teaspoon cayenne pepper
Salt
Freshly ground black pepper
4 tablespoons (½ stick) butter
2 tablespoons vegetable oil
2 small onions, chopped
2 green bell peppers, seeded and chopped
1 garlic clove, finely chopped
1 tablespoon curry powder
¾ teaspoon ground mace
1 28-ounce can Italian plum tomatoes, with juice
4 cups cooked rice
½ cup currants or raisins

⅓ cup toasted, blanched, slivered almonds, for garnish

Cut the chicken into 8 serving pieces; rinse them and drain in a colander. Mix together the flour, paprika, cayenne, and salt and pepper to taste. Dredge the slightly damp chicken pieces in the flour, coating on both sides, and place on wax paper.

Meanwhile, heat the butter and oil in a large 12-inch chicken fryer or skillet. Place the chicken in the hot fat, skin side down, and fry until the chicken is deep golden brown; turn. When the other side is browned, remove from the pan. Add the onions, peppers, garlic, curry powder, and mace to the pan and cook until the onions are soft but not browned, about 3 to 5 minutes. Add the tomatoes and their juice. Return the chicken to the pan, skin side up, cover, and simmer until tender, about 30 minutes. Transfer the chicken onto hot rice on a very large serving platter. Stir the currants into the sauce and pour over the chicken or pass in a gravy boat. Garnish with the toasted almonds.

RAY'S
CHICKEN-N-DUMPLINGS
SERVES 8

After the War Between the States, the South underwent great changes. Rebirth was slow and prosperity seemed to return even more slowly. Families were large (in part to provide help with all the daily chores); cash money was scarce, and feeding everyone was a challenge. Chicken and dumplings was standard fare at the dinner table because one chicken could flavor a large stockpot; depending on how many people were to be fed, a little more flour, lard, and water worked miracles. This recipe has been adapted using shortening instead of lard and chicken stock and buttermilk in place of the water. The result is a light, flavorful dumpling that would make Ray's Great-Grandma Maude proud. Serve it on the old family china and you have a typical Sunday dinner.

> 1   *3-pound frying chicken*
> 2   *quarts water*
> 1   *onion, quartered*
> 1   *carrot, quartered*
> 1   *celery stalk, quartered*
> 1   *bay leaf*
> 10 *peppercorns*
> 2   *teaspoons salt*
> 1   *sprig thyme*
> 1   *sprig rosemary*
> DUMPLINGS
> 3   *cups all-purpose flour*
> ½   *teaspoon soda*
> ½   *teaspoon salt*
> 5   *tablespoons shortening*
> ¼   *cup chicken stock*
> ⅔   *cup buttermilk*
> 1   *tablespoon chopped fresh thyme*
>   *Salt*
>   *Freshly ground black pepper*

Place the chicken in a heavy 5-quart stockpot with water to cover. Add the onion, carrot, celery, bay leaf, peppercorns, salt, thyme, and rosemary. Bring to the boil, lower to a simmer, and gently cook 1 to 1½ hours, skimming any scum that may rise to the top.

Remove the chicken from the stockpot. When slightly cooled, remove the meat from the carcass and reserve. Return the skin and bones to the stockpot and simmer 1 hour longer. Strain the stock, discarding the solids. Return the stock to the stockpot. Skim off as much of the fat as possible.

To make the dumplings, combine the flour, soda, and salt. Lightly cut in the shortening until the flour resembles coarse meal. Add the ¼ cup chicken stock, buttermilk, and thyme and stir to make a stiff dough. Turn the dough onto a lightly floured surface and knead gently 5 to 6 times. Pat the dough into a round, wrap in plastic wrap, and chill for 1 hour.

Bring the strained stock to a simmer. Roll the chilled dough out ⅛ inch thick on a lightly floured surface, moving the dough after each roll to make sure it doesn't stick to the surface. Cut the dough into 4 × 1-inch pieces, and drop them, one at a time, into the simmering stock, stirring often so the dough doesn't stick together. Cook gently 10 to 12 minutes, until the dumplings are firm yet tender. Add the reserved chicken meat to the pot and serve at once. Season with salt and lots of freshly ground pepper.

BEEF POT ROAST IN A BARBECUE SAUCE
SERVES 4 TO 6

Some would say there is no such thing in the South as barbecued beef. Indeed, this is oven-cooked beef, braised in its own juices and a barbecue sauce. It's good and it's foolproof.

2 medium onions, chopped
1 3½- to 4-pound boneless beef chuck roast
1 cup beef stock or bouillon
3 garlic cloves, crushed or chopped
2 8-ounce cans tomato sauce
¼ cup dark brown sugar, packed
1 teaspoon Hungarian paprika
1 teaspoon dry mustard
1 tablespoon finely chopped fresh rosemary
1 tablespoon finely chopped fresh thyme
½ cup fresh lemon juice
½ cup ketchup
½ cup red wine vinegar
2 tablespoons Worcestershire sauce

Preheat the oven to 350°F.

Sprinkle the onions over the bottom of a large heavy pot or Dutch oven. Place the meat on top of the onions, cover, and bake 1½ hours, adding some stock if the pan juices begin to dry up.

Mix the garlic, tomato sauce, brown sugar, paprika, mustard, rosemary, thyme, lemon juice, ketchup, vinegar, and Worcestershire sauce in a bowl. Pour the sauce over the meat, cover, and continue to bake, basting every 20 minutes, until the meat is tender, about 1½ hours longer. Remove the lid for the last ½ hour of cooking.

Slice the meat and arrange on a serving platter. Spoon some sauce on the top and serve the remaining sauce on the side.

MARGARET ANN'S "SUNDAY BEST" ROAST CHICKEN
SERVES 4

Sundays are when the Southern home cook shines, and Sunday dinner wouldn't be Sunday dinner without chicken! Perfect for a midafternoon dinner, roast chicken can also be made ahead in the morning or the night before if need be and reheated. The vegetables flavor the stock well, giving the cream sauce a delicious richness; don't leave out the turnips, as they add a welcome touch of sweetness.

1 3½- to 4-pound roasting or frying chicken
1 to 2 bunches of your favorite herbs for stuffing (tarragon, sage, thyme, or rosemary)
1 to 1½ cups chicken broth or stock, homemade or canned
2 yellow squash, cut in 2-inch chunks
2 turnips, peeled and cut in 2-inch chunks
8 small red potatoes
2 medium Vidalia onions, peeled and quartered
2 large carrots, peeled and cut into 1-inch pieces
1 red bell pepper, seeded and quartered
1 green bell pepper, seeded and quartered
¾ cup heavy cream
3 tablespoons all-purpose flour
Salt
Freshly ground black pepper

Preheat the oven to 400°F.

Rinse the chicken and pat dry. Tuck the wing tips under the body of the chicken. Stuff the cavity with the herbs and tie the legs together. Place the chicken in a roasting pan

large enough to hold the chicken and the vegetables, which will be added later. Pour the broth around the chicken and place in the oven. Roast for 20 minutes per pound, basting every 15 to 20 minutes.

Forty-five minutes before the chicken is done (which may be after only 15 minutes or so), remove the pan from the oven and scatter the squash, turnips, potatoes, onions, carrots, and peppers around the chicken. Return to the oven and continue cooking and basting until done.

Remove the chicken and vegetables to a serving platter, tent with foil, and set aside. Strain the pan juices into a heavy saucepan.

Whisk together the cream and flour in a small bowl until smooth. Gradually whisk the thickened cream into the pan juices, bring to a boil, and cook, whisking over medium heat for 2 or 3 minutes. Season to taste with salt and pepper.

Serve the chicken surrounded by the vegetables, with some of the sauce poured over the vegetables. You may need to put some of the vegetables in a separate serving dish if your platter is not very large. Pass the remaining sauce in a gravy boat.

Succulent roast chicken surrounded by roasted vegetables is a meal in one.

HAM AND GREENS SPOON BREAD
SERVES 4 TO 6

Like most spoon breads, this is not a bread at all but a light soufflé full of good things to eat.

   ¼ cup (½ stick) butter
   2 garlic cloves, chopped
   1 onion, chopped
   1 10-ounce package (1½ cups)
      frozen turnip, collard, or kale
      greens, thawed and squeezed dry
   3 ounces smoked country ham, diced
   1 teaspoon salt
   ½ teaspoon freshly ground black pepper
   1 cup cornmeal
   1 cup milk
   4 large eggs, separated
   ¼ cup freshly grated imported
      Parmesan cheese
   ¼ cup grated Swiss cheese

Preheat the oven to 350°F. Butter a 2-quart soufflé dish.

In a skillet, melt 2 tablespoons butter over medium heat. Add the garlic and onion and cook until soft, 5 to 7 minutes. Stir in the greens and ham and set aside.

In a heavy medium saucepan, combine 2 cups water with the salt and pepper and bring to the boil over moderately high heat. Stir in the cornmeal. Reduce the heat and cook 1 to 2 minutes, stirring with a wooden spoon, until the sauce base is very thick (the consistency of mashed potatoes) and almost comes together in a ball, leaving the bottom of the pan clean. Remove from the heat and beat in the remaining 2 tablespoons butter and the milk. Beat in the egg yolks. Add the greens and ham mixture and the cheeses.

In another bowl, beat the egg whites until stiff but not dry. Stir one-quarter of the egg whites into the cornmeal batter to lighten it, then fold the batter into the remaining whites. Pour the batter into the buttered dish and bake in the middle of the oven for 50 to 55 minutes, until puffed and lightly browned. It will be soft in the center and crusty around the edges. Serve immediately.

BAKED STUFFED SWEET POTATOES WITH COLLARD GREENS
SERVES 8

The best sweet potatoes in Georgia are those that are dug up after the first frost and stored. They are really special all on their own, but even better this way.

   4 medium sweet potatoes, unpeeled
   6 slices bacon
   1 10-ounce package frozen collard
      greens, blanched, drained, and
      chopped, or 1 cup cooked collards
   4 scallions or green onions, sliced
   ¼ cup (½ stick) butter, softened
   ½ cup heavy cream
   ½ cup freshly grated Parmesan cheese
   ½ teaspoon cayenne pepper
   Salt
   Freshly ground black pepper
   1 cup finely grated Swiss cheese

Preheat the oven to 350°F.

Pierce the sweet potatoes with a knife several times. Bake 1 to 1¼ hours until soft. When cool slice each potato in half and hollow out with a spoon, reserving the potato flesh in a large mixing bowl.

Meanwhile, in a large skillet, fry the bacon until crisp. Remove with a slotted spoon and drain on paper towels, reserving the fat. When cool, crumble the bacon. Add the drained greens to the bacon fat. Sauté briefly over medium heat, then transfer to a medium bowl. Add the crumbled bacon and scallions and mix well. With a hand mixer or potato masher, whip the sweet potatoes until smooth, adding the butter, cream, Parmesan, cayenne, and salt and pepper to taste. Fold the bacon-onions-greens mixture into the potatoes. Divide the mixture evenly among the 8 potato shells, mounding the mixture; top with Swiss cheese. (The potatoes can be made ahead to this point and even frozen.) Bake the potatoes until the cheese is melted and the potatoes are heated through, about 20 to 30 minutes.

BLACK-EYED PEA AND CORN SALAD
SERVES 8 TO 10

I'm always grateful for new ways to use up garden vegetables. With a snappy hot dressing, red onion, and bell peppers combined with cowpeas (black-eyed), a touch of the familiar gets a new upbeat note. And it's so pretty! This salad requires advance preparation.

>   1   pound dried black-eyed peas,
>   washed and picked over
>   1   2-inch piece fatback, salt pork,
>   or bacon
> 2½   cups Silver Queen corn kernels, cut
>   from 5 ears
>   ¼   pound bacon
>   1   large red onion, cut into ¼-inch dice
>   3   red bell peppers, roasted,
>   peeled, seeded, and cut into
>   ¼-inch dice (page 99)
>   5   scallions or green onions, white and
>   green parts, cut into ¼-inch slices
>   Salt
>   Freshly ground black pepper

HOT DRESSING
>   1   cup apple cider vinegar
>   1   teaspoon sugar
>   1   tablespoon Dijon mustard
>   1   garlic clove, finely chopped
>   2   to 3 tablespoons chopped fresh basil
>   2   to 3 tablespoons chopped fresh thyme
>   2   to 3 tablespoons chopped fresh parsley
>   1   cup chicken stock

Cover the peas with water and soak 7 to 8 hours or overnight. Drain. Place the peas and fatback in a 5-quart stockpot with water to cover and bring to the boil. Cover, reduce the heat, and simmer for 25 minutes, until the peas are firm but not mealy. Drain.

In a medium saucepan, combine the corn with ¼ cup boiling water. Return to the boil, then reduce the heat and cook over medium heat until the kernels are crisp-tender, about 6 to 8 minutes; drain. In a skillet, cook the bacon until very crisp. Transfer to paper towels with a slotted spoon, reserving the fat in the skillet. When cool, crumble the bacon.

Combine the drained corn and peas in a large mixing bowl. Add the red onion, roasted peppers, scallions, salt and pepper to taste, and the crumbled bacon.

To make the hot dressing, add the vinegar, sugar, and mustard to the bacon drippings in the frying pan and bring to the boil over high heat. Reduce by half, about 3 to 4 minutes, then add the garlic, basil, thyme, and parsley. Cook a minute or two, until the garlic is soft, then add the chicken stock. Return to the boil once more and cook until reduced by half, 5 to 7 minutes. Pour the hot dressing over the pea-corn mixture and toss. Refrigerate overnight. Serve cold or at room temperature.

NOTE: To quick-soak peas, cover with 3 times the quantity of water and bring to the boil. Cover. Set aside for 1 hour. Drain.

VERONICA'S SPICY CONFETTI CORN AND RICE
SERVES 6 TO 8

Although this dish has a southwestern flavor, it uses ingredients that are popular throughout the South.

- 1 cup uncooked long-grain white rice
- 2 cups chicken stock or water
- 2 green bell peppers (about ¾ pound)
- 2 red bell peppers (about ¾ pound)
- 4 ears fresh corn or 2 cups frozen kernels
- 2 tablespoons olive oil
- 3 tablespoons butter
- ½ cup finely chopped scallions or green onions
- 2 tablespoons ground cumin
- 1 tablespoon finely minced fresh thyme
- 1 tablespoon finely minced garlic
- ¼ teaspoon red pepper flakes
- Salt
- Freshly ground black pepper

Combine the rice and stock or water in a 2- to 3-quart saucepan and bring to the boil. Stir once or twice, then lower the heat to a simmer, cover with a tight-fitting lid or heavy-duty foil, and cook 15 minutes. If the rice is not quite tender or the liquid not absorbed, cook 2 to 4 minutes longer.

Core and seed the peppers. Cut them into very thin strips or dice—either shape works nicely in this dish. If using fresh corn, scrape the kernels from the ears. In a frying pan, heat the oil and butter over medium heat; add the peppers, corn, scallions, cumin, thyme, garlic, and red pepper flakes; season to taste with salt and pepper. Cook 3 to 4 minutes, shaking the frying pan and stirring. Stir the vegetables into the cooked rice and serve.

CARROT AND ORANGE SALAD WITH BENNE SEEDS
SERVES 4 TO 6

Benne seeds are also called sesame seeds. Simple and refreshing, this is "real good" anytime, but particularly as a winter salad.

- 1 orange, peeled and sliced
- 1 pound carrots, peeled and grated
- 3 tablespoons fresh orange juice
- 1 tablespoon red wine vinegar or raspberry vinegar
- Sugar
- Salt
- Freshly ground black pepper
- 1 teaspoon benne (sesame) seeds
- 1 to 2 tablespoons salad oil

In a large serving bowl, combine the orange, carrots, orange juice, vinegar, sugar, and salt and pepper to taste. Mix well. Quickly toast the seeds in the oil in the microwave or in a small pan on top of the stove. Sprinkle the oil and seeds over the salad and toss to combine. Chill until serving.

LEFT: *The spicy corn salad.* OPPOSITE: *The piquant Carrot and Orange Salad.*

BAKED GREEN BEANS
SERVES 4

This is a very new way of treating our favorite Southern vegetable, green beans. They look terrible but taste wonderful, particularly with Tomato Conserve (page 87).

> 1 to 1½ pounds green beans, trimmed
> 2 to 3 tablespoons olive oil
> Salt
> Freshly ground black pepper

Preheat the oven to 400°F.

Place the beans in a baking dish. Drizzle with the olive oil and toss lightly. Sprinkle with salt and pepper, and bake until the beans are shriveled and browned, about 30 to 45 minutes. Serve hot or at room temperature.

POTATO-ONION CASSEROLE
SERVES 6 TO 8

This alternative to scalloped potatoes is lower in calories but still a very special side dish that's full of flavor.

> 4 large baking potatoes (2 to 2½ pounds), peeled and sliced ⅛ inch thick
> 1 to 2 garlic cloves, finely chopped (optional)
> 1 large (about ¾ pound) Vidalia onion, sliced ⅛ inch thick
> 3 to 4 tablespoons finely chopped fresh thyme
> Salt
> Freshly ground black pepper
> 1¼ cups freshly grated imported Parmesan cheese
> 1 cup chicken broth or stock, preferably homemade

Preheat the oven to 375°F.

Generously grease an 8 × 11-inch baking dish or spray with nonstick spray. Layer the ingredients in the baking dish in the following order: one-fourth of the potatoes; one-third of the garlic, onion, thyme, salt, and pepper mixed together; and one-fourth of the Parmesan cheese. Repeat 2 more times, and end with a fourth layer of potatoes and cheese. Pour the chicken broth into the pan around the sides until it comes about halfway up the sides. Bake until the potatoes and onions are tender, about 1 hour.

RAY'S WHITE LOAF BREAD
MAKES 2 LOAVES OR 60 FINGER ROLLS

There are times when tender white bread is the only bread that will do. For pimiento cheese sandwiches, for instance—as well as peanut butter ones—and for the first tomato sandwich of the season, it would be a sacrilege to use any other kind.

This loaf rises beautifully, its golden crust towering out of the pan, to make giant slices of soft, airy bread and freezes well.

> 2 packages active dry yeast
> 2 tablespoons sugar
> ½ cup warm water (105°F. to 115°F.)
> ¾ cup milk, scalded and cooled to 105°F. to 115°F.
> ½ cup (1 stick) butter, at room temperature
> 2 teaspoons salt
> 4 eggs, lightly beaten
> 5 to 7 cups bread flour
> 1 tablespoon butter, melted

Grease two 9 × 5-inch loaf pans.

Dissolve the yeast and sugar in the warm water. In a large bowl, pour the milk over the butter and salt and stir. Cool 5 or 10 minutes, then add the eggs, yeast, and 3 cups flour, beating with an electric mixer, by hand, or in a food processor until smooth. Add as much additional flour as necessary to make a soft dough that is not sticky. Turn out onto a floured board and knead until the dough bounces back when you touch it. Place in an oiled plastic bag or an oiled bowl, seal or cover with plastic wrap, and let rise in a warm place until doubled, about 1 hour. Punch down the dough and divide in 2. Roll each piece into a 9 × 12-inch rectangle. Starting at a short edge, gently roll the dough. Tuck the ends under and place in one of the pans. Repeat with the second piece of dough. Let rise, uncovered, until doubled, about 1 hour.

Preheat the oven to 375°F. Brush the loaves with the melted butter. Slash the tops. Bake 30 minutes, or until the bottom sounds hollow when tapped. Turn out on a rack.

FINGER ROLLS: After the dough has risen the first time, punch down and divide into sixty 2-inch pieces. Roll each piece into a cylinder 3½ to 4 inches long. Brush the tops with a glaze made by mixing an egg yolk with 2 tablespoons water and sprinkle with poppy seeds, if desired. Place on a lightly greased baking sheet, 1½ inches apart, and let rise until doubled. Bake for 15 minutes, or until golden brown; cool on wire racks.

SALLY LUNN ROLLS OR BREAD
MAKES 18 ROLLS OR 1 LOAF

This angel-light bread derived from an old English recipe is almost a cake, it's so spectacular, light, and delicious. A reader once wrote me, scolding me for not having ever visited Sally Lunn's home in England after I said the recipe might be traced back to a street hawker of baked goods calling "Soleil Lune" (Sally Lunn being an anglicized pronunciation of the words *sun* and *moon* in French). Still, most Southerners consider it a homegrown recipe since we've eaten it all of our lives on special occasions. It may be baked in a tube or bundt pan or scooped into muffin tins and baked into rolls.

2 *packages active dry yeast*
½ *cup sugar*
1 *cup milk (105°F. to 115°F.)*
4 *eggs*
3 *teaspoons salt*
4 *cups bread flour*
¾ *cup (1½ sticks) butter, melted*

In a small bowl, combine the yeast, sugar, and warm milk, and let stand until dissolved. Beat the eggs with an electric mixer until light. Add the yeast mixture and the salt. Add the flour to the egg mixture, alternately with the melted butter, beginning and ending with flour. Beat well with the mixer after each addition and at the end; the batter will be thick. Cover with plastic wrap and let rise in a warm place until doubled in volume, about 1 hour.

Before using, beat the dough down with the mixer on the lowest speed.

Preheat the oven to 350°F.

Butter a 10-inch tube or bundt pan. Turn the batter into the prepared pan. Cover with plastic wrap and allow to double again, about 30 minutes. Place the pan on a cookie sheet and then in the oven. Bake 30 to 40 minutes, until a toothpick comes out clean. Cool in the pan about 10 minutes, then turn out and cool on a wire rack.

NOTE: Both the bread and rolls freeze well.

ANGEL BISCUITS
MAKES 20 TO 25 BISCUITS

Angel biscuits are a traditional old-time Southern specialty aptly named because they are as light as clouds! They are also known as bride's biscuits. Because the dough contains yeast, these can be made ahead and you may bake up a few biscuits at a time from the dough over a period of a week. They also freeze well; no one would even guess if you baked the whole batch and froze them.

These wonderful biscuits are adapted from the *Pirate's House Cookbook,* compiled by my former assistant Sarah Gaede.

1 package active dry yeast
¼ cup sugar
3 tablespoons warm water
   (110°F. to 115°F.)
1 teaspoon baking soda
1 tablespoon baking powder
1 teaspoon salt
6 cups white soft wheat all-purpose
   flour or cake flour
1 cup vegetable shortening
2 cups buttermilk
   Additional flour

Dissolve the yeast and a pinch of the sugar in the warm water. Sift the baking soda, baking powder, salt, and the remainder of the sugar with the flour. Cut the shortening into the dry ingredients with 2 forks, a pastry cutter, or your fingers until the size of garden peas. Add the yeast mixture to the buttermilk and stir into the flour mixture until all of the flour is barely moistened to make a sticky dough. Cover with plastic wrap and refrigerate overnight or up to a week before using.

When ready to cook, preheat the oven to 425°F. Lightly grease a baking sheet. Place about 1 cup additional flour on the work surface. Place the sticky dough on top of the flour and sprinkle with more flour. Pat out into a round ⅓ inch thick and then fold over to a height of ⅔ inch. Using a 2½-inch biscuit cutter, cut out the biscuits. Place the biscuits, their sides touching, on the greased baking sheet. Bake 10 to 12 minutes, until lightly tinged with brown.

REFRIGERATOR BISCUIT MIX
MAKES 4 BATCHES OF 12 BISCUITS

This biscuit mix is ideal for a busy cook. It will keep several months in a tightly covered container in the refrigerator. Simply combine one part milk or buttermilk with two parts mix for any quantity of biscuits from 6 to 60!

10 cups self-rising flour
 3 teaspoons salt
 4 teaspoons baking powder
 2 cups shortening

Sift together the flour, salt, and baking powder. With a pastry cutter, 2 knives, or your fingers, cut in the shortening until it resembles a coarse meal. Store in the refrigerator in an airtight container until ready to use.

NOTE: To make 12 biscuits, preheat the oven to 500°F. Measure out 2½ cups biscuit mix. Add 1¼ cups milk or buttermilk. Mix just until you have a wet dough.

Turn out onto a lightly floured surface (such as a tea towel) and knead gently 3 to 4 times. Roll or pat the dough to ½-inch thickness. Using a 2-inch cutter, cut the dough into 12 rounds. Place them on an ungreased cookie sheet with their sides barely touching. Bake until golden, about 8 to 10 minutes.

Margaret Ann's "Burnt Sugar" Caramel Cake

Makes 1 Cake

When Southern cooks had to cook for large families regularly, they probably thought this icing was easy to make, but these days, a homemade cake is a special treat. The first time you make this cake, take care and count it as a learning experience—it's tricky but worth it. David's grandmother, Ma-Ma, made the caramel in an iron skillet and I still frequently do, and although we never could get Ma-Ma's recipe down exactly the way she made it, thanks to Margaret Ann this recipe is very close to the traditional favorite. "Burnt sugar" is the affectionate colloquialism normally used for caramel—it's not really "burnt" at all.

4½ cups cake flour
1 tablespoon baking powder
1½ teaspoons salt
3 cups sugar
1½ cups (3 sticks) butter, softened
1½ cups heavy cream
8 egg whites
½ cup water
1 tablespoon vanilla extract

CARAMEL ICING
6 cups sugar
⅓ cup water
¾ cup light Karo syrup
2¼ cups milk
¼ teaspoon baking soda
3 tablespoons butter
1 teaspoon vanilla extract
1 to 2 tablespoons heavy cream, to
thin icing, if needed

Preheat the oven to 350°F.

Grease and flour three 9-inch round cake pans. Cut 3 rounds of wax paper to fit the cake pans, grease and flour the rounds, and add them to the pans.

Combine the flour, baking powder, salt, and sugar in a mixer bowl. Mix on low speed to combine. Add the butter and 1 cup heavy cream and beat for 1½ minutes. Scrape down the batter from the sides of the bowl. In a small bowl, mix the remaining ½ cup heavy cream, 4 egg whites, the water, and vanilla and add this mixture in 3 batches to the bowl, beating for 20 seconds after each addition.

In another mixing bowl, beat the 4 remaining egg whites to soft peaks. Fold into the batter and pour the batter into the prepared pans. Bake 25 to 30 minutes, or until the cakes spring back when pressed in the center. Cool on wire racks.

To make the icing, put 1 cup sugar, the water, and Karo syrup in a heavy 12-inch iron skillet and stir to combine. Cook over low heat until the sugar is dissolved, about 15 to 20 minutes. Turn up the heat and boil until a nice caramel color is obtained, about 15 to 20 minutes. Meanwhile, dissolve the remaining 5 cups sugar in the milk with the baking soda in a deep Dutch oven; then bring to the boil over medium heat. Cover your hand with a towel and pour the caramel into the boiling milk and sugar mixture; it will pop and spatter before settling into a rolling boil. Add the butter and continue cooking over medium heat, stirring frequently, until the mixture reaches soft-ball stage (238°F. on a candy thermometer). This should be measured in the center of the pot and the thermometer should not touch the bottom of the pan. Remove the icing from the heat, stir in the vanilla, and cool for 10 minutes. Stir vigorously by hand until the icing is almost room temperature and beginning to lose its shine, and still soft enough to spread but not runny, about 15 to 20 minutes. This is a hard thing to determine, so watch carefully.

Spread the icing between the cake layers,

then frost the top and sides. If the icing begins to thicken while you are frosting the cake, whisk in the cream, a teaspoon at a time.

SNAP BANANA PUDDING
SERVES 8 TO 10

Easy, fast, gooey, and delicious. Fun for children to make, but interesting enough for grown-ups.

¼ cup all-purpose flour
1½ cups plus ⅓ cup sugar
¼ teaspoon salt
4 eggs, separated
2 cups milk
1 cup heavy cream
3 teaspoons vanilla extract
48 gingersnaps
8 bananas, sliced

Preheat the oven to 425°F.

Combine the flour, 1½ cups sugar, and the salt in a heavy saucepan. Beat the egg yolks with the milk and add to the saucepan. Add the cream and cook over medium heat, stirring constantly until smooth and thickened, about 12 minutes. Stir in 2 teaspoons vanilla.

In a buttered 2-quart baking dish, layer a third of the gingersnaps with a third of the sliced bananas and a third of the custard. Repeat 2 more times.

Beat the egg whites at room temperature until soft peaks form. Add the remaining ⅓ cup sugar a little at a time, and continue beating until stiff peaks form. Fold in the remaining 1 teaspoon vanilla. Spread the meringue over the custard, sealing the edges first and working to the center. Bake until golden brown, 10 to 12 minutes. Cool slightly, then chill 3 to 4 hours before serving.

PECAN PIE
SERVES 8

Pecan pie is more than a pie—it's an institution! It's supposed to be sweet enough to give a bit of a jolt, yet not so sweet as to be cloying. The crust is to melt in your mouth, and make you remember the first pie you ever ate. And the pecans—they should be beautiful halves, meaty, just right for a little give and crunch between your teeth before a burst of flavor and then an easy glide down your throat. This pie does all that—with the bonus of a bit of orange.

4 eggs
⅔ cup brown sugar, packed
3 tablespoons butter, melted
¾ cup dark corn syrup
Grated peel of 1 orange (no white attached)
1 teaspoon vanilla extract
½ teaspoon salt
1½ cups pecan halves, chopped
1 recipe Basic Piecrust (page 192)
1½ cups pecan halves

Preheat the oven to 325°F.

In a large bowl, combine the eggs, brown sugar, butter, corn syrup, orange peel, vanilla, and salt. Whisk together by hand. Stir in the chopped pecans. Pour into the unbaked piecrust. Neatly arrange the perfect pecan halves in spirals or in rows over the top of the filling. Bake until the filling is set and the pastry is nicely browned, 45 to 50 minutes. Serve slightly warm or at room temperature.

NOTE: This pie freezes well.

The Holidays

CHRISTMAS IN THE SOUTH IS A TIME OF camellias and occasional bouts of walking weather mixed in with days of nasty, mean rain that drops the temperature and chills the bones. On those rare instances when it snows over the holidays it is not unusual to see pansies poking their heads up through the snow.

In these changeable times I alternate between covering my pansies and camellia bushes at night with sheets and old tablecloths to protect them from the threat of freeze, and sitting in the sun like a lazy cat, albeit with jacket and gloves. I've been known to have the convertible top down and the car heater on while delivering Christmas goodies.

At Thanksgiving the turkey reigns supreme, but in the South, Christmas Day is for ham. The holiday feast might also include a goose, or quail, but there will most assuredly be a ham on the table. Unless there is a country ham lurking in the closet (an increasingly daunting undertaking for the novice cook), the tendency more

A stuffed country ham and Hot Curried Dried Fruit make for a memorable holiday meal.

and more is to use a prepared one. The accompanying vegetables—turnip casserole, yam soufflé, as well as the traditional ones—cram the table. Soft yeast rolls make a special treat.

It is much like a Sunday family dinner, only more so. The desserts command, with little treats available from under the tree—bourbon balls, divinity, and pralines so sweet they'll satisfy any sweet tooth—there for eating all day long.

If Christmas Day is a family time, Christmas Eve is a time when elegance may appear for those not waiting for Santa, and for me it rivals the day itself. Elaborately set tables full of game, a buffet table laden with ambrosia and hot curried fruit, and a ham filled with grits and greens precede midnight church services or follow the children's service.

At Amanda and George Olmstead's on Christmas Eve, a misty, mean rain can make it impossible to find the curb for parking, but that doesn't daunt any of us. The house is always full when I arrive. There are dozens of children of all ages, the most dangerous being at knee level, chasing each other gleefully. Even their velvet garments (bought a little big so they can be worn for several years) hardly slow them down.

The grown-ups sip various potions, from iced tea to eggnog or bourbon and branch water. We fill up our plates with ham and fixings and catch up with people we haven't seen since last year—but meant to. There is always a cousin or two in the crowd, and it is a time to exchange information about births, deaths, and divorces. At last, when we feel warm and cozy enough, it is time to go home to the world of ribbons and paper and those undone tasks that will make the morrow the best it can be.

GRITS AND GREENS
SERVES 8

This is a really wonderful and unusual dish that can be used as a dip or as a vegetable side dish! If you have any tiny Poke Sallet (page 58) volunteering in your yard, don't throw it away. Cook the tiny leaves and stems, but avoid the toxic berries and the root.

> 3 cups milk
> 1 cup heavy cream
> 1 cup quick grits
> 6 tablespoons (¾ stick) butter
> 1 pound greens (spinach, turnip greens, or poke sallet leaves), washed, veined, and stemmed
> 1½ cups freshly grated imported Parmesan cheese
> Salt
> Freshly ground black pepper
> Poke sallet stems the size of young asparagus, blanched in boiling water for 5 minutes, for garnish

Combine the milk and cream, preferably in a heavy nonstick saucepan, and heat nearly to the boil. Stir in the grits and cook 5 to 10 minutes, stirring as necessary to prevent scorching. Remove from the heat and stir in 2 tablespoons butter.

Place the greens, still wet from washing, in a large frying pan; cook over medium-high heat until wilted, about 5 minutes. The water clinging to the leaves should be sufficient, but add up to several tablespoons water if necessary. Drain the greens and refresh in cold water. Drain the greens thoroughly, squeezing to remove all water. Melt the remaining 4 tablespoons butter in the frying pan over medium heat. Add the drained greens and sauté briefly. Add to the grits. Stir in the grated Parmesan cheese and season to taste

with salt and pepper. Transfer to a serving dish and garnish with poke sallet stems, if desired. This dish may be made ahead and reheated over low heat or in the microwave.

AMBROSIA
SERVES 8 TO 10

Ambrosia is a gift from the gods—a salad as well as a dessert. I love it served in a cut glass bowl. Coconut made a real foothold here in the land of the sweet tooth when it was used as ballast in the early ships coming to the South for cotton. Some people prefer toasting the coconut.

> 1 3- to 3½-pound ripe pineapple, peeled, cored, and cut into about 10 ½-inch slices, or 1 20-ounce can sliced pineapple, drained
> 10 seedless oranges
> 2 large, firm, ripe bananas, cut into ½-inch slices, about 1½ cups
> 1½ cups grated fresh or frozen coconut, or 1 3½-ounce can flaked coconut
> ¼ cup maraschino or fresh cherries, stemmed and halved

Place the sliced pineapple in a large bowl. Peel the oranges with a small, sharp knife, removing the skin and all the white pith. Slice the oranges thinly, and add the slices and the juice to the pineapple. Toss the sliced bananas, grated coconut, and cherries gently but thoroughly with the fruit in the bowl. Serve ambrosia in a large deep platter or bowl.

Chili at Christmas

For a French cook, Christmas means buche de Noel, to a British cook it means plum pudding. But for me, a Southern Christmas means chili.

This modern ritual of mine began in the early 80s, when the Brewers started a Christmas tree farm on Cedar Lane. Around the 15th of November each year, the sign goes up announcing the opening of the Mt. Pleasant Christmas Tree Farm. Immediately Ann Brewer's phone starts ringing with requests to come out to tag a tree even

though she doesn't officially start selling them until November 30.

School buses drive up, unloading small children who are taken on hayrides by the teenagers Ann hires for the season. Sometimes Ann and her loyal coworker Arci May will entertain 50 children at a time, offering a drink of Kool-Aid, cookies, and popcorn. They might have decorated a tree with candy canes waiting for someone to find it on a tree hunt. Often a tree is selected for

Steaming mugs of Chili warm the cold hands and empty stomachs of our group of Christmas tree inspectors.

a school, to be strung with popcorn, bread shapes, Cheerios, and/or cranberries for the birds.

Although the ring of children's laughter on Cedar Lane is a joyous sound, I take equal pleasure in selecting a tree for myself. I pack a thermos full of chili and invite a couple of young friends and we ride that hay wagon until we find just the right pine or cedar. It takes a couple of bowls of chili and maybe a swig or two of (nonalcoholic) cider before the decision is made.

CHILI
SERVES 4

This is a pretty traditional recipe. For something unusual, I add the bell peppers. This version doesn't call for beans, but of course they can be added.

> 6 tablespoons butter
> 1 tablespoon oil
> 1 onion, chopped
> 1 garlic clove, chopped
> 1 pound lean ground beef
> 2 bell peppers, 1 green and 1 red or both green, seeded and chopped
> 5 tablespoons flour
> 1 teaspoon brown sugar (optional)
> 1 teaspoon paprika
> 4 teaspoons Creole seasoning
> 3 cups canned Italian plum tomatoes, with the juice
> Salt
> Freshly ground black pepper

Melt 3 tablespoons of the butter with the oil in a large pan. Add the onion and garlic, and cook until soft, about 5 to 7 minutes. Add the remaining 3 tablespoons of butter, and stir in the ground beef. Brown the meat, and drain if necessary. Add the peppers if using, and toss together. Stir in the flour, brown sugar, paprika, and Creole seasoning. Add the tomatoes, breaking them up with a wooden spoon. Bring to a boil, then reduce the heat and simmer, uncovered, over low heat for 30 to 45 minutes. Season to taste with salt and pepper. May be made ahead several days or frozen and reheated.

HAM STUFFED WITH GRITS AND GREENS
SERVES 6 TO 8

This ham makes a regal presentation, each slice a magnificent spiral of rosy flesh laced with white cheesy grits and flecks of the dark greens. The combination of the South's three premiere foods makes this the perfect centerpiece for a holiday feast.

1 6- to 7-pound half ham
  Double recipe Grits and Greens
    (page 139)
4 eggs, lightly beaten

Preheat the oven to 325°F.

Remove the bone from the ham or have your butcher do it for you. With a sharp knife, remove enough extra meat to create a pocket large enough to stuff. Chop the extra meat and stir it into the Grits and Greens mixture. Add the eggs and mix well. Stuff the greens mixture into the ham, and sew it closed or tie it at 1-inch intervals with kitchen twine. Wrap the tied ham with cheesecloth and place it upright (i.e., the small end down and the cut side up) in a deep, ovenproof mixing bowl. Bake for about 15 minutes per pound. Remove from the oven and cool slightly. Turn the oven temperature to broil. Remove the cheesecloth and place the ham on a baking sheet. Run the ham under the broiler just to brown the fat.

BOURBON ROAST TURKEY
SERVES 12 TO 14

Bourbon adds a lovely hint of flavor and color to the crisp skin of this turkey. Bourbon is such a staple in many Southern homes that it is usually available for cooking. However, unsweetened apple juice or cider substitute just fine.

1 12- to 14-pound turkey
1 large onion, chopped
4 medium carrots, peeled and chopped
1 tablespoon dried rosemary
½ cup (1 stick) unsalted butter, melted
2 cups chicken stock
¼ cup bourbon or unsweetened apple
    juice
3 tablespoons all-purpose flour
  Salt
  Freshly ground black pepper
  Sprigs of fresh parsley, sage, or
    rosemary, for garnish

Preheat the oven to 350°F.

Remove the giblets and neck from the turkey, and set aside for another use. Rinse the turkey under cold running water, drain well, and pat dry with paper towels.

Toss the onion, carrots, and rosemary in a medium bowl, and mix well. Stuff the vegetable mixture into the neck and body cavities of the turkey, and close the cavities with skewers and string. Tie the legs together and tuck the wings under the body. Place the turkey, breast side up, on a rack in an open roasting pan. Brush all over with ¼ cup melted butter. Pour the chicken stock into the roasting pan and roast the turkey for 1 hour; cover with foil and roast another 1½ hours.

Stir the remaining ¼ cup melted butter and the bourbon together in a small bowl. Uncover the turkey, brush with the bourbon mixture, and roast, uncovered, 30 minutes longer, or until the breast skin is crisp and golden and the juices run clear when the thigh is pierced with a fork, and the internal temperature reaches 180°F.

Remove the turkey from the pan to a serving platter. Scrape the roasting pan to loosen the brown bits; pour the pan juices into a 4-cup glass measure and let stand until the fat rises to the surface. Skim off 3 tablespoons fat from the liquid and place in a 2-quart saucepan; skim off and discard the remaining fat. Add enough water to the remaining pan juices to measure 3 cups; set aside. Heat the reserved fat over medium heat; add the flour and cook, stirring constantly for 2 minutes, until the mixture is golden. Gradually add the reserved liquid and bring to the boil, stirring constantly. Reduce the heat to low and simmer 5 minutes longer. Season to taste with salt and pepper.

Serve the turkey garnished, if desired, with herb sprigs and accompanied by gravy.

THE PATIO'S GRILLED QUAIL ON GREENS
SERVES 6

Guests are always dazzled by the elegant combination of game and greens. Sometimes I cook the leaves whole, other times I chop them up. The quail may be halved, quartered, or left whole and spatchcocked, with the backbone removed and spread flat. Semiboneless European-style quails with the breastbone removed are readily available, and they quarter easily. The original recipe served at the Patio Restaurant calls for balsamic vinegar.

MARINADE
- ¼ cup olive oil
- 2 tablespoons soy sauce
- 1½ tablespoons red wine vinegar
- 1 teaspoon salt
- 1 teaspoon paprika
- ¼ teaspoon garlic powder
- ¼ teaspoon onion powder
- ¼ cup water

8 quail

GREENS
- 8 cups water
- 5½ ounces salt pork
- 2 cups sliced onion
- 8 to 12 cups chicken stock
- ½ teaspoon salt
- ½ teaspoon pepper
- 1 large bunch collards, washed, stemmed, and chopped, or 2 1-pound packages frozen chopped thawed collards, 7 or 8 leaves reserved for garnish
- 1½ cups Mary's Brown Sauce (page 146)

In a large bowl, mix together the olive oil, soy sauce, vinegar, salt, paprika, garlic powder, onion powder, and water. Toss the quail in this marinade and refrigerate for 24 to 48 hours, stirring occasionally.

In a large pot, bring 8 cups water to the boil. Add the salt pork and cook, uncovered, for approximately 1½ hours, until the liquid is reduced to 1 cup. Add the onion and 8 cups chicken stock and simmer 20 minutes. Add the salt, pepper, and greens and any more stock needed to cover, and simmer until the greens are tender, 25 to 30 minutes for frozen greens. Discard the salt pork.

When ready to serve, drain the quail and place on a hot grill, turn when brown, and repeat until brown all over—about 15 to 20 minutes total for commercial, 30 minutes for game. While the quail is grilling, reheat the greens and sauce if necessary.

Arrange a portion of greens in the center of a plate. Place quail on greens and spoon a few tablespoons of sauce over each serving.

QUAIL WITH
COUNTRY HAM

SERVES 12 AS A FIRST COURSE
OR 4 AS A MAIN COURSE

This recipe is particularly nice for quail that has been skinned (removing the feathers is a tedious process that many hunters prefer to avoid) because the ham serves as a protective coating that keeps it moist. Presliced biscuit ham is thinner than a steak but not as thin as a conventional ham slice. If slicing yourself, aim for ¼- to ½-inch-thick slices of cured but not cooked country ham.

Quail range in size according to their age and feed, so cooking times vary; the times below are a good estimate for game quail.

> 2 to 3 tablespoons vegetable oil
> 2 to 3 tablespoons butter
> 12 whole quail
> Salt
> Freshly ground black pepper
> 12 pieces "biscuit thin" country
>   ham slices
> ½ cup Madeira wine

Preheat the oven to 350°F.

In a large skillet, heat the oil and butter over high heat until "singing" hot. Season the quail with salt and pepper. Add the quail to the fat and quickly brown on all sides. Remove the quail from skillet and wrap each in a piece of country ham. Place the wrapped quail in a 13 × 9-inch casserole dish, pour the Madeira over the quail, cover, and bake for 30 minutes. Transfer the quail to a serving platter and, if desired, reduce the liquid in the casserole dish by half over high heat, about 10 minutes. Pour the sauce over the quail and serve immediately.

MARY'S BROWN SAUCE
MAKES ABOUT 1 QUART

1 *cup peeled and finely chopped carrots*
1 *teaspoon chopped fresh thyme*
1 *cup finely chopped onion*
1 *cup finely chopped celery*
5 *cups beef stock or beef bouillon*
2 *cups burgundy wine*
½ *cup (1 stick) plus 1 tablespoon butter*
½ *cup all-purpose flour*
1 *garlic clove, mashed*
   Freshly ground black pepper

Combine the carrots, chopped fresh thyme, onion, celery, stock, and wine in a small saucepan. Bring to the boil, then reduce the heat and simmer until reduced by about half, half an hour to an hour, watching to be sure that all the liquid does not evaporate; strain. You should end up with 3 to 3½ cups.

In a large saucepan, melt ½ cup butter until it sizzles. Whisk in the flour to make a roux and cook over moderate heat for 15 minutes, whisking as necessary.

In a small skillet, melt 1 tablespoon butter. Add the garlic and sauté for 2 or 3 minutes, until slightly golden.

Whisk the reduced stock into the roux. Add the garlic and pepper. Simmer, stirring occasionally, until thick enough to coat a spoon. Strain if desired. Freeze leftover brown sauce.

CINDY'S SOUTHERN CORN BREAD DRESSING CUSH
SERVES 12

As a young woman, Cindy Morgan worked for me when I owned and ran a restaurant in Social Circle, Georgia. Now she is a grown woman—an airline flight attendant with a husband and a baby. She shared this recipe when we met by accident at a swimming pool in Hawaii and started talking about our favorite recipes. She has also doubled the recipe and stuffed it under the skin of the turkey before roasting. The term *cush* is the ancient word for what we now call dressing. It's been thought to be Indian in derivation. Others say that the Gullahs' Nigerian and Angolan ancestors brought *kushkush* with them from Africa. Research suggests that the original word came from the Arabian couscous and was passed into African dialects. Cush is the shortened form of the Gullahs' fried, sweetened cornmeal.

5 *cups crumbled corn bread*
4 *cups toasted bread cubes*
1½ *cups chicken broth*
½ *cup (1 stick) butter*
1½ *cups chopped onion*
1⅓ *cups chopped celery*
1 *green bell pepper, seeded and chopped*
⅓ *cup chopped parsley*
½ *teaspoon dried sage*
½ *teaspoon dried thyme*
   Salt
   Freshly ground black pepper
2 *eggs, beaten*
2 *hard-cooked eggs, chopped*
1 *pint raw oysters (optional)*

Preheat the oven to 400°F.

Soak the corn bread and bread cubes in the broth. Heat 2 to 3 tablespoons butter in a large frying pan. Add the onion, celery, and

Thanksgiving

Thanksgiving is walking weather in Georgia. Just-planted pansies greet me as I stride briskly home from Thanksgiving services, usually with just a jacket thrown over my shoulders or a light cape covering my arms. The house is bursting with aromas by the time I return home, the turkey—half-done and covered lightly with foil when I left for services—richly bronzed. Sitting in church, I was occasionally reminded by a voice in the back of my head how foolish it is to leave the house with something in the oven. But the gratitude for all the good in my life wins out over the nagging and is its own prayer, keeping my house safe while I am where I should be.

How can anyone not feel grateful for a table as abundant as the one I have on Thanksgiving? There are sweet potatoes from south Georgia, layered with white turnips, white potatoes, tarragon, and a cheesy cream sauce. Though her son and I have long since parted, my mother-in-law still comes to dinner, bringing her homemade tomato conserve to put over the green beans. I offer both corn bread and biscuits because who could decide between them? And field peas—preferably lady peas and butter beans, snapped and picked through in the summer, then frozen.

Ambrosia—oranges and coconut laced together and always served in a crystal bowl—cuts the richness of the meal and is served at the same time as the turkey and fixings in my home. Piled high on diners' plates, it runs into the mashed potatoes and green beans, adding a sweet citrus undercurrent. The curried fruit brings back the memories of previous Georgia Thanksgivings and Aunt Lawson's smile—it's her favorite.

Caramel cake and even coconut cake are top contenders for dessert, along with the traditional pecan pie.

When all is finished, the football game beckons some, others walk out into the sunshine and stroll the afternoon away. It's a good day, Thanksgiving in Georgia.

green pepper, and cook until tender. Add the breads to the cooked vegetables. Melt the remaining butter, and add to the mixture with the parsley, sage, thyme, and salt and pepper to taste. Add the eggs after tasting. As an option, drain the raw oysters, simmer until their edges curl, and add to the dressing. Place the dressing in a greased casserole dish and bake, uncovered, for 45 minutes, or use as a stuffing under the turkey skin or in the cavity.

Country Hams

The fall-time ritual of putting up a whole hog is still practiced by some traditionalists in the South. In the years past, "putting up" (the colloquialism for salting and curing) was an important way of ensuring an ample supply of meat for the winter. Today most of us go the easy route and buy a succulent country ham, and the tangy pink meat is an irreplaceable part of many Southern holiday celebrations.

Of the country hams, Smithfield hams are the most exalted. They are aged longer than traditional hams (a minimum of 180 days and up to nine months), and utilize the "long cut," which includes the loin and entire shank. Until 1968 Smithfields were fed only peanut feed, but now they may be fed a feed mix that includes peanut oil (an oily pig will not shrink as much as a corn-fed one). Most Smithfield hams come from animals raised between Moultrie, Georgia, and the Smithfield, Virginia region.

The usual curing process for Smithfield and other country hams starts by hand rubbing a mixture of nitrate and salt into the meat. About 40 days of refrigeration follow, after which the hams are washed, then hung and oak- or hickory-smoked above 90 degrees for ten days, which kills trichinae.

Provided federal regulations and procedures have been followed, both Smithfield and country hams are perfectly safe to eat without further cooking, like a prosciutto ham. Once the mold exterior has been scrubbed thoroughly, they may be sliced and eaten, for example, as in figs with country ham. Still, many people prefer to cook the hams whole, and many country and Smithfield hams are also cooked where they are cured. One source for country, Smithfield, and cooked country and Smithfield hams is V. W. Joyner, Smithfield, Virginia.

If you have any doubts that your country ham has been cured in accordance with federal regulations, make sure to cook the ham until the internal temperature registers 160°F. on a meat thermometer. (Trichinae are killed at 140°F.)

Country hams and Vidalia onions are brought up from the Southern cellar to brighten holiday tables. The onions have been carefully stored since spring, knotted into hose to keep them from molding.

HOT CURRIED DRIED FRUIT
SERVES 8

Curried fruit makes a regular appearance on Thanksgiving and holiday tables all over the South. It suits our desire for sweet-sour condiments and side dishes. Usually it is made with canned fruit, although dried fruit is used as well.

Margaret Ann Surber, who has worked with me for nearly fifteen years, off and on, has one of the finest palates I know. She developed this dish, remembering the curried fruit her mother, Jean Sparks, served on holidays. The dried cherries are a recent arrival in many grocery and gourmet stores. If you prefer a non-alcoholic dish, substitute additional broth for the sherry.

> 2 pounds mixed dried fruit (figs, apricots, apples, peaches, raisins, cherries)
> ½ cup sherry (optional) or chicken broth or stock
> ½ cup (1 stick) butter
> ½ cup light or dark brown sugar, packed
> 4 teaspoons curry powder
> 1 teaspoon cumin
> 1 cup chicken broth or stock

Macerate the fruit overnight in the sherry, stirring occasionally. The fruit should absorb most of the liquid. Preheat the oven to 350°F.

In a small skillet, melt the butter; stir in the brown sugar, curry powder, and cumin and cook briefly. Stir the butter mixture into the fruit, mixing well. Place the fruit in a large 9 × 13-inch or 1-quart casserole, and pour the chicken stock over it. Bake for 45 minutes to 1 hour, stirring every 10 to 15 minutes to prevent burning. Serve warm, cold, or at room temperature.

BRUSSELS SPROUTS WITH MUSTARD SAGE SAUCE
SERVES 6

This easy and delicious sauce is made by boiling cream until it is thick. (It can also be used with cauliflower, green beans, chicken, pasta, rice, and fish.) Cutting the Brussels sprouts speeds their cooking so they'll stay green and bright. The sage gives an earthy aroma and flavor that contrasts nicely with the crunchy sprouts. Frozen Brussels sprouts can be used if you are desperate. This can be reheated in the microwave in 3 to 4 minutes.

> 1 tablespoon butter
> 1 onion, chopped
> 2 tablespoons red wine vinegar
> ½ cup chicken stock
> 1 tablespoon chopped fresh sage
> 2 tablespoons Dijon mustard
> 1½ cups heavy cream
> Salt
> Freshly ground black pepper
> 2 pounds small Brussels sprouts

In a heavy saucepan, melt the butter over low heat. Add the onion and cook until soft, 5 to 8 minutes. Stir in the vinegar, stock, sage, and Dijon mustard, bring to the boil, and cook until the liquid is reduced to about 3 tablespoons, 8 to 10 minutes. Stir in the cream, return to the boil, then reduce heat and simmer until the sauce is reduced and thick, about 5 minutes. Season to taste with salt and pepper.

Cut an X in the bottom of each Brussels sprout. Bring a large pan of salted water to the boil, add the sprouts, and cook uncovered over high heat about 7 minutes, or until just tender. Drain. Add the sprouts to the thickened sauce and toss to coat evenly. May be made ahead and reheated.

YAM SOUFFLÉ
SERVES 4 TO 6

This very pretty, light recipe came from Frances Baker, one of my longest-time cooking students. She's loyal, stays in touch, and comes back having cooked the recipes—flattering to any teacher! As a bonus, she shares her recipes with me!

Add a teaspoon of cinnamon, nutmeg, or ginger to the yams for a variation. If you can't find canned yams, sweet potatoes will do fine.

2 28-ounce cans yams
3 large eggs, lightly beaten to mix
1 cup sugar
1 teaspoon vanilla extract
½ teaspoon salt

TOPPING

1 cup chopped pecans
½ cup sugar
1 teaspoon vanilla extract
¼ cup all-purpose flour
2 tablespoons butter, melted
¼ cup flaked coconut

Preheat the oven to 375°F.

Drain the yams, reserving about 1½ cups liquid. In a large bowl, mash the yams with 1 cup reserved liquid, adding more if needed for a smooth consistency. Add the eggs, sugar, vanilla, and salt; mix well and pour into a greased casserole.

In a small bowl, mix the pecans, sugar, vanilla, flour, butter, and coconut. Crumble over the top of the casserole and bake for 30 to 35 minutes. Serve hot.

NOTE: This dish can be made in advance and frozen.

SALAD OF BEETS AND LEEKS
SERVES 2

This pretty salad is a real pick-up in the late fall and winter when we need color on the plate. But, oh, if you can get a fresh homegrown beet in the summer, that is when it's at its best—near perfection.

1 leek, julienned, using the white and enough of the green to make 2-inch strips

VINAIGRETTE

¼ cup red wine vinegar
½ cup olive oil
2 teaspoons Dijon mustard
Salt
Freshly ground black pepper

½ teaspoon grated orange peel (no white attached)
1 large beet, cooked and peeled, or 3 to 4 canned beets
6 to 8 lettuce leaves, washed and dried
Strips of orange peel, for garnish

Bring a small pot of water to the boil. Add the julienned leek, return to the boil, and cook until tender, about 2 to 3 minutes. Whisk together the vinegar, oil, mustard, salt and black pepper to taste, and the grated orange peel. Julienne the beet or grate coarsely in a food processor or by hand.

Place the lettuce leaves on individual salad plates and arrange the leek and beets decoratively on top. Spoon the vinaigrette over the vegetables and garnish with the orange peel strips.

RAY'S TOTALLY ORIGINAL BOURBON BALLS
MAKES 3 TO 4 DOZEN

Ray Overton has always loved musical evenings. He's a teddy bear of a man who is an actor at heart. When friends drop by during the holidays, he loves to light a fire, play the piano, and sing a tune, setting the stage for an evening of good food and wine. After Christmas carols, he passes around bourbon balls made from his own secret recipe. They have a little spicy kick that makes them especially unusual and good. Like the music, the glow of the mahogany, and the warmth of the fire, the bourbon balls spell joy for him.

To make rum balls, substitute rum for the bourbon.

> 2 *cups finely ground gingersnap cookies*
> 2 *cups finely ground graham crackers*
> 1½ *cups confectioners' sugar*
> 1 *cup ground pecans*
> 1 *cup flaked coconut*
> ½ *cup raisins*
> 1 *tablespoon grated orange peel*
>   *(no white attached)*
> 3 *tablespoons honey or corn syrup*
> ½ *teaspoon vanilla extract*
> ⅓ *cup bourbon*
> 2 *tablespoons butter, melted*
>   *Additional confectioners' sugar*

Puree the gingersnaps, graham crackers, ¾ cup confectioners' sugar, the pecans, coconut, raisins, orange peel, honey, vanilla, bourbon, and butter in a food processor or mixer until it comes together in a ball. Roll by tablespoons into 1½-inch balls. Roll them in the remaining confectioners' sugar. Let them stand for 2 or 3 days in an airtight container to mellow before serving.

NOTE: These may be frozen.

Savannah Pralines
MAKES 24

I can't imagine a world without pralines—nuts trapped in a candy so sweet and rich it nearly sets your teeth on edge, yet you find yourself craving them! Be sure to use a pot or saucepan large enough to accommodate the bubbly mixture.

1 cup buttermilk
1 teaspoon baking soda
3 cups sugar
1 cup (2 sticks) unsalted butter, melted
2 tablespoons light corn syrup
  Pinch salt
1 teaspoon vanilla extract
3 cups broken pecans

Combine the buttermilk and baking soda in a large heavy pot. Add the sugar, butter, corn syrup, and salt and cook over low heat until the sugar is dissolved, about 5 minutes. Bring the mixture to the boil and simmer until the mixture reaches 236°F. on a candy thermometer (soft-ball stage), 10 to 12 minutes. Remove from the heat and let stand until lukewarm, 110°F. Stir in the vanilla and pecans, and beat with a wooden spoon just until the mixture begins to thicken. Working quickly, drop mixture by tablespoons onto wax paper and let stand until firm. Store in an airtight container or freeze.

Divinity
MAKES 36 CANDIES

This is perfect for a holiday candy dish or a bake sale. It is best to make the candy on a sunny, dry day; use 1 tablespoon less water on humid days. Divinity freezes well and will keep for days if tightly covered. Use a heavy stand mixer for best results.

2½ cups sugar
½ cup light corn syrup
½ cup water
3 egg whites
1 teaspoon vanilla extract
½ cup chopped walnuts or pecans

In a heavy saucepan, heat the sugar, corn syrup, and water over low heat until the sugar is dissolved. Brush down any sugar crystals with a brush dipped in water. Continue cooking, without stirring, to the hard-ball stage, 260°F. In a large mixer bowl, beat the egg whites until stiff peaks form. Pour the hot sugar syrup slowly over the egg whites in a steady stream, whipping constantly. Add the vanilla and beat until the mixture holds its shape and loses its glossy sheen, about 10 minutes. Fold in the chopped nuts. Drop the candy by tablespoons onto wax paper–covered racks and allow to dry at room temperature. The candy should hold its shape. Store in an airtight container or freeze.

Pecan-Rolled Chocolate Orange Truffles
MAKES ABOUT 60 BALLS

These bite-size truffles are just the right size to satisfy a chocolate craving without going overboard. The orange peel and extract provide the taste of a liqueur—but without any alcohol. This is a very soft mixture, using more cream than usual to give it a smooth silky texture. For this reason, it is very delicate. Freezing the truffles and serving them in paper candy cups makes eating them much easier.

1 cup heavy cream
1 pound bittersweet chocolate, broken
  into bits, or semisweet bits

4 tablespoons butter, softened
Grated peel of 2 oranges (no white attached)
2 teaspoons vanilla extract
½ cup pecans, chopped
1 cup ground pecans for coating
2 tablespoons sugar

In a very large saucepan over medium-high heat, bring the cream to the boil and boil until reduced by half, 10 to 12 minutes. Remove from the heat and stir in the chocolate until melted and smooth. Add the butter, orange peel, and vanilla. Add the chopped nuts. Pour the mixture into a lightly greased 9-inch-square cake pan. Refrigerate the mixture until cool and firm, about 2 to 3 hours. With a melon baller, scoop out the mixture into small balls about the size of marbles, or you may cut the chocolate into 1-inch squares and form into balls by rolling gently between the palms of your hands. In a small bowl, mix together the ground pecans and sugar. (It is easier and less messy if the truffles are dipped into the pecan mixture, shaped in your hands, and then dipped a second time.) Refrigerate or freeze until firm.

NOTE: The truffles will keep 1 month refrigerated or 3 months frozen.

SURPRISE CHIFFON PIE
MAKES ONE 9-INCH PIE

Under this fluffy pumpkin chiffon is a layer of rich mincemeat—a splendid choice for those who can't decide between the two traditional favorites. It's a little tricky getting the egg whites whipped and incorporated before the filling is set, so work quickly and be organized. This recipe was given to me years ago by Chris Everitt of Covington, Georgia,

1 package unflavored gelatin
3 tablespoons cold water
1¼ cups plain or brandy- or rum-flavored mincemeat
1 prebaked Basic Piecrust (page 192)
½ cup packed light brown sugar
¼ teaspoon salt
¼ teaspoon ground ginger
¼ teaspoon cinnamon
¼ teaspoon grated nutmeg
1 cup pumpkin puree
2 egg yolks
¼ cup milk or half-and-half
2 egg whites
¼ teaspoon cream of tartar
¼ cup sugar

Sprinkle the gelatin over the cold water in a very small pan and set aside.

Spread the mincemeat over the bottom and sides of the cooled piecrust.

Mix the brown sugar, salt, ginger, cinnamon, nutmeg, pumpkin, egg yolks, and milk or half-and-half in a saucepan. Bring to the boil over medium heat, stirring constantly. Remove from the heat and place the pan in a bowl of ice water to cool. Meanwhile, in another saucepan, melt the softened gelatin over low heat. When dissolved, whisk it into the pumpkin mixture. Cool the mixture, stirring constantly, until it mounds when dropped from a spoon.

Beat the egg whites with cream of tartar until stiff. Add the sugar and continue beating until stiff and glossy. Stir ¼ of the egg whites into the pumpkin mixture to lighten, then fold in the remaining egg whites. Pour into the mincemeat-lined crust. Chill until set.

Hot Weather Food

ABOUT THE TIME OF YEAR THE FIREFLIES start to flicker in the early evening and the gardenias and magnolias add their perfumes to the sultry summer air, it becomes too hot to cook in the heat of the day. July, August, and September can be scorchingly hot months in the South, but suntan days in February can be had as well. So hot weather food is year-round fare and many Southern standards can be served hot, cold, or at room temperature depending on the day.

When the sun is at its hottest, the wise seek the shade of a water oak, crepe myrtle, or giant magnolia (frequently called a "slave" tree, as it gave shade to those working in the fields during the brutal midday sun) if a large open porch with a cross breeze and a ceiling fan is not at hand. Large hats that cast a shadow are not the province of the gardener alone. We become languid

LEFT: *Homemade Peach Ice Cream bursting with fresh fruit.* RIGHT: *A pastoral picnic spot.*

157

and our pace slows up and our sensuality peaks as we relish the sound of the crickets in the dusk and sit, occasionally dozing or rocking, sipping iced tea or Coca-Cola from sweating glasses. The air is lush and heavy as we listen to the ice cream churn and small children giggling.

By late summer when the crepe myrtle sheds its flowers in a pink carpet, it is too hot to do anything but pick at one's food until the evening comes. The heat penetrates your bones and the ground beneath your feet and you think you will never be cool again. This is when I start waking extra early and sit with the whippoorwills calling to me as I sort through recipes and drink hot tea in the cool of the morning and plan my cooking day. The night air can be so cool that when it hits the hot ground it causes a fog that covers the land two or three feet deep. Watching the fairylike ground fog rise and disappear, I do my major cooking and baking.

I sauté sausage or pork tenderloin early in the day, to be tucked inside a biscuit, then pulled out at the lake just after a swim. Curried slaw and deviled eggs are made and refrigerated to be served cold from the cooler or refrigerator, and cantaloupe and fruit are cut up for a cooling addition to a pool party.

I love this cooking-ahead time, a time when the rest of my world is slumbering, and I can bring my own music, the sound of water boiling, the butter singing, the knife cutting and shredding, the mixer beating. I'm ready for picnics and parades, with the Fourth of July a blazingly important day, a grand day for barbecues. In Covington, as in most small Southern cities, there is always a large parade on the Fourth, with banners and bands and children singing and laughing, with ribs and slaw and ice cream and all the cakes in the world.

And there is roast pig. Martha Washington roasted a pig every Fourth of July and pig is still traditional. There are those that cook their barbecued meats during the day. But the wisest cook them overnight, low and slow, first toasting the pig with a mint julep or two, then sitting in the cool night air and watching the fire and enjoying the night sounds, telling stories of eccentric cousins and others long dead, taking the pig off the fire in the early morning, then going to sleep while the air is still cool, to be refreshed and awake for the cutting up and serving of the pig during the day.

ABOVE: *Cooling Tomato Aspic.* RIGHT: *The chilled Green and Golden Salad.*

Jellied Delights

A word on aspics. These molded salads .are a rooted tradition in the South that long predates the fashion of serving mixed greens for starters. They are meant to cool and refresh and slide down one's throat. With a sweating glass of tea nearby, they herald the next course or serve as a side dish on a delicate plate. We love them, and they have never gone out of style.

MARTHA SUMMEROUR'S TOMATO ASPIC

SERVES 6 TO 8

This is the ideal make-ahead salad; the flavors marry, producing a better and deeper-tasting aspic the longer it sits. The onion will taste better if grated by hand rather than in a food processor.

3 *envelopes unflavored gelatin*
¼ *cup water*
1 *quart tomato juice*
2 *to 3 tablespoons lemon juice*
1 *tablespoon grated onion*
1 *tablespoon salt*
1 *tablespoon vinegar*
¼ *teaspoon cayenne pepper*

BASIL MAYONNAISE
1 *cup mayonnaise*
3 *tablespoons finely chopped fresh basil*
    Freshly ground black pepper
2 *tablespoons lemon juice*
    Fresh basil leaves, for garnish

In a small saucepan, soak the gelatin in the ¼ cup water for 10 minutes. Oil a 1-quart mold or 8 half-cup molds or ramekins and set aside.

In a metal bowl, combine the tomato juice, lemon juice, grated onion, salt, vinegar, and cayenne pepper.

Place the gelatin over low heat and, when liquefied, slowly add it to the tomato juice mixture, stirring well. If the aspic is needed in a hurry, place the metal pan over a bowl of ice and water, and stir the mixture constantly until it is thick. Then put the mixture into the desired mold and chill. Otherwise, pour the aspic directly into the molds and chill.

In a small bowl, whisk together the mayonnaise, basil, pepper, and lemon juice. Chill several hours or overnight until ready to serve.

At serving time, unmold the aspic onto a serving platter or individual plates. Garnish with fresh basil leaves and pour some sauce over the aspic, passing the rest separately.

VERONICA'S GREEN AND GOLDEN SALAD
SERVES 4 TO 6

This dramatically beautiful salad is good for eating inside or outdoors—spring or fall, as a simple lunch, side dish, or a starter. I myself could make an entire meal of asparagus alone. Serve chilled or at room temperature.

1½ to 2 pounds small asparagus spears
(about 36)
2 medium avocados
2 large oranges
2 teaspoons fresh lemon juice

CITRUS VINAIGRETTE
½ cup salad or olive oil
¼ cup red wine vinegar
¼ cup orange or lemon juice
2 teaspoons Dijon mustard
Salt
Freshly ground black pepper
½ teaspoon grated orange peel
(no white attached)

Trim the bottoms of the asparagus. If the asparagus is thicker than a pencil, peel from the bottom up to the first of the little offshoots. Place the spears in a frying pan, add boiling water to cover, and cook over medium-high heat until done, usually 3 to 5 minutes for small spears, 5 to 8 minutes for large ones. Alternatively, steam the asparagus for the same amount of time. When done, immediately plunge the spears into ice-cold water to stop the cooking. Drain and cut in thirds.

Peel the avocados and cut into bite-size pieces. With a sharp knife, peel the oranges, then free the segments from the membranes. Remove the seeds and cut the oranges into bite-size pieces. Gently toss the avocados, oranges, and asparagus together in a mixing bowl. Stir in the lemon juice.

To make the vinaigrette, whisk the oil into the vinegar and add the orange or lemon juice, the mustard, salt and pepper to taste, and the orange peel. Pour the vinaigrette over the salad and toss to mix well.

CREAM OF GAZPACHO SOUP WITH SHRIMP
SERVES 6 TO 8

Gazpacho, a layered tomato, onion, cucumber, oil, tomato juice, and breadcrumb recipe found in *The Virginia Housewife*, 1860 edition, took a good turn when it was combined with vinegar. With our temperatures moderate—or downright hot—so much of the year it is an often-used recipe here.

I frequently use canned tomato juice because I like the stronger flavor it gives and see no sense in wasting my meager portion of just ripe tomatoes on something to be whirred around in a food processor or blender.

The breadcrumbs thicken the soup and the sour cream lightens the color to a beautiful pink. It's stunning with either a sprinkle of coarsely chopped shrimp or a rim of whole shrimp on the edges of the bowl.

1 *large onion, cut in chunks*
2 *garlic cloves*
1 *green bell pepper, cut in chunks*
1 *red bell pepper, cut in chunks*
1 *medium cucumber, peeled and seeded*
5 *cups tomato juice, fresh or canned*
5 *tablespoons red wine vinegar*
⅓ *cup fresh or dry breadcrumbs*
½ *cup sour cream*
1 *teaspoon Tabasco sauce*
Salt
Freshly ground black pepper
GARNISHES
1 *medium onion, coarsely chopped*
1 *tomato, seeded and coarsely chopped*
½ *red bell pepper, coarsely chopped*
½ *green bell pepper, coarsely chopped*
1 *pound shrimp, cooked and peeled*
½ *cup sour cream*
½ *cup chopped parsley*

Puree the onion, garlic, bell peppers, and cucumber in a blender or food processor. Add the tomato juice, vinegar, and breadcrumbs and process again. Stir in the sour cream and the Tabasco sauce. Season to taste with salt and pepper. Chill or, if desired, transfer to a saucepan and heat over medium-low heat just until hot. Ladle into bowls and pass the garnishes separately. Serve with toast sticks.

COLESLAW
SERVES 4 TO 6

This recipe from Elizabeth Burris is colorful and makes just enough for a family dinner. (It also doubles easily if you're feeding a crowd.) The curry powder adds real zing.

2 *pounds green cabbage, shredded*
  (about 7 cups)
1 *medium carrot, shredded*
1 *cup mayonnaise*
1½ *tablespoons sugar*
2 *tablespoons red wine vinegar*
1 *teaspoon grated onion*
¾ *teaspoon celery seed*
¼ *teaspoon dry mustard*
⅛ *teaspoon curry powder*
  Salt
  Freshly ground black pepper

Combine the cabbage and carrots in a large bowl. In a smaller bowl, combine the mayonnaise, sugar, vinegar, onion, celery seed, dry mustard, curry powder, and salt and pepper to taste and mix well. Pour over the vegetables and toss gently. Cover and chill.

DEVILED EGGS
SERVES 6

A summer picnic in the South without deviled eggs, kept cold in the cooler until the last minute, is unheard of. And, of course, they are a good use for any Easter eggs that have been kept refrigerated and need to be used.

6 *eggs*
¼ *cup mayonnaise*
½ *teaspoon Dijon mustard*
2 *tablespoons finely chopped green*
    onions or scallions
1 *tablespoon finely chopped capers*
  Cayenne pepper
  Salt
2 *teaspoons finely chopped fresh*
    thyme, for garnish

To hard-cook eggs, bring a large pan of water to the boil. Prick the shells at the large end with an egg pricker or needle. Place the egg on a spoon and gently roll it off onto the bottom of the pan.

Roll the eggs for a few seconds to center the yolk. Reduce the heat and simmer 11 minutes. Remove the eggs to cold water briefly, then drain. Roll them on the counter to crack the shells, then peel them, starting at the large end. Slice the eggs in half lengthwise and place the yolks in a small mixing bowl. Mash them well with a fork or whisk; add the mayonnaise, mustard, green onions, capers, and cayenne pepper and salt to taste. Mix well. Spoon or pipe decoratively back into the halves. Garnish with finely chopped thyme.

POTATO SALAD
SERVES 6 TO 8

This potato salad is so good I've never had any leftovers. You may think that it sounds silly to have all these stages of preparation for oil and vinegar and refrigerating, and then mayonnaise and refrigerating, and then last-minute sour cream, but I will tell you that it really does make a difference in putting this over the edge!

8 *to 10 new potatoes*
¼ *cup vegetable oil*
¼ *cup apple cider or wine vinegar*
6 *to 8 ribs celery, diced*
1 *large onion, diced*
  Salt
  Freshly ground black pepper
1 *cup mayonnaise*
2 *tablespoons sour cream*

Bring a large quantity of water to the boil, add the scrubbed potatoes, return to the boil, and boil until tender, abut 10 to 15 minutes. Drain. While hot, peel and cube the potatoes. Place in a large bowl and toss with the oil and vinegar. Add the celery and onion, season to taste with salt and pepper, and refrigerate 2 to 4 hours or overnight. The potatoes will soak up some of the oil and vinegar. Stir in the mayonnaise and refrigerate another 2 hours until the flavors blend. Just before serving, stir in the sour cream.

CANTALOUPE AND ORANGE SALAD

SERVES 4 TO 6

Cordele, Georgia, is called "The Melon Capital of the World." Farmers line up in pick-up trucks at the market to show off their melons and have them weighed. One of the farmers taught me that melons, like tomatoes, can be ripened after picking by leaving them in a sunny place for several days until ripe and soft and the green webbing turns pale peach. We developed this recipe to use a cantaloupe that had ripened to the point of perfection. It features a lovely vinaigrette that does nicely served on delicate vegetables as well as on fruit. The salad is also very portable, as it may be made ahead.

4 oranges, ripe, flavorful, and juicy
1 medium ripe cantaloupe

HONEY-MINT VINAIGRETTE
1 tablespoon finely chopped fresh mint
1 tablespoon finely chopped onion
1 teaspoon finely chopped fresh
   rosemary
¼ cup vegetable oil
¼ cup white wine vinegar
1 tablespoon honey

With a sharp knife, remove all the rind and pith from the oranges. Cut along the membranes to free the segments and cut them into bite-size pieces. Place in a large mixing bowl. Cut the cantaloupe in half, scoop out the seeds, then either scoop out with a melon baller or just cut into bite-size pieces and add to the oranges.

To make the vinaigrette, combine the mint, onion, rosemary, oil, vinegar, and honey in a blender or food processor; blend thoroughly. Pour the vinaigrette over the fruit and toss to coat lightly.

BLACK-EYED PEAS WITH BACON AND CREAMY TARRAGON-GARLIC VINAIGRETTE
SERVES 6 TO 8

This dish is a cool, light, refreshing way to use peas when they are at their peak and we have so many leftovers. It's not necessary to use an exact weight or measure—just take what you have and add a good vinaigrette, garlic, herbs, and bacon. You'll love it.

CREAMY TARRAGON-GARLIC
VINAIGRETTE
¾ cup olive oil
¼ cup white wine vinegar
4 garlic cloves, finely chopped
1 teaspoon dried tarragon, crushed, or
    1 tablespoon finely chopped
    fresh tarragon
    Salt
    Freshly ground black pepper

4 cups cooked or canned black-eyed peas
8 slices bacon, crisply fried and
    crumbled
1 teaspoon dried thyme or 1 tablespoon
    finely chopped fresh thyme
    Salt
    Freshly ground black pepper

To make the vinaigrette, whisk the olive oil, vinegar, garlic, and tarragon together. Season to taste with salt and pepper.

In a large bowl, toss together the peas, bacon, and thyme with the vinaigrette. Add salt and pepper to taste. Serve chilled or at room temperature.

ELLIOTT MACKLE'S BEETS AND GREENS
SERVES 4 TO 6

This innovative recipe sings with the addition of ginger. It's very colorful as well as exciting in flavor.

10 ounces washed and trimmed beet or
    turnip greens
2 teaspoons butter
2 garlic cloves, chopped
1 teaspoon finely chopped fresh ginger
1 pound cooked beets or 1
    16-ounce can beets, drained and
    coarsely chopped
    Juice of 1 lemon
    Salt
    Freshly ground black pepper

Bring a large pot of lightly salted water to the boil. Add the greens and cook until limp, about 5 minutes. Drain and chop coarsely.

Melt the butter in a skillet; add the garlic, ginger, and greens and sauté 1 to 2 minutes. Stir in the chopped beets, lemon juice, and salt and pepper to taste. Heat through for 1 or 2 minutes. Serve hot or at room temperature.

REJANE'S CEVEACHE
SERVES 4 TO 6

Ceveache (also spelled seviche) has been served in the South and featured in cookbooks since the earliest Colonial days, probably working its way here from England via Spain. I particularly like to prepare it with catfish, but any firm white fish will do.

1 pound firm white fish (such as
    catfish), cut into chunks
¼ cup olive oil
2 garlic cloves, peeled and crushed

1½ cups fresh lemon juice (about
        10 lemons)
½ inch piece fresh ginger, peeled and
        finely chopped
1 small hot red or green pepper, seeded
        and finely chopped
½ teaspoon coarse salt
6 to 8 scallions, white part only, thinly
        sliced
2 tablespoons chopped fresh dill
¼ cup finely chopped red bell pepper
        (optional), for garnish

½ cup milk
1 egg, slightly beaten
2 cups all-purpose flour
3 teaspoons garlic salt
2 teaspoons paprika
2 teaspoons freshly ground black pepper
½ teaspoon poultry seasoning
1 2½- to 3-pound frying chicken,
        cut up
    Shortening or butter

Place the fish, oil, garlic, lemon juice, ginger, hot pepper, and salt in a large bowl. Toss to mix and marinate in the refrigerator for at least 6 hours. When ready to serve, stir in the scallions and dill. Taste for seasoning. Garnish

SUPER CRISP COUNTRY FRIED CHICKEN
SERVES 4

Fried chicken is surely the South's most famous dish. The milk and egg batter makes it extra crispy. This recipe calls for frying the chicken in shortening, as it is so easy to handle and gives a crisper bird, but many prefer butter, as my great-uncle Harry Keiser does. In 1991, when he turned ninety-nine years of age, he pulled me aside to lecture me, saying butter was the only proper fat to fry chicken in, as it makes the bird deeply colored, delicious, and memorable. I agree, but it is more difficult because it burns, it's more expensive, and the chicken is not so crisp. If you do use butter, add a little oil to keep it from burning or, if you prefer, use clarified butter (page 11).

For extra spicy chicken, increase the black pepper to 3 teaspoons and the poultry seasoning to 1 teaspoon.

Combine the milk and egg in a medium bowl.

Combine the flour, garlic salt, paprika, pepper, and poultry seasoning in a paper or plastic bag. Add a few pieces of the chicken to the bag at a time and shake to coat. Dip the chicken in the milk-and-egg mixture, then shake a second time in the flour mixture.

To skillet-fry, place enough shortening in the skillet to come ½ to 1 inch up the sides of the pan. Heat the shortening to 365°F. in an electric skillet or over medium-high heat in a large heavy skillet. Brown the chicken on all sides, then reduce the heat to 275°F. or medium-low heat and continue cooking until the chicken is tender, about 30 to 40 minutes, turning the chicken several times. Drain on paper towels.

To deep-fry, heat 2 or 3 inches of the shortening to 365°F. in a deep fryer or deep saucepan. Fry the chicken for 15 to 18 minutes, or until the meat near the bone is no longer pink. Drain on paper towels.

TENDERLOIN OF PORK IN HERBED BUTTERMILK BISCUITS

SERVES 4 TO 6

I love pork tenderloin and this makes an un-usual and unexpected treat—perhaps even better than the all-time favorite, sausage and biscuits—especially as a tuck-along for picnics, boating, and hiking.

> 1 tablespoon butter
> 1 tablespoon vegetable oil
> 2 ½- to ¾-pound tenderloins of pork
> 12 Herbed Buttermilk Biscuits
> (page 59)

Preheat the oven to 400°F.

Heat the butter and oil in a large oven-proof skillet until sizzling. Add the tenderloins and brown all over. Place in the oven and roast until the internal temperature reaches 140°F., 20 to 30 minutes.

Slice the tenderloins thinly. Split the biscuits and fill with 2 or 3 slices of pork. Serve at room temperature.

ABOVE: *Pork-filled biscuits and deviled eggs.*
OPPOSITE: *Barbecued ribs await the crowd observing the Independence Day Parade.*

BARBECUED PORK RIBS WITH FOURTH OF JULY BARBECUE SAUCE

SERVES 4

I suppose there are those who would eat beef ribs on the Fourth of July, but not a *true* Southerner. This sauce keeps several weeks in the refrigerator.

BARBECUE SAUCE
> 2 tablespoons butter
> 1 medium onion, chopped
> 1 cup apple cider vinegar
> 1 cup water
> ¼ teaspoon ground cloves
> ¼ teaspoon cayenne pepper
> 1 teaspoon chili powder
> ¼ teaspoon dry mustard
> 1 cup ketchup
> ¼ cup tomato paste
> 2 tablespoons light brown sugar, packed
> 1 teaspoon prepared mustard
> 3 tablespoons Worcestershire sauce
> 3 garlic cloves, chopped
>
> 4 pounds pork spareribs (4 racks)

To make the barbecue sauce, melt the butter in a heavy saucepan or Dutch oven over medium heat. Add the onion and sauté until softened and slightly golden, 5 to 7 minutes. Add the vinegar, water, cloves, cayenne, chili powder, dry mustard, ketchup, tomato paste, brown sugar, prepared mustard, Worcestershire sauce, and garlic and cook over medium heat 20 to 30 minutes. Bring a large pot of water to the boil. Add the ribs and simmer for 30 minutes; drain and pat dry. Place the ribs on a hot grill and cook until brown on both sides, approximately 5 minutes per side. When cooked, brush them with barbecue sauce and return them to the grill briefly. Drench them with additional sauce and serve.

Pit Barbecue

The Bentleys—Gwen and Jimmy—are masters of hospitality and pit barbecue. Jimmy's menu is traditional and when we say barbecue, we mean pork. In fact, it's not much different from Martha Washington's traditional Fourth of July at Mount Vernon: mint juleps for blessing the pig, hickory-smoked barbecued pork, barbecue sauce, Brunswick stew, whole dill pickles, Ocilla slaw, home-baked bread, crisp potatoes, homemade cakes, ice-cold beer, and freshly brewed ice tea with side-yard mint. Of course, the barbecue is the centerpiece of the event, and is a major undertaking. Here's how to duplicate it yourself.

Select a site that's free of overhanging tree limbs for at least 30 feet above the flame. Dig a 12- to 14-inch-deep pit 3 feet wide by 5 feet long. (This chore requires two people and a six-pack of cold beer, according to Jimmy.)

Build a fire in the pit from oak, hickory, nut, or fruit wood about an hour before starting to cook. This dries the inside of the pit and heats the walls and bottom. Spread out the coals. There should be no flames and the fire should be just hot enough to allow you to hold your hand over the pit 8 to 10 seconds. Build a separate campfire next to the pit to supply coals throughout the night.

Buy a whole hog, because it looks handsome over the pit. A pig of about 90 pounds will feed 80 to 100 people when dressed with its head and feet removed; figure ¾ pound of fresh pork per person. (There is more waste with a whole hog, so it is more economical and simpler, if less romantic, to cook 12 to 14 pounds of fresh hams and shoulders.) The pig should be slaughtered 2 days before cooking to ensure that it is well drained and thoroughly chilled, and the butcher should have sawed the backbone through the center, leaving the skin intact.

The Bentleys have made an H-shaped wooden rack with an additional crossbar of hardwood poles 2 to 3 inches in diameter. Two of the poles are seven feet long; the other two are 3½ feet long, with wire attached to support the meat while it is cooking. The hog is spread-eagled and attached securely with strong hog or poultry wire—meat side down and skin side up—tied at the legs, along the belly, across either end, and down the center.

Give support to the rack by placing two iron pipes across the pit under the rack. Place a large sheet of heavy plastic or cardboard along one side of the pit to hold the pig and to swab when the rack is turned.

Once the pig is on the pit, the Bentleys bless it with mint juleps and sit around the campfire all night, cooking the pig slowly, basting and turning throughout the night. A solution of 1 quart water to 3 tablespoons salt, 1 cup natural red apple cider vinegar, and 1 teaspoon freshly ground black pepper is used for the basting. Make a swab from cheesecloth and a three-foot tree limb. In the morning, cut up the pig to be ready to serve around noon—with plenty of barbecue sauce.

To cook a shoulder of pork on the fire, reduce the swabbing liquid considerably and smoke/grill for about 4 to 6 hours until tender.

"N.C.-STYLE" BARBECUE SAUCE
MAKES ABOUT 6 CUPS

North Carolina barbecue sauce is a thin, slightly fiery version, good for grilled shoulder ribs. Its flavor is best after it has mellowed for six months, and it will keep indefinitely in the refrigerator.

½ tablespoon light brown sugar, packed
2 cups apple cider vinegar
1 teaspoon salt
1 teaspoon cayenne pepper
2 tablespoons freshly ground
    black pepper
1 cup ketchup
2 cups water
    Tabasco sauce

In a large heavy saucepan, combine the brown sugar, vinegar, salt, peppers, ketchup, water, and Tabasco to taste. Stir well and bring to the boil. Reduce the heat and simmer 15 minutes. Pour into pint jars and refrigerate until ready to use.

Beef or Pork?

To most Southerners barbecue means pork and nothing else. In his book The Sass Menagerie, my friend Bob Steed wrote, "The reason Texans think that barbecue is beef is because you can't ride a horse and steal a pig at the same time." Of course, he didn't consider Texans Southerners, and I think some are.

COUNTRY-STYLE BARBECUED RIBS WITH BENNIE'S DISAPPEARING MARINADE
SERVES 4

Country-style ribs are the blade ends of the pork loin, butterflied. There are approximately 2½ to 3 ribs per pound. Plan on 2 to 3 ribs per person. This white sauce is named after a friend of Lee Hopper's, a young man who was chef at the Georgia Governor's Mansion and a good friend of mine. It disappears in the cooking, leaving delicious ribs behind.

MARINADE
1 cup lemon juice
1 cup red wine vinegar
½ cup vegetable oil
1½ tablespoons salt
1½ tablespoons onion salt
1½ to 2 tablespoons freshly
    ground black pepper
1½ tablespoons celery salt
1 tablespoon chopped fresh marjoram
1 tablespoon chopped fresh oregano
1 tablespoon chopped fresh thyme
1 tablespoon chopped fresh basil
3 tablespoons soy sauce
3 tablespoons Worcestershire sauce
5 large garlic cloves

3 pounds country-style back ribs

In a food processor, combine the lemon juice, vinegar, oil, salt, onion salt, pepper, celery salt, marjoram, oregano, thyme, basil, soy sauce, Worcestershire sauce, and garlic; process until well blended.

Pour the marinade over the ribs and marinate several hours or overnight. Heat the grill. Drain the meat, place it on the hot grill, and cook 8 to 10 minutes. Turn and brown the other side, 6 to 8 minutes.

POUND CAKE
MAKES 1 LOAF

This cake is great with summer fruits, by itself, or toasted for breakfast. The shortening makes it a bit lighter than the usual pound cake. And, oh yes, it's delicious with peach ice cream or even store-bought lemon yogurt.

½ cup (1 stick) butter
¼ cup vegetable shortening
1¼ cups sugar
3 large eggs
2 cups cake flour or soft wheat flour
½ teaspoon baking powder
1 teaspoon vanilla extract
½ cup milk

Cut a piece of wax paper to fit the bottom of a 9-inch loaf pan and grease and flour the paper. Set side.

Preheat the oven to 350°F.

In a mixer bowl, beat together the butter, shortening, and sugar until light and fluffy. Add the eggs 1 at a time, beating well after each addition.

Sift together the flour and baking powder and add to the butter and egg mixture in thirds, alternating with the milk, beginning and ending with the dry ingredients. Pour into the prepared loaf pan and bake 1 to 1¼ hours or until a toothpick inserted into cake comes out clean. If the top of the cake browns too quickly, cover loosely with aluminum foil.

NOTE: This cake freezes well.

*Fresh Pound Cake
topped with
Quick Caramel
Pecan Ice Cream.*

Ice Cream Facts

In the days before refrigeration, cold, icy winters were welcome, for without them there could be no ice cream in summer! Christine Meadows, curator of Mt. Vernon, tells me that in the winter George and Martha Washington harvested "rim" ice from the edges of the river as well as ice floes from the center to store in their icehouse for the hot months. The ice was hauled up to an opening in the top of the icehouse in baskets, then rammed in to form a seal. In the spring and summer the ice was chipped out as needed from a lower door near the cool earth, ready to be used in ices and ice creams.

PEACH ICE CREAM
SERVES 6 TO 8

Although there is ongoing debate about which state produces the best peaches, there is no question that peach ice cream is the favorite Southern ice cream. It's always good over apple pie, but try it over bread pudding, peach cobbler—anything!

6 pounds peaches, peeled and chopped (about 10 cups)
4 cups heavy cream
2 teaspoons vanilla extract
1 tablespoon ground ginger

Place half of the peaches in a large mixing bowl. Puree the remaining peaches in a blender or food processor and add to the chopped peaches. Add the cream, vanilla, and ginger; stir to mix well. Place in a hand-cranked freezer churn or an electric ice cream maker, and churn until cold and thick. Let mellow at least 30 minutes in the freezer before serving.

QUICK CARAMEL PECAN ICE CREAM
MAKES 1 QUART

This luscious, crunchy praline topping transforms plain, store-bought ice cream. It's also wonderful over pies and cobblers.

1 cup water
1½ cups sugar
¾ cup pecans, coarsely chopped
1 quart vanilla or chocolate ice cream, softened

Oil a baking sheet.

In a small, heavy-bottomed pan, gently heat the water and sugar until the sugar dissolves. Brush down the sides of the pan with cold water to remove the crystals. Raise the heat to medium-high, bring to the boil, and boil until the mixture is a pale golden brown. Stir the pecans into the mixture until well coated. Continue cooking to achieve a rich, tawny caramel. Pour at once onto the oiled baking sheet and let cool until hard.

Crush the caramel in a mortar and pestle or with the end of a rolling pin in a bowl, leaving some large pecan pieces. Stir into the softened ice cream and return to the freezer for at least 1 hour before serving.

DENICE SKREPCINSKI'S KEY LIME BARS
SERVES 24 TO 30

These tart bars on a tender crust are a serious rival to Key lime pie, and they are very easy to prepare.

1½ cups all-purpose flour
1 cup graham cracker crumbs
¾ cup (1½ sticks) butter, softened
½ cup confectioners' sugar
2 cups sugar
½ cup lime juice (from Key limes, if possible)
4 large eggs
Grated peel of 1 lime (no white attached)
Confectioners' sugar for dusting

Preheat the oven to 350°F.

Mix together 1¼ cups flour, the graham cracker crumbs, butter, and confectioners' sugar to form a soft dough. Press the dough into an ungreased 13 × 9 × 2-inch baking pan and bake until lightly browned, about 20 to 25 minutes.

While the crust is baking, beat together the sugar, lime juice, remaining ¼ cup flour, eggs, and lime peel until well mixed. Pour over the hot crust and return the pan to the oven. Bake until set, an additional 20 minutes. Cool on a wire rack and then cut into bars. The center will be soft like a custard. Sift confectioners' sugar over the top.

NOTE: These bars freeze well.

BARBECUE BUNS
MAKES 10 BUNS

The debate over what kind of bread is best with barbecue is as intense as that regarding what kind of barbecue (inside meat or outside with the skin; sliced or chopped). Some like their buns buttered and toasted. Others like French bread, plain or toasted, or a side of hush puppies instead.

1 package active dry yeast
½ cup warm water (105°F. to 115°F.)
¼ cup sugar
¼ cup milk
½ tablespoon salt
¼ cup butter, melted
1 egg, beaten
2½ to 3 cups bread flour

Dissolve the yeast in a large bowl with the water and sugar. Add the milk, salt, butter, and egg. Stir in the flour, 1 cup at a time, to make a soft dough. Turn out onto a floured board, and knead until smooth and elastic, 8 to 10 minutes, or knead in the mixer or food processor, adding more flour if necessary. Place the dough in a greased plastic bag or in a greased bowl, turning the dough to grease all over; cover with plastic wrap and let the dough rise in a warm place until doubled in bulk, about 1 hour.

Preheat the oven to 375°F.

Punch down the dough and divide in half. Form each half into five 3-inch balls. Place them 3 inches apart on greased baking sheets and press each ball to flatten. Let them rise again until doubled, about 30 minutes.

Bake the rolls until done and golden brown, 15 to 20 minutes. Remove them from the pan and place on a rack to cool. These may be frozen.

The Sweet Tooth

The Southerner's reputation for having a sweet tooth is well deserved. No meal is considered complete without a taste of something sweet at the conclusion. In local diners and buffets in small Southern town hotels, the desserts are proudly displayed in glass cases or on tall pedestals, where they promise a sweet conclusion to even the most humble repast. In fact, in a Southern cafeteria, frequently the dessert is at the front end of the buffet and is the first food on your tray!

Some of the finest Southern sweets are to be found at local bake sales. There, gathered under one shade tree, are the foods that figure most prominently in the fantasies and memories of the Southern palate. Children, like little bees, swarm right to the sugar. Certain women are renowned throughout their communities for their baking—with a few men these

LEFT: *Homemade Toasted Coconut Cake, Yogurt Praline Cake, and Cream Cheese Brownies Supreme.* RIGHT: *Strawberry Jam.*

days joining their ranks as well. Signature cakes are remembered from funerals and anniversaries and church suppers—we all know who makes the best cakes and the best pies. These in particular are searched out when the sale time comes, ready to be taken home and eaten, or better yet, saved in the freezer to be pulled out for visiting relatives (and perhaps raved on as one's own).

Tender crusted pies, whether ready for the freezer or to be eaten warm from the oven, often combine the tart and sweet as in a buttermilk pie or tangy lemon/lime meringue. When berries and cherries are at their seasonal peak, there is no simpler or more spectacular way to showcase their charms than a flaky latticed pie.

Little bites of cookies and candies are some of my favorite treats. I could eat an entire batch of Benne Seed Wafers by myself. I truly am addicted to them as well as to Ray's Oatmeal Chocolate Chippers, about which I lie to myself and say since they have oatmeal they are healthier than, say, the shock of sugar in peanut brittle. But then, what does have the crunch and delight of peanut brittle besides peanut brittle?

COCA-COLA CAKE
MAKES 1 CAKE

My friend Judy Walz brought this to a church covered dish party we had in my home and it was the hit of the evening. It has everything in it that children love—Coca-Cola, chocolate, nuts, and miniature marshmallows! Let them make it themselves for the next family occasion.

2 cups all-purpose flour
2 cups sugar
1 cup (2 sticks) butter
1 cup Coca-Cola
3 tablespoons cocoa powder
½ cup buttermilk
1 teaspoon baking soda
2 eggs
1 teaspoon vanilla extract
1½ cups miniature marshmallows

FROSTING
½ cup (1 stick) butter
3 tablespoons cocoa powder
6 tablespoons Coca-Cola
1 1-pound box confectioners' sugar, sifted
1 cup chopped pecans
1 teaspoon vanilla extract

Preheat the oven to 350°F. Butter a 9 × 11-inch oblong pan.

Sift the flour and sugar together into a large mixing bowl. Combine the butter, Coke, cocoa, and buttermilk in a saucepan and bring to the boil. Pour the Coke mixture over the flour mixture; add the baking soda, eggs, vanilla, and marshmallows and mix well.

Pour the batter into the buttered pan and bake until a toothpick inserted in the center comes out clean, about 45 minutes. Let the cake cool for 10 minutes or so.

To make the frosting, combine the butter, cocoa, and Coke in a saucepan and bring to a boil. Remove from the heat, and fold in the sugar, pecans, and vanilla. Spread the frosting on the still warm cake.

NOTE: For more servings, the cake can be baked in a 9 × 13-inch sheet cake pan, decreasing the baking time by 10 to 12 minutes. However, you will need to increase your frosting by at least half to compensate for the extra surface.

BENNE SEED WAFERS
MAKES 3 DOZEN

These delicious communion wafer–sized nibbles are a tradition in Savannah, Georgia, where they are baked by Girl Scouts in the ancestral home of Juliette Gordon Low, the founder of the Girl Scouts. Benne is the African word for sesame seeds.

6 tablespoons (⅔ stick) butter, at room temperature
¾ cup light brown sugar, firmly packed
1 egg
½ teaspoon vanilla extract
½ cup plus 2 tablespoons all-purpose flour
¼ cup toasted benne seeds
⅛ teaspoon baking powder

Preheat the oven to 325°F.

Beat together the butter and sugar until light and fluffy. Add the egg and vanilla and beat to combine. Add the flour, benne seeds, and baking powder and mix thoroughly. Line a pan with wax paper, parchment paper, or foil, and drop or pipe the cookie dough onto the paper by ½ teaspoons 2 inches apart. Bake 10 to 15 minutes. Cool on a rack until the cookies release from the paper. Store in a tightly sealed tin or freeze.

MARGARET ANN'S CHOCOLATE BUTTERMILK CAKE

MAKES ONE 3-LAYER CAKE OR THREE 1-LAYER CAKES

This is a rich, chocolaty yet light cake. It leaves everyone begging for more!

CAKE

3 cups cake flour

½ cup cocoa powder

2 teaspoons baking soda

1 teaspoon salt

1 cup (2 sticks) butter, at room temperature

2 cups sugar

2 eggs

1 teaspoon vanilla extract

2 cups buttermilk

ICING

½ cup (1 stick) butter

6 ounces semisweet chocolate

1 tablespoon vanilla extract

¾ cup heavy cream

6 cups sifted confectioners' sugar

Chocolate Curls, for garnish

Preheat the oven to 350°F.

Grease and flour three 9-inch round cake pans. Cut rounds of wax paper to fit the pans, grease and flour them, and add to the pans.

Combine the flour, cocoa, baking soda, and salt; set aside. Beat the butter and sugar together until light and fluffy. Add the eggs 1 at a time, beating well after each addition. Add the vanilla. Add the dry ingredients alternately with the buttermilk, beginning and ending with the dry ingredients. Pour into the 3 pans and bake 25 to 35 minutes, or until a toothpick inserted into the center of the cakes comes out clean. Cool in the pans on racks for 10 minutes. Remove from the pans and cool completely on wire racks. (The cake can be frozen at this point.)

To make the icing, melt the butter and chocolate in a heavy saucepan. In a food processor or mixer, combine the chocolate mixture, vanilla, and cream. Slowly beat in the confectioners' sugar until the frosting is well mixed and the desired consistency. If too thick, add an additional tablespoon of cream; if too runny, add a little more confectioners' sugar. Place strips of wax paper on a serving plate and put the first layer on them (they will protect the plate from drips). Spread some of the icing on top; repeat with the remaining layers. Spread the sides with icing and smooth the top.

Garnish the iced cake with chocolate curls.

CHOCOLATE CURLS

4 ounces white chocolate

4 ounces bittersweet chocolate

2 tablespoons solid vegetable shortening

Place the white and dark chocolates in separate small heavy saucepans. Add 1 tablespoon shortening to each pan. Stir both over very low heat until melted and smooth. Pour each mixture into small square plastic containers and freeze until firm, about 30 minutes.

Remove the blocks of chocolate from the containers and, using a cheese slicer or vegetable peeler, scrape across the surface of each to make curls.

Alternately, when the chocolate is melted, spread it thinly on a chilled marble slab (preferably straight from the freezer). With a sharp knife held at an angle, ease under the very hard chocolate and roll to make a curl.

Students from the Covington Elementary school man the annual bake sale.

Praline
Cake

Chocolate

Strawberry

TOASTED COCONUT CAKE
MAKES 1 CAKE

This is a killer cake—it's a show-off dessert, just right for large family parties or special occasions. Coconut cake is an important cake in the South. It's seen at all the best church suppers, sold at bake sales and top department stores. If you prefer not to toast the coconut, that's okay too.

CAKE

1 cup (2 sticks) butter, at room
   temperature
2 cups sugar
4 eggs, separated
2 teaspoons vanilla extract
3 cups all-purpose flour
2 teaspoons baking powder
1 teaspoon salt
1 cup milk
2 cups shredded coconut

ICING

1 cup sugar
   Pinch salt
½ cup water
3 egg whites
1 teaspoon vanilla extract
4 cups shredded coconut, toasted

Preheat the oven to 350°F.

Grease and flour three 9-inch round cake pans. Cut rounds of wax paper to fit the bottom of the pans, grease and flour the rounds, and add them to the pans.

Beat the butter and sugar together until light and fluffy. Add the egg yolks one at a time, beating well after each addition. Add the vanilla and beat again. Combine the flour, baking powder, and salt. Alternate adding the flour mixture and the milk to the butter mixture, beginning and ending with the dry ingredients. Beat the egg whites until stiff peaks form and fold them into the batter. Fold in the coconut.

Divide the batter among the 3 pans, and bake until golden and the edges begin to pull away from the sides of the pan, about 25 to 30 minutes. Let cool 5 minutes in the pans, then turn the cakes out onto oiled racks.

To make the icing, combine the sugar, salt, and water in a heavy saucepan. Cook over low heat until the sugar is dissolved, then raise the heat to high, insert a candy thermometer, and boil. When the syrup reaches 225°F., begin beating the egg whites to soft peaks. When the syrup reaches 240°F., beat it into the egg whites in a stream; continue to beat until cool. Beat in the vanilla.

To assemble the cake, place 1 layer on a platter, cover with icing, and sprinkle with toasted coconut. Repeat with the next layer. Place the third layer on top and spread the top and sides of the cake with icing. Press the remaining toasted coconut onto the sides of the cake.

YOGURT PRALINE CAKE
MAKES 3 LAYERS

This cake is one of our favorites—a very light cake with a rich caramel-nut icing that's almost like candy. We spent a lot of time perfecting this icing, which is a challenge to make but so good it is worth the trouble.

Denice Skrepcinski deserves special mention for this cake, the serendipitous by-product of a rainy afternoon the apprentices spent testing recipes for yogurt pralines when nothing had worked out right. We are all savers around here, so the failed praline mixture wound up in the refrigerator. When drop-in guests arrived, I pulled out some layers of a cake, spied the praline mixture, and iced the cake with it. It was so good I knew we had to include it in this book; the trick then was to get the yogurt mixture to "fail" again. Denice took on the mission, with delicious results.

Southern Bakers

Pick up any Southern cookbook and it will be weighted with sweets. In fact, in years past sweets were served with every course. Now, we might want a little sweet with our meat, such as pepper jelly, but we mostly save the sweets for the end of the meal. I think Southerners are among the best bakers in the world. One can only marvel at the enormous effort that must have been made preairconditioning to achieve the flaky creations that satisfy our cravings.

CAKE

1 cup (2 sticks) unsalted butter, at
    room temperature
3 cups sugar
6 eggs
2⅔ cups all-purpose flour
¼ teaspoon baking soda
1 teaspoon salt
1 cup sour cream
1 tablespoon vanilla extract

YOGURT PRALINE ICING

3½ cups sugar
1 teaspoon baking soda
1½ cups plain low-fat yogurt, drained
¼ cup light corn syrup
1 tablespoon vanilla extract
¼ cup (½ stick) unsalted butter
3 to 5 cups pecan halves

Preheat the oven to 350°F. Grease and flour three 9-inch pans. Cut rounds of wax paper to fit the bottoms of the pans, grease and flour the rounds, and add them to the pans.

Beat the butter until light. Gradually beat in the sugar until the mixture is light and fluffy. Add the eggs one at a time, beating well after each addition. Sift together the flour, baking soda, and salt. Mix one-quarter of the flour mixture into the eggs, then one-third of the sour cream, and combine thoroughly. Repeat, alternating the flour and sour cream, ending with the flour. Stir in the vanilla. Divide the batter among the prepared pans. Tap the pans lightly on the counter top several times to remove any air bubbles. Bake until the cake springs back when touched, about 25 to 35 minutes. Cool on cake racks for 10 minutes, then carefully remove the cakes from the pans. Remove the paper. (You may freeze the layers at this point once they are thoroughly cooled. Wrap them in plastic wrap and then in foil.)

To make the icing, mix the sugar and baking soda together in a heavy 5-quart 12-inch saucepan. Blend in the yogurt and the corn syrup. Cook over low heat until the sugar is dissolved, about 10 minutes. Bring to the boil, then simmer 15 to 20 minutes without stirring, or until the syrup reaches 238°F. on a candy thermometer (measured in the center of the pot—do not let the thermometer touch the bottom the pan) or forms a soft ball in cold water. Remove from the heat. Stir in the vanilla and butter. Cool slightly, about 10 minutes. Beat vigorously, about 5 to 10 minutes, or until just beginning to thicken, then cool to room temperature.

Ice the cooled layers and press pecan halves decoratively onto the sides and top of cake while the icing is still soft.

CREAM CHEESE BROWNIES SUPREME
MAKES 24

Olive Ann Burns was a cousin of my mother-in-law, Celeste Sigman Dupree. When I married David, Olive Ann and her husband, Andy, lived next door to Celeste and Jimmy on Rumson Road. In her book, *Cold Sassy Tree*, Olive Ann perfectly captured the desire of the South to have an abundance always available like these fudgy brownies. I love the contrast of cream cheese and chocolate and find them a wonderful treat for sitting and reading.

> 4 ounces unsweetened chocolate
> ½ cup (1 stick) unsalted butter
> 2 cups sugar
> 6 eggs
> 2 teaspoons vanilla extract
> 1¼ cups all-purpose flour
> 1 teaspoon baking powder
> 1 teaspoon salt
> 1 pound cream cheese, softened

Preheat the oven to 350°F. Grease a 13 × 9 × 2-inch baking pan.

In a saucepan or microwave melt the chocolate and butter. Blend in the sugar, 4 eggs, and 1 teaspoon vanilla. Stir in the flour, baking powder, and salt.

In a mixer, beat the cream cheese and the remaining 2 eggs and 1 teaspoon vanilla until light and fluffy. Pour half the brownie mixture into the baking pan. Spoon the cream cheese mixture on top. Pour the remainder of the brownie mixture on top of the cream cheese layer. With a knife, make swirls through the mixtures for a marbled effect. Bake 30 minutes. Cool slightly, then cut into bars.

ABOVE: *The Red Grandma's Cookies.* OPPOSITE: *The perfect afternoon pick-me-ups: hot tea, a good book, and luscious Cream Cheese Brownies.*

THE RED GRANDMA'S COOKIES
MAKES 3 DOZEN

By a very strange coincidence, both of Carr Kaufmann's grandmothers purchased the very same winter coat but in different colors. At age four the only way he could differentiate them was by the color of their coats; one was green and one was red. Thus these are the "red" grandma's cookies.

> 1 cup (2 sticks) butter, softened
> ½ cup sugar
> 1⅔ cups all-purpose flour
> ⅔ cup finely chopped unsalted almonds
>   Confectioners' sugar

Preheat the oven to 300°F. Grease a cookie sheet.

In a large bowl, beat the butter and sugar together until light in color. Gradually add the flour and almonds and mix until just blended.

Roll level tablespoons of dough into balls and place about 1 inch apart on the cookie sheet. Bake for 30 to 35 minutes, until very slightly brown.

Transfer the cookies to a rack to cool, then sprinkle with confectioners' sugar.

Flour

Flour is different in every geographic region. Cake flour, such as Swansdown, is a good substitute for the all-purpose soft wheat flour used throughout the South. However, if you wish to order soft wheat flour, you may order it through White Lily, 218 Depot, Knoxville, TN 37901.

Self-rising flour is all-purpose or cake flour with salt and baking powder added to it. It is used primarily for biscuits, but recipes for quick breads and some cakes call for it as well. To make your own, add ½ teaspoon salt and 1½ teaspoons baking powder to each cup of all-purpose or cake flour.

MAYBELL'S LACY PECAN AND ORANGE COOKIES
MAKES ABOUT 4 DOZEN

Maybell is a Southern woman who loves pampering herself and her loved ones. She keeps these delicate, orange-flavored lace cookies on hand in the freezer. These wonderful cookies may be formed into cups, too!

2 cups pecans
2 cups all-purpose flour
½ cup granulated sugar
½ cup light brown sugar, packed
½ teaspoon salt
1 cup light corn syrup
1 cup (2 sticks) unsalted butter, at
   room temperature
1 teaspoon finely chopped orange peel
   (no white attached)
½ teaspoon vanilla extract

Preheat the oven to 350°F.

Place the pecans in a food processor fitted with a metal blade and process until finely chopped. Place on a baking sheet. Bake until golden, up to 10 minutes, stirring occasionally, or brown in the microwave. Place the pecans in a bowl and toss with the flour.

In a large heavy saucepan, combine both sugars, the salt, corn syrup, and butter. Cook over moderately low heat, stirring constantly, until the butter is melted and the ingredients are incorporated; remove from the heat. Stir in the flour and pecans, then add the orange peel and vanilla and mix well. Set aside to cool slightly before baking.

Line 2 or more baking sheets with parchment paper. Drop the batter by tablespoons leaving at least 3 inches between the cookies; each sheet will only hold 4. Take care at this point to shape the batter carefully so you will produce nice round cookies.

Bake until the cookies are golden and most of the bubbling has stopped, about 6 to 8 minutes. Remove the baking sheet from the oven and let sit 2 to 3 minutes, or until the cookies are firm enough to remove. Working quickly, ease each cookie off with a spatula and transfer to a rack to cool. Continue with the remaining batter in the same manner. If the cookies become too firm to remove from the baking sheet, return them to the oven until warm and softened enough to move.

The cookies may be stored in an airtight container at room temperature for several days or they may be frozen. Defrost at room temperature.

If making cups, mold the still warm cookies onto the back of custard cups, pressing the cookie gently over the cup. Let cool completely, then fill the cookie cups with a scoop of ice cream or mousse.

MARGARET ANN SURBER'S ANGEL FOOD CAKE
MAKES ONE 9-INCH SQUARE CAKE OR ONE 10-INCH ROUND CAKE

Centuries before it was embraced by those on low cholesterol diets, angel food cake was prized for its lightness and tenderness.

To measure the flour for this special recipe of Margaret Ann's, sift it, then spoon it into a dry measuring cup. I prefer using cake flour or the Southern flours that have 9 to 10 percent protein because they make a lighter cake. Recently I discovered square angel food pans, which make a nice change.

- 1¾ cups egg whites (about 12 large eggs)
- 1 teaspoon cream of tartar
- ¼ teaspoon salt
- 1¼ cups sifted cake or all-purpose flour
- 1 teaspoon ground ginger
- ½ teaspoon freshly grated nutmeg
- 1¾ cup sugar, processed in a food processor until very fine
- 2 teaspoons vanilla extract

Preheat the oven to 300°F. Grease and flour a piece of wax paper to fit the removable bottom of a 9-inch square or 10-inch round tube pan. Do not grease or flour the pan sides.

Place the egg whites in a large mixer bowl. Sift the cream of tartar over the whites, add the salt, and beat the whites to soft peaks using the whisk attachment. Meanwhile, sift the flour with the ginger and nutmeg. With the mixer on the lowest speed, gradually whisk in the sugar, then gradually whisk in the flour mixture. Fold in the vanilla. Pour the batter into the prepared pan and smooth the top. Bake until pale brown and springy to the touch, about 1 to 1¼ hours.

NOTE: The cake can be frozen.

MICROWAVE PEANUT BRITTLE
MAKES 1½ TO 2 POUNDS

Here's a fast version of a traditional recipe. The volume increases more in the microwave, so be sure to use a very large bowl to keep the mixture from boiling over. Lightly grease the inside of the bowl with butter before adding the ingredients so the mixture will pour out of the bowl more easily.

- 2 cups sugar
- 1 cup white corn syrup
- ¼ teaspoon salt
- 2 to 3 cups raw peanuts
- 2 tablespoons butter
- 2 teaspoons baking soda
- 1 tablespoon vanilla extract

Grease a 12 × 15-inch jelly roll pan. In a 2-quart microwavable bowl, stir together the sugar, corn syrup, salt, and peanuts. Cook on high power for 4 minutes. Stir well and continue cooking on high for 4 more minutes. Stir in the butter until well blended. Cook on high power until the peanuts have turned a golden brown, 3 to 5 minutes longer. Remove the mixture from the microwave and add the baking soda and vanilla. Quickly stir the mixture until it turns a light brown color. Quickly pour it onto the prepared pan and let the brittle cool completely. Break it into pieces and store in an airtight tin.

RAY'S OATMEAL CHOCOLATE CHIPPERS
MAKES 60

These gooey chocolate cookies are crumbly, delicate, and decadent.

- 1 cup (2 sticks) unsalted butter, at room temperature
- ¾ cup granulated sugar
- 1 cup dark brown sugar, firmly packed
- 1 teaspoon salt
- 1 teaspoon vanilla extract
- ½ teaspoon almond extract
- 2 large eggs
- 1½ cups unsifted all-purpose flour
- 1 teaspoon baking soda
- ½ teaspoon ground cinnamon
- ¼ teaspoon ground nutmeg
- ¼ teaspoon ground cloves
- ¾ cup rolled oats
- 2 cups chopped pecans
- 12 ounces semisweet chocolate chips
- ½ cup raisins

Preheat the oven to 350°F. Lightly grease a large cookie sheet.

In the large bowl of an electric mixer, beat the butter until light. Add both sugars, the salt, and the vanilla and almond extracts and beat well. Add the eggs and beat well. In a separate bowl, sift together the flour, baking soda, cinnamon, nutmeg, and cloves; stir in the rolled oats. With the mixer on low speed, add about half the flour mixture to the butter and sugar, mixing just until incorporated. Add the remaining flour mixture and stir briefly. Stir in the pecans, chocolate chips, and raisins. Drop by ½ tablespoons onto the cookie sheet and bake until golden, about 10 to 12 minutes. Cool on a wire rack. Store in an airtight container or freeze.

PEANUT BRITTLE
MAKES 2 POUNDS

Here is the traditional version of this world famous confection.

- 2 cups sugar
- 1 cup white corn syrup
- 1 cup hot water
- 3 cups roasted unsalted peanuts with skins
- 1 tablespoon baking soda, sifted

Grease a 12 × 15-inch jelly roll pan. Combine the sugar, corn syrup, and hot water in a 4-quart saucepan with a heavy bottom and cook over low heat until the sugar is dissolved. Bring to the boil and cook over high heat until the syrup reaches the soft-ball stage, 238°F. on a candy thermometer.

Add the peanuts and continue to boil and bubble until the mixture reaches the hard-crack stage (300°F.), stirring constantly to prevent burning. Remove from the heat and quickly add the baking soda, stirring just to combine; the candy will bubble and pucker. Quickly pour the mixture onto the prepared cookie sheet, spreading to the edges of the pan so that the mixture is the same thickness. Allow it to cool and then break it into pieces and store in an airtight container.

ABOVE: *Ray's Oatmeal Chocolate Chippers.*
RIGHT: *Traditional Peanut Brittle.*

CHERRY LATTICE PIE
SERVES 4 TO 6

There is nothing quite like a cherry pie to lend color to a pie safe, and it's tart yet sweet, with a beautiful crust.

2 recipes Basic Piecrust (page 192)
2 pounds preserved or 2 16-ounce cans pitted tart red cherries, drained, juice reserved
½ cup sugar
1½ tablespoons cornstarch
1 teaspoon fresh lemon juice
1 teaspoon almond extract
3 to 4 drops red food coloring
2 tablespoons milk

Preheat the oven to 375°F.

Roll out the pastry into 2 rounds ⅛ inch thick or less. Line a 9-inch pie plate with one round. Reserve the second round for the top. Chill both rounds.

To make the filling, combine the drained cherries and ½ cup reserved juice in a large saucepan. In a small bowl, combine the sugar and cornstarch. Slowly stir in ¼ cup additional cherry juice, the lemon juice, and almond extract. Bring the cherries to a boil and slowly stir in the juice and starch mixture. Add the food coloring and reduce the heat to low. Stir until the mixture has thickened. Let the mixture cool to room temperature. Pour the cherry filling into the unbaked pie crust. Cut the second round into ½-inch strips. Place 5 strips across the filling, spacing them evenly apart. Fold every other strip back. Next, begin placing the remaining strips across in the opposite direction. Place 1 strip across. Replace the folded strips and fold back the alternating strips. Put on another cross strip. Continue in this manner until the entire pie is covered. Trim the pastry and press the edges with a fork. Brush the top of the lattice and the outside edge with milk. Bake until the pie is golden brown, 35 to 40 minutes.

STRAWBERRY JAM
MAKES EIGHT ½-PINT JARS

Strawberries grow in all the Southern states, and when they are fresh and ripe it is hard to know which state yields the best. Thickened with sugar, this spread has the consistency of honey, and is ambrosia to the Gods when spread on a hot biscuit or loaf bread.

1½ to 2 quarts fresh strawberries
½ teaspoon unsalted butter
1 1¾-ounce box powdered fruit pectin
7 cups sugar

Rinse and drain the strawberries. Remove the green stems and crush the berries with a potato masher or quickly pulse in a food processor without pureeing them, leaving some pieces of fruit. Measure 5 cups crushed strawberries into an 8-quart stockpot. Add the butter and fruit pectin. Bring the mixture to a full rolling boil, stirring constantly to prevent scorching. (A rolling boil is one that does not stop even when stirred.) Add the sugar quickly and bring back to the rolling boil, again stirring all the time. Boil the mixture for 1 minute. Remove from the heat and skim off any foam on top. Fill sterilized jars (see Note) immediately to within ⅛ inch of the top. Wipe the rims of the jars and quickly cover with the flat lids. Screw the bands on tightly. Invert the jars for 5 minutes, then turn upright and allow to cool for 1 hour. Check the seals after 1 hour. Store in a cool dark place and then in the refrigerator when opened.

NOTE: To process jars and lids for "putting up" or canning, place them on a rack in a large pot. Place the flat lids in a small pan. Cover both with water and bring to the boil. Boil for 10 to 15 minutes. Drain jars and place in a 200°F. oven until ready to use. Always wipe the rims of the jars after filling. It's a good idea to check the seal after 1 hour.

ICED CURRANT POPPY SEED RING
SERVES 8

This glazed ring makes a stunning presentation and has a delightful aroma and flavor. The softness of the currants along with the crunch of the poppy seeds and the slightest hint of lemon makes this a Danish worth waking up for. This can be frozen for 2 to 3 months.

SWEET DOUGH

1 package active dry yeast
1 teaspoon sugar
½ cup warm water (105° to 115°F.)
½ cup buttermilk
¼ cup brown sugar
½ cup butter
½ teaspoon salt
1 teaspoon vanilla extract
  Grated peel of 1 lemon (no white attached)
3½ to 4½ cups bread flour

FILLING

1 cup currants
¾ cup walnuts, chopped
5 tablespoons poppy seeds
½ cup (1 stick) butter, softened
½ cup brown sugar
1 teaspoon cinnamon
½ teaspoon grated nutmeg
¼ cup flour
  Grated peel of 1 lemon (no white attached)

CREAMY GLAZE

1 cup confectioners' sugar
2 tablespoons butter, softened
¾ teaspoon vanilla extract
2 to 3 tablespoons heavy cream

In a small cup, mix together the yeast, sugar, and warm water. Stir until dissolved. In a large bowl or the work bowl of a food processor, mix together the buttermilk, brown sugar, butter, salt, vanilla, and lemon peel. Add the yeast mixture and 2½ cups of the flour. Mix or process until smooth. Add more flour, ½ cup at a time, turn out onto a board, and knead until the dough is smooth and elastic. Place in an oiled bag and let double, about 1 hour.

Meanwhile, combine the currants, walnuts, poppy seeds, butter, brown sugar, cinnamon, nutmeg, flour, and lemon peel in a bowl.

When the dough has doubled, punch the dough down and on a floured board, roll into a rectangle 10 inches wide by 16 inches long. Spread the filling to within 1 inch of the edges of the rectangle. Roll up lengthwise, pinching the seam to seal. Shape the dough into a ring, joining the ends of the ring securely. Place on a well greased baking sheet. Slash the ring in 10 places almost to the center and twist each cut section clockwise, exposing the filling. If desired, oil a 3-ounce ramekin and place in the center of the ring to keep ring open during baking. Let rise again until double, about 45 minutes to 1 hour. Preheat the oven to 375° F.

Bake the ring for 25 to 30 minutes or until golden. Remove from the oven, remove center ramekin, and place on a rack to cool. In a small bowl, mix together the confectioners' sugar, butter, vanilla, and 1 to 2 tablespoons of the heavy cream, stirring until smooth and thick but still pourable; add additional cream to thin glaze, if necessary. Drizzle on cooled ring and serve at once.

BASIC PIECRUST
MAKES ONE 9-INCH PIECRUST

- 1¼ cups all-purpose soft wheat flour
- ½ teaspoon salt
- ¼ cup solid vegetable shortening
- ¼ cup (½ stick) unsalted butter
- 3 to 6 tablespoons ice water

Mix the flour and salt together in a bowl. Cut in the shortening and butter with a pastry blender or fork until the mixture resembles cornmeal. Add the ice water a little at a time, tossing the mixture with the pastry blender or fork until it is moist and holds together. Gather the dough into a ball and flatten slightly. Wrap in plastic wrap and place in the refrigerator for at least ½ hour or longer if possible.

Flour a board or wax paper. Using a floured or stockinged rolling pin, roll the pastry out ⅛ inch thick or less and at least 1½ to 2 inches larger than your pan. Fold the round in quarters. Place the pastry in a 9-inch pie pan and unfold. Trim the pastry 1 inch larger than the pie pan. Fold the overhanging pastry under itself, then either press the tines of a fork around the edge to form a pattern or use your thumbs to flute the dough all around. Chill the shell for 30 minutes before baking.

To prebake (or "bake blind"), preheat the oven to 425°F. Crumple a piece of wax paper, then spread it out to the edges of the pan. Fill the paper with raw rice or dried peas (they can be used repeatedly) to keep the crust from bubbling up and to support the sides. Bake for 20 minutes. Carefully remove the paper and rice or peas. If the filling requires no cooking, bake the pie shell 10 minutes more; otherwise, add the desired filling and continue baking according to the filling directions.

An antique pie safe holds an array of baked offerings.

LEMON/LIME MERINGUE PIE
MAKES ONE 9-INCH PIE

If you like lemon meringue pie, you'll love it with the addition of lime. It's unbelievably delicious. I do love the ease of graham cracker crusts, as well as their flavor.

GRAHAM CRACKER CRUST
- 2 *cups graham cracker crumbs*
- 2 *tablespoons confectioners' sugar*
- ½ *teaspoon ground ginger*
- 6 *tablespoons (¾ stick) butter, melted*

FILLING
- 1 *cup sugar*
- ½ *cup cornstarch*
- ¼ *teaspoon salt*
- 1 *cup water*
- 5 *egg yolks*
- 2 *tablespoons butter*
- ¼ *cup fresh lemon juice*
- ¼ *cup fresh lime juice*
- 1 *tablespoon grated lemon peel (no white attached)*
- 1 *tablespoon grated lime peel (no white attached)*

MERINGUE
- 6 *egg whites*
- ½ *teaspoon cream of tartar*
- ½ *cup sugar*

Preheat the oven to 350°F.

In a bowl, mix the graham cracker crumbs, the confectioners' sugar, ginger, and butter, stirring with a spatula or wooden spoon until the butter is evenly mixed into the crumbs. Press the mixture evenly onto the bottom and sides of a 9-inch pie plate and bake for 10 minutes. Cool on a rack.

To make the filling, whisk together the sugar, cornstarch, and salt in a medium saucepan. Gradually stir in the water until well mixed. Cook over medium-high heat, whisking until thick. Reduce the heat and cook, stirring or whisking, for another 2 minutes. Remove from the heat and quickly beat in the egg yolks one at a time. Return to the heat and cook, stirring constantly, 2 more minutes. The sauce should be very thick. Add the butter, juices, and grated peel to the hot mixture. Allow to cool slightly before pouring into the crust.

To make the meringue, combine the egg whites and cream of tartar in a mixing bowl and beat to soft peaks. Gradually add the sugar, 1 tablespoon at a time, beating until the mixture forms stiff peaks. Spread the meringue over the filling, being sure to spread it all the way to the outside of the crust to seal in the filling and prevent shrinkrage. Bake until the meringue is golden brown, 15 minutes. Cool before serving.

STRAWBERRY PIE
SERVES 6 TO 8

This is really easy for a knock-em-dead pie. The pecan base is a variation of the French frangipane base often seen in classic recipes, but the combination of fresh strawberries and pecans make it uniquely Southern.

- 1 *cup very finely chopped pecans, packed*
- 1 *cup sifted confectioners' sugar*
- 1 *egg white*
- 1 *whole egg*
- 2 *tablespoons (¼ stick) unsalted butter, melted*
- 1 *teaspoon grated lemon peel (no white attached)*
- 1 *Basic Piecrust (page 192)*
- 1 *quart strawberries, halved*
- ⅓ *cup red currant jam, melted and strained (optional)*

Preheat the oven to 400°F.

In a bowl, blend together the pecans, sugar, egg white, and whole egg to form a paste. Beat in the butter and lemon peel until smooth. Pour the filling into the unbaked piecrust. Bake until the mixture bounces back when touched lightly, 15 to 20 minutes. Let the pie cool. Arrange the strawberries decoratively on top of the cooled pie. If desired, brush with warm melted red currant jam for a shiny glaze.

APPLE CINNAMON LIFESAVER PIE
SERVES 6 TO 8

We call this lifesaver pie because it helped pull Veronica, one of my assistants, through a lengthy illness. She was in the hospital during her senior year of high school with hepatitis and had a relapse. She was cranky and bratty about being sick for so long, and she so much hated the hospital food at that point that she refused to eat it. Her mom lovingly baked her one of these apple pies every day until she was well. That, with a quart of cold milk, pulled her through. Maybe we should call it Loving Mother Pie.

2 recipes Basic Piecrust (page 192)
6 to 8 Granny Smith apples
    (about 2 pounds), peeled, cored,
    and sliced 1 inch thick
1 tablespoon fresh lemon juice
1 tablespoon bourbon (optional)
¼ cup sugar, or to taste depending on
    the tartness of the apples
2 tablespoons ground cinnamon,
    or to taste
½ teaspoon ground cloves
    Pinch salt
2 to 3 tablespoons butter
2 to 3 tablespoons milk

Preheat the oven to 450°F.

Flour a board or wax paper and, using a floured or stockinged rolling pin, roll out one of the pastry balls ⅛ inch thick or less and at least 1½ to 2 inches larger than the pie pan. Fold the round in quarters. Place the pastry in a 9-inch pie pan and unfold it. Trim the pastry. Place it in the freezer or the refrigerator for 30 minutes before baking.

Place the apples in a large mixing bowl, add the lemon juice and optional bourbon, and toss to coat. Alternate mixing in the sugar, cinnamon, and cloves, tossing to coat evenly. Add a pinch of salt. Pour half the mixture into the unbaked chilled piecrust and dot with half the butter. Add the rest of the apple mixture and dot with the remaining butter.

Roll out the remaining ball of dough about ⅛ inch thick. Brush the edges of the bottom crust with water. Drape the top round over the apple mixture. Crimp the edges of the top and bottom crusts decoratively and brush all over with the milk. Make 1 or 2 slits in the crust for steam vents.

Place the pie in the middle of the oven on a cookie sheet, as some of the juices may run out. Bake 10 minutes, then reduce the heat to 375° F. and continue baking until golden brown, another 45 to 50 minutes.

Cabin Cuisine

HEN FRUSTRATION BESETS ME, I HEAD for the woods. There are cabins all over the South, both private and state owned, that beckon those of us who cannot stay too long in the city; for us, a great canopy of trees overhead and a trail beneath our feet help to sort things out. These cabins can be simple mountain shacks with little more than a fireplace, plenty of warm quilts, and perhaps a bit of electricity for lights and a refrigerator, providing a place for games of poker and a venison steak; or glamorous homes on the bayou, with all the amenities and a houseboat at the dock for the overflow. Southerners pride ourselves on our cabins, for these cabins and fish camps are not

LEFT: *Packets of fish and vegetables cook right in the open fire.* RIGHT: *The welcoming hunting lodge.*

for the catching and cooking of fish and game alone; a special camaraderie results when people come together to feel close to nature and each other.

When cooks and hunters come together, the combination of primitive facilities and sophisticated palates often creates culinary magic. When the bounty of the fisherman or the hunter is presented to the cook, it arouses the most basic of human feelings about food—the provider meets the expediter, the keeper of the fire. Sometimes the cook and the hunter are one, making the game and the hunter part of the same respectful system and honoring the game as the gardener does the earth. Fishing camps and hunting cabins become sacred places where the catch is cooked, blessed, and eaten.

My meals with hunters and fishers have all been wondrously different. I've spent peaceful evenings sitting in front of the fireplace with my friends the Clines, adding a packet of just-caught, foil-wrapped trout to the potatoes in the fire and reveling in the smoky aromas as the flames flicker and the sun goes down. I've spent an afternoon standing over a sink with Tom and Susan Puett, skinning dozens of quails, then feeding a crowd.

Cabin cuisine runs the gamut from deep-fried catfish cooked over an open fire at a fish camp to packing a venison steak (kept in the freezer for such occasions) for a dear one to carry to the hunting cabin, thus ensuring the first night's card game goes well.

Not so many fresh vegetables show up in cabins, perhaps because game goes so well with potatoes or wild rice. Rat or cheddar cheese is usually to be found in any cabin, and I've learned that broccoli, cabbage, Brussels sprouts, onions, and carrots keep well and are easily obtained in country stores year-round. Combined in sturdy stir-frys or hearty casseroles, they round out the day's catch. In the cabins, grilling and frying prevail—it's the quality of time and the freshness of the game that heighten appreciation of the cuisine.

Whether gathering places for large groups or solitary places for those who need to feel close to nature or each other, there is a special camaraderie that pervades these sanctuaries, for everyone is part of a shared experience, be they hunter, fisher or cook, successful or not. The experience is one that provides lifelong bonds for families in which sons and daughters hunt with fathers and mothers, one that is larger than the total of the participants.

MARY HATAWAY'S GOLDEN SQUASH SOUP
SERVES 12

This beautiful soup makes both an elegant starter and a great soup-in-a-mug for your favorite fish camp because it is so refreshing hot or cold. The combination of butternut squash and apples is a smooth one, with the herbs giving a bit of a subtle undercurrent. It's particularly good in the fall but works year-round and it freezes well.

2 *pounds butternut squash, peeled, seeded, and coarsely chopped*
2 *pounds Golden Delicious apples, peeled, cored, and coarsely chopped*
2 *cups finely chopped onions*
¾ *cup fresh breadcrumbs*
7½ *cups chicken stock*
1½ *teaspoons salt*
1 *teaspoon dried or 1¾ teaspoons fresh rosemary*
1 *teaspoon dried or 1⅓ teaspoons fresh oregano*
¾ *teaspoon white pepper*
1½ *cups heavy cream*

Mix the squash, apples, onions, breadcrumbs, stock, salt, rosemary, oregano, and pepper in a large pan. Simmer 1½ hours, or until the squash and apples are very soft. Puree by hand

or in a food processor. Return to the pan and whisk in the cream. Adjust the seasonings and reheat or chill and serve cold.

MARINATED VENISON STEAK
SERVES 4

Most of my venison comes as gifts from hunters. However, farm-raised venison is now readily available through mail-order and specialty purveyors, and you are assured of getting the cut you want and that it will be tender. Wild game is much riskier, dependent on the skill of the hunter dressing the meat.

MARINADE
½ *cup soy sauce*
½ *cup dry sherry or tawny port*
½ *cup olive oil*
1 *medium onion, finely sliced*
4 *garlic cloves, chopped*
10 *juniper berries, crushed*
2 *teaspoons powdered ginger*
1 *teaspoon grated orange peel (no white attached)*
Salt
Freshly ground black pepper

2 *pounds venison saddle or round steak*

To prepare the marinade, mix the soy sauce, sherry, oil, onion, garlic, juniper berries, ginger, orange peel, and salt and pepper to taste. Pour over the steaks and refrigerate for 1 to 2 hours. Grill 3 to 5 minutes per side, depending on the thickness of the steaks.

LEFT: *A steaming mug of squash soup.* RIGHT: *Marinated venison steaks complete the hunter's meal.*

Quail
Tips

The native Southern quail is the bobwhite, an all-white-meat bird, although the pharoah quail (a combination of dark and light meats) is farm-raised here in some places. I love the skin of quail, but hunters often remove the skin rather than pluck it. If I am concerned about having the skin for presentation, I buy my quail in the grocery store or follow the cardinal rule for cooks: Know your hunter. However, many recipes will accommodate skinned birds.

A good way to freeze quail (as well as shrimp) is to surround them with water before freezing in a milk carton or freezerproof plastic bag.

ELLIOTT MILLER'S QUAIL AND WILD RICE
SERVES 6

Elliott Miller is a wise and wonderful friend who has taught me an enormous amount about the hunt as well as about cooking the catch. He embraces the cooking of the catch with the same enthusiasm as he does the hunting cycle, where the game is honored and blessed. Elliott contributed this dish to a game dinner I hosted for TV chef Jeff Smith. Dried cranberries can be found in specialty stores.

6 *quail*
1 *teaspoon ground cumin*
1 *teaspoon fennel seed*
½ *cup red wine*
2 *cups chicken broth*
 Freshly ground black pepper
1 *cup wild rice*
2 *garlic cloves, chopped*
1½ *teaspoons chopped fresh rosemary*
½ *cup olive oil*
⅓ *cup balsamic vinegar*
½ *cup dried cranberries*

Place the quail, cumin, fennel, and red wine in a nonreactive skillet with the broth to cover.

Season with black pepper. Bring to the boil, reduce the heat, and simmer until very tender, about 30 minutes. When done, remove the quail. Add the wild rice to the broth, adding water if needed to make 3 cups liquid for 1 cup rice, and cook until the rice is done, about 45 minutes.

Meanwhile, remove the quail from the bone and place the shredded meat in a large bowl. Add the chopped garlic, rosemary, olive oil, vinegar, and dried cranberries. When the rice is tender, drain well and add to the quail mixture. Serve hot or cold.

NOTE: This dish can be frozen.

LEMON TROUT IN FOIL
SERVES 2 TO 4

The Georgia/Carolina mountains are host to many streams that are seeded with trout regularly, so access to trout fishing is easy and the fish abundant.

The trout can be baked or cooked on a fireplace grill or in the oven and will remain tender and moist for 15 minutes or so until the foil is opened. I assemble the packets beforehand and cook them when guests arrive. Vary the herbs to change the flavor.

At the Fish Camp

The rituals and customs of the fish camp are well established, and each locality has its own. The memory of a visit to one camp in particular always makes me smile.

My TV crew and I had been invited to join Otto and his large and happy family at his Louisiana fish camp. The family had all worked together to prepare a delicious duck feast, with the men primarily doing the cooking and the women the toting and setting. We walked in, weary after a full day, and were greeted by wonderful aromas and much conviviality. Dozens of family members had gathered for the evening, and women were boisterously setting an immense table that easily sat twenty-five or thirty as well as two or three smaller tables.

When it came time to be served, we, as guests, were first in the line to dish up the rice and duck, which Otto served with great flourish. We seated ourselves randomly at the large table, where a grand blessing was said by Otto.

As we bowed our heads over the food we could feel the family sneaking glances at us, and I was bemused. Should we, too, offer up a prayer? I looked past Cynthia, my producer, to the man next to her, then the man next to him, and a light went on in my head; unwittingly we had seated ourselves at the men's table! We acknowledged our gaffe as soon as the prayer was over, offering to move; but the men waved us down and told us it was a wonderful new experience having women at the same table at the fish camp, even if it broke family tradition. During the evening, several of the men joined the women's table, their chairs rocked back on the outside, to join in with their gossip, seeing if it differed from that of the men's table.

2   *trout fillets (about 1 pound)*
1   *medium onion, thinly sliced*
3   *medium mushrooms, thinly sliced*
1   *lemon, thinly sliced*
2   *tablespoons fresh lemon juice*
1   *tablespoon butter*
2   *tablespoons fresh herbs (thyme, dill, or your choice), finely chopped*

Preheat the oven to 400°F.

Place the fillets on a large sheet of foil.

The foil should extend 5 inches beyond the fillets at each end. Layer the onion, mushrooms, and lemon slices on top of the fillets; sprinkle with lemon juice and dot with butter. Sprinkle with herbs. Place a second sheet of foil over the fillets. Fold the edges over 3 times on each side to seal the foil packet. Measure the packet at the thickest point and bake for 12 minutes per inch.

FRIED CATFISH
SERVES 4

One of my favorite things to do with guests from out of state is to take them out for a catfish fry. Fried catfish, never served without hush puppies, is the specialty of many country restaurants, like the one on the Jackson Highway in Covington, Georgia, where I've been going for many years. Still, I sometimes fry catfish at home or in the mountains, particularly when a mom or dad and a small child grab poles, go down to the lake or pond, and catch a mess. Fresh fried catfish can't be beat!

4 *catfish, in 6- to 8-ounce fillets*
   or whole
¼ *cup buttermilk*
¾ *cup all-purpose flour*
¾ *cup cornmeal*
   Salt
   Freshly ground black pepper
   Vegetable oil for frying

Soak the catfish fillets in buttermilk for at least 30 minutes or overnight. In a shallow dish, combine the flour, cornmeal, and salt and pepper to taste. Drain the catfish and dredge in the flour and cornmeal mixture. Measure the thickness of the fish. In a heavy skillet, heat 1½ inches oil to 360°F. Fry the catfish on each side for 5 minutes per inch of thickness until golden brown. Drain on paper towels and serve hot.

Freshly caught
catfish is quickly
fried and served
with its tradition-
al accompaniment,
Hush Puppies.

Hush Puppies

Fried fish and hush puppies were a central part of the supper in 1969 on Ocracoke Island, North Carolina, that I shared with my former husband, David, on our wedding day, and I still think them a magical combination.

Together with our families we congregated at the Ocracoke Inn. The inn's long pine wooden tables were gleaming, and the smells and sounds of foods frying from the kitchen were seductive. The requisite hot sauce was on the table next to the oleanders. Platters of hot, freshly fried fish, moist inside, crunchy-fried outside, were accompanied by Southern vegetables and bowls of cool coleslaw. And, of course, there were heaping plates of hush puppies to complete the meal.

The origins of this Southern staple are obscure, but at least one story often repeated in Southern folklore traces them to the hunting and fishing camps so popular in the South of yesteryear as well as today. Amid the bountiful, boisterous eating that comes from catching one's own and cooking it in the open came the frying of a cornmeal batter to go with the crisp fried fish.

Dogs, sniffing around the campfire, were tantalized by the smells and excited by the festivities. To quiet them, a cook fried up the last of the fish batter, thick from sitting, and tossed it to the "dawgs," crying out, "Hush, puppy." On the next fishing expedition, the cook dipped some onions into his thick cornmeal batter, shaped the mixture into balls, and ate the "hush puppies" himself.

The important thing is, of course, the hot, fish-flavored fat—always at 350° F. The shape is debatable—round, thick, long, or thin? If no fish has been fried in the fat, add a bit more salt to the batter!

HUSH PUPPIES
MAKES 20 TO 25

Marjorie Kinnan Rawlings's *Cross Creek Cookery*, published in 1942, calls hush puppies "a concomitant of the hunt," and says, "fresh-caught fried fish without hush puppies are as a man without a woman."

1¼ cups cornmeal
½ cup self-rising flour
1 teaspoon salt
2 medium onions, finely chopped
1 egg
1 cup milk
dash of Tabasco
3 to 4 cups vegetable oil

Combine the cornmeal, flour, salt, and onions. Whisk together the egg, milk, and Tabasco and stir into the cornmeal mixture. Heat 2 to 3 inches of oil in a skillet to 350°F. Drop the batter into the hot oil by tablespoons. Fry until golden brown on all sides, about 3 to 4 minutes. Drain on paper towels and serve hot.

HOT AND SPICY STIR-FRIED COLESLAW
SERVES 16

This is a very pretty as well as tasty vegetable accompaniment, especially for game. It can easily be cut in half.

 3 tablespoons peanut or vegetable oil
 2 cups thinly sliced cabbage
 2 cups grated carrots
 4 cups seeded and thinly sliced green
   and red bell peppers
   Freshly ground black pepper
 1 teaspoon salt
10 dashes Tabasco sauce
 2 tablespoons soy sauce

Heat the oil in a large skillet over high heat until it sizzles. Add the vegetables, pepper, salt, Tabasco sauce, and soy sauce. Sauté for 5 minutes, stirring well and frequently.

BUTTERMILK CORN BREAD MUFFINS
MAKES 24

You may use white or yellow cornmeal for these muffins, depending on personal preference. Some feel the sugar is heresy—but it sure is good if you want a sweet corn bread, and the very hot oven gives them crusty sides.

 3 eggs, beaten to mix
 3 cups buttermilk
 2 tablespoons sugar (optional)
 2 teaspoons salt
 ¼ cup (½ stick) unsalted butter
 3 cups cornmeal
 1 cup all-purpose flour
 2 tablespoons baking powder
 1 teaspoon baking soda

Preheat the oven to 500°F. Grease 24 muffin cups and place in the oven to heat.

In a mixing bowl, combine the eggs, buttermilk, sugar, and salt. Melt the butter in a small pan and whisk into the buttermilk mixture. Quickly stir in the cornmeal, flour, baking powder, and baking soda, mixing just until combined. Measure 2 heaping tablespoons of batter into each muffin tin. Bake 15 to 20 minutes, until lightly browned.

NOTE: The baked muffins can be frozen.

POTATO PACKET
SERVES 2

You are more liable to find an abundance of starches than fresh vegetables at a cabin. Cheese and sausage are standard in a hunter's pantry.

 1 pound new potatoes (creamers),
   washed and cut into ½-inch cubes
 ½ cup grilled sausage links, cut
   into ¼-inch slices
 ½ cup grated Cheddar cheese

Preheat the oven to 350°F.

Tear off 2 pieces of foil 15 inches long. Lightly grease one sheet of foil. Place the potatoes in a single layer in the center of the foil. Sprinkle the sausage over the potatoes and top with the cheese. Lightly grease the second sheet of foil and place it, greased side down, on top of the mixture. Fold the edges of the foil over 3 times. Bake or grill until the potatoes are tender, about 30 minutes.

liking. Season to taste with salt and pepper. Squeeze lemon juice over the vegetables and sprinkle with parsley.

CHARRED BRUSSELS SPROUTS, CARROTS, ONIONS, AND GARLIC
SERVES 4 TO 6

Baked and caramelized Brussels sprouts are quite different from steamed or boiled. They have a nutty flavor with a crisp center. The charred garlic, onions, and carrots enhance the Brussels sprouts with their color and caramelized flavor.

 1 *pound Brussels sprouts, X cut in*
    bottoms and outer layers removed
 6 to 8 *garlic cloves, peeled*
 2 *medium onions, cut in wedges*
 2 *carrots, peeled and julienned*
 3 to 6 *tablespoons olive oil*
    Salt
    Freshly ground black pepper
 1 to 2 *tablespoons fresh lemon juice*
 3 *tablespoons chopped fresh parsley*

Preheat the oven to 425°F.

Toss the Brussels sprouts, garlic, onions, and carrots with the olive oil and arrange in an oiled pan in a single layer. Bake 30 to 45 minutes, stirring occasionally, or until the vegetables are crisp, tender, and charred to your

BROCCOLI SALAD
SERVES 6

I first ate this at the home of Judy Walz, who got the recipe from our mutual friend Sue Kreutzberg … which is the way recipes go in the South. Broccoli has a long history here. I particularly enjoyed coming across references to it in George Washington's journals when I did some research at Mount Vernon. He and his gardener were prone to give it dreadful misspellings but did give explicit directions about its planting.

 1 *bunch broccoli*
 ¼ *pound Swiss cheese, grated*
 2 *green onions or scallions, including*
    some of the tops, chopped
 ½ *cup mayonnaise*
 ¼ *cup sugar*
 1 *tablespoon apple cider vinegar*
 ½ *pound bacon, crisply fried and*
    crumbled

Wash the broccoli and cut the tops into bite-size florets. Reserve the stems for another use. Combine the broccoli in a bowl with the Swiss cheese and green onions.

In a small bowl stir together the mayonnaise, sugar, and vinegar to make a dressing, and add it to the broccoli mixture. Let the salad marinate overnight or up to several days. Just before serving, stir in some of the bacon and sprinkle the rest on top.

ABOVE: *Oven-charred vegetables.*
RIGHT: *Sturdy Broccoli Salad.*

Bibliography

America Cooks—The General Federation of Women's Clubs Cookbook. Ann Seranne, editor. New York: G.P. Putnam & Sons, 1967.

Bland Farms. *They Only Make You Cry When They're Gone!* (A collection of Vidalia onion recipes.) Self-published.

Child, Lydia Maria. *The American Frugal Housewife.* Cambridge, MA: Applewood Books, originally 1832.

DeBolt, Margaret Wayt. *Savannah Sampler Cookbook.* With Emma R. Law. Norfolk, VA: The Donning Co., 1978.

Dull, Mrs. S. R. [Henrietta Stanley Dull]. *Southern Cooking.* New York: Grosset & Dunlop, 1941.

Egerton, John. *Side Orders.* Atlanta: Peachtree Publishers, 1990.

_____. *Southern Food.* New York: Alfred A. Knopf, 1987.

Flower Committee, Independent Presbyterian Church. *Hints from Southern Epicures.* Savannah, Ga: By the author, n.d.

Fox-Genovese, Elizabeth. *Within the Plantation Household: Black and White Women of the Old South.* Cherry Hill, NC: University of North Carolina Press, 1988.

Frank, Dorothy C. *The Peanut Cookbook.* New York: Clarkson Potter, Inc.,1976.

Gaede, Sarah R. *The Pirate's House Cookbook.* Memphis, TN: Wimmer Bros., 1982.

Harris, Jessica B. *Iron Pots and Wooden Spoons.* New York: Atheneum, 1989.

Huntsville Heritage Cookbook. Huntsville, AL: The Grace Club Auxiliary, Inc., 1967.

Jefferson, Thomas. *Writings.* Merrill D. Peterson, ed. New York: The Library of America, 1984.

Junior Associates of the Atlanta Music Club, Inc., Staff, ed. *Atlanta Cooks for Company.* Atlanta: By the author, 1968.

Junior Charity League of Monroe, Louisiana, Inc., Staff, ed. *The Cotton Country Collection.* Memphis, TN: S. C. Toof and Company, 1972.

Junior League of Baton Rouge, Inc.,Staff, ed. *River Road Recipes.* Baton Rouge, LA: By the author, 1959.

Junior League of Nashville, Inc., Staff, ed. *Nashville Seasons.* Memphis, TN: S. C. Toof and Company, 1984.

Junior League of Tallahassee, Inc., Staff, ed. *Thymes Remembered.* Tallahassee: By the author, 1988.

Lewis, Edna. *In Pursuit of Flavor.* New York: Alfred A. Knopf, 1988.

_____. *The Taste of Country Cooking.* New York: Alfred A. Knopf, 1985.

The Linley Heflin Cookbook. rev. Margaret Ann Surber. Birmingham, AL: By the author, 1962.

Lupo, Margaret. *Southern Cooking from Mary Mac's Tea Room.* Atlanta, GA: Marmac Publishing Co., 1983.

Lustig, Lillie S.; Sondheim, S. Claire; and Rensel, Sarah. *The Southern Cookbook of Fine Old Recipes.* Reading, PA: Culinary Arts Press, 1939.

Miller, Joni. *True Grits. The Southern Foods Mail-Order Catalogue.* New York: Gloria Norris Books, 1990.

The National Society of the Colonial Dames of America of the State of Georgia. *Georgia Heritage Treasured Recipes.* By the author, 1979.

Neal, Bill. *Bill Neal's Southern Cooking.* Chapel Hill, NC: University of North Carolina Press, 1985.

_____. *Biscuits, Spoonbread, and Sweet Potato Pie.* New York: Alfred A. Knopf, 1990.

Price, Fran. "The One and Only Cook," *The Richmond News Leader,* Wednesday, March 27, 1991.

Randolph, Mrs. Mary. *The Virginia Housewife: or, Methodical Cook.* Philadelphia, PA: E. H. Butler & Co., 1860.

Rawlings, Marjorie Kinnan. *Cross Creek Cookery.* New York: Charles Scribner's Sons, 1942.

Rhett, Blanche S.; Gay, Lettie; Woodward, Helen; and Hamilton, Elizabeth. *Two Hundred Years of Charleston Cooking.* Columbia, SC: University of South Carolina Press, 1976.

Rutledge, Sarah. *House and Home; or, The Carolina Housewife.* "By a Lady of Charleston." Fourth edition. Charleston, SC: Walker, Evans & Cogswell, n.d.

Washington, Martha. *A Booke of Cookery.* Transcribed and noted by Karen Hess. New York: Columbia University Press, 1981.

_____. *A Booke of Sweetmeats.* Transcribed and noted by Karen Hess. New York: Columbia University Press, 1981.

Acknowledgments

I'm particularly blessed by the people who work with me to develop and test the recipes in my books, and who help with my television shows. • A very talented and creative cook named Margaret Ann Sparks Surber came into my life in 1976, when she worked with me at Rich's Cooking School. I'm very grateful for all the touches of perfection and original recipes she contributed to this book, and for the years she has worked for me. • Ray Overton has also dedicated himself to these recipes. With Ray I just can get started talking about a long-remembered meal, or something that would satisfy a craving, and the next thing I know he has duplicated the very recipe. • I wouldn't be doing a Southern cookbook if it weren't for Kate Almand, Grace Reeves, and Martha Summerour who, each in her own way, made me recognize that authentic Southern cuisine was worth saving and putting into print. • Richard Lands shows up every week to proofread, checking research and facts, making sure the recipes are adaptable for use in my television show. • Sue Hunter encouraged me to follow my dream, and helped immeasurably with editing the copy from its rough form. • My editor, Pam Krauss, was enormously helpful every step of the way. • I am grateful for all the apprentices, students, and friends who gave their recipes for us to adapt, including Frances Baker, Ann Brewer, Gary Brier, Elizabeth Burris, Carl Campbell, Shirley Corriher, Aunt Lawson Duncan, Celeste Dupree, Ma-Ma Dupree, Mr. and Mrs. Joe Elliott, Sarah Gaede, Harper, Mary Hataway, Sue Hunter, Maude Jones, Carr Kaufmann, Sue Kreutzberg, Dorothy Lander, London Cordon Bleu, Ruby Lands, Edna Lewis, Margaret Lupo, Elliott Mackle, Brian McElheny, Rejane Mittelstadt, Barbara Morgan, Cindy Morgan, Neeley Oliver, The Patio, Paul Prudhomme, Grace Reeves, Patti Scott, Candy Sheehan, Alyssa Skrepcinski, Denice Skrepcinski, Jean Sparks, Bob Steed, Cynthia Stevens, Marion Sullivan, Martha Summerour, Margaret Ann Surber, Terry Thompson, Elizabeth Tilden, Becky Turner, Jean Van den Berg, and Judy Walz. • Frank Turner, city manager of Covington, Georgia, led me to Ann Brewer, who helped oversee our photographic efforts, coordinating keys and cars, making hot meals for hungry photo crews, putting us up for the night when it was too late to drive back to Atlanta. I'm grateful to her, the people of Covington, and the following: Mr. and Mrs. E. E. Callaway, Mrs. Kenneth L. Carson, Mr. and Mrs. Kenneth Cox, Don Davison, William L. Dobbs, Falconwood Stables, William D. Fortson, Joyce Hairston, Arsie Mae Hardman, Claude Jordan, Patricia Mayfield, Alexander G. Morehouse, Patrick's Feed and Seed Store, Trey Polk, J. W. Richardson, Debbie Rushton, Beth Sexton, Mr. and Mrs. Billy S. Smith, Laura Soltis, Mr. and Mrs. E. Phillip Stone, Frank B. Turner, and Roy Varner. • When we went to Charleston my brother James Gordon (Chuck) Meyer and his wife, Linda, were invaluable. Mrs. Jerry Bennett Taylor pointed us to some lovely baskets. In Savannah, Bailee Kronowitz spent the day with us, directing us to oyster beds and special homes. • On Edisto, Philip Bardin, chef of the Old Post Office, and Karen Lindsay, his herbalist, were enormous helps; as were Susan and Jim Rice, Pierre and Julee LaMunion, and Bruce and Tecla Earns. Christine Meadows, curator at Mt. Vernon, made my research there possible.

Special thanks as well to: Tom Eckerle, a particularly gifted photographer who was able to capture my mental image of food and transform it into pictures. He and his assistants were tireless in their efforts. Cynthia Jubera was the head food stylist for much of this book, with help from Marion Sullivan and Ray Overton. Other people who helped with the photography were The Joyner Company of Smithfield, Virginia, Sue Hunter, Maria Capolino, Denice Skrepcinski, Patti Scott, Rejane Mittelstadt, Will Deller, Margaret Ann Surber, Sarabeth Lassiter, Elizabeth Tilden, Veronica Love, and John Christianson of Russo's Seafood in Savannah. The invaluable Kay Calvert spends hours here each week on the computer checking recipes and details. Audrey and Pierre-Henri Thiault have also lent their support.

The following homes were used: Usher House, home of Dr. and Mrs. Robert Faulkner; Swanscombe, home of Mr. and Mrs. William Thomas Craig; Thomas/Stone House, home of The Reverend and Mrs. Jack Atkinson; Chestnut Grove, home of Mr. and Mrs. James Watterson; Mr. and Mrs. Pierce Cline; Patrick Feed and Seed, Mr. Gary Patrick; Little Red School House, home of the Service Guild of Covington; Covington Woman's Club, Mrs. Sharon Frey, President; Celeste Sigman Dupree; Dr. and Mrs. Jordan Callaway; Mr. and Mrs. Robert R. Fowler III; Regency Hall, home of Mr. Terry Thompson and Mr. Arvin F. Spell III; Mount Pleasant Plantation, home of Mrs. Oby T. Brewer, Jr.

The children in the Christmas Tree Hay Ride picture were Walker Jordan, Lucye Jordan, and Bonner Jordan. The children in the Bake Sale picture are Nicole Craver, Katie Cunard, Michelle Jackson, Judson Rhodes, Seth Rhodes, and Demetries Smith.

Index